LILLIAN EICHLER WATSON

One of the most widely read authorities on social usage in the world, Lillian Watson is author of the fabulous best seller, the original *Book of Etiquette*, and a dozen more inspirational and self-improvement books.

Light from Many Lamps fulfills a lifetime's ambition —to select from the world's storehouse of wisdom those quotations that can be of most help in our troubled times.

And to make her selections more meaningful, Lillian Watson has given the reader many stories of how the thoughts and ideas came to be written. In short biographies, she conveys the kinship we share with the people—both humble and famous—whose words offer moral, spiritual, and ethical guidance across the years.

This is a book of infinite riches. Keep it handy to dip into as needed, to enjoy in small stimulating portions. It is an unfailing source of comfort and inspiration for every member of the family.

Light
From Many
Lamps

Edited by
Lillian Eichler Watson

PUBLISHED BY POCKET BOOKS NEW YORK

POCKET BOOKS, a Simon & Schuster division of GULF & WESTERN CORPORATION
1230 Avenue of the Americas, New York, N.Y. 10020

ISBN: 0-671-83507-6

First Pocket Books printing June, 1976

10   9   8   7   6   5   4

POCKET and colophon are trademarks of Simon & Schuster.

Cover photo by Matt Tepper

Printed in the U.S.A.

ACKNOWLEDGMENTS

Much of the material in this volume is copyright by other publishers, and may not be reprinted or reproduced without the permission of the owners. A complete list of the holders of the copyright, or their agents, follows. Any errors are accidental and will be corrected in future printings upon advice to the editor or publisher.

ALEXANDER L. ABBOTT for quotation from *The Other Room* by Lyman Abbott, copyright 1905.

AMERICAN MAGAZINE for quotation from "If I Were Starting Out Today" by Karl T. Compton, copyright 1950, *American* magazine.

D. APPLETON & COMPANY for quotation from *Viva Mexico* by Charles M. Flandrau.

BERNARD BARUCH for quotations from his speeches.

BOBBS-MERRILL CO., INC. for quotation from *A Fortune to Share* by Vash Young, copyright 1931; by special permission of the publishers.

CREATIVE AGE PRESS for quotation from *Victory in My Hands* by Harold Russell and Victor Rosen, copyright 1949; by permission of Creative Age Press.

CURTIS PUBLISHING COMPANY for quotation from "What Is Civilization?" by Will Durant, reprinted by special permission from the author and *The Ladies' Home Journal;* copyright 1946, The Curtis Publishing Co. For quotation by Chester W. Nimitz from "If I Were Twenty-One" by Gretta Palmer, reprinted by special permission of Mr. Nimitz and *The Ladies' Home Journal;* copyright 1947, The Curtis Publishing Company. For quotation by Mary Roberts Rinehart from "Face Your Danger In Time" by Gretta Palmer, reprinted by special permission of Mrs. Rinehart and *The Ladies Home Journal;* copyright 1947, The Curtis Publishing Company. For quotation from "I Owe My Career to Losing a Leg" by Alexander P. de Seversky, reprinted by special permission from the author and *The Ladies' Home Journal;* copyright 1944, The Curtis Publishing Company. For quotation from "The Front Line Is in Our Hearts" by Robert E. Sherwood, reprinted by special permission from the author and *The Ladies' Home Journal;* copyright 1941, The Curtis Publishing Company.

CURTIS BROWN LTD. for quotation from *Ways of Escape* by Philip Gibbs, copyright 1933 by William Heineman, Ltd.; permission granted by Curtis Brown Ltd.

THOMAS Y. CROWELL COMPANY for quotation from *The Durable Satisfactions of Life* by Charles W. Eliot, copyright 1910, Thomas Y. Crowell & Company. For quotations from *The Happy Life* by Charles W. Eliot, copyright 1896, Thomas Y. Crowell & Co. For quotation from *Guide-Posts in Chaos* by Channing Pollock, Thomas Y. Crowell Co. publishers; reprinted by permission; copyright 1942 by Channing Pollock.

THE JOHN DAY COMPANY for quotations from *Being an American* by William O. Douglas, copyright 1940, The John Day Co. For quotation from *On the Wisdom of America* by Lin Yutang, copyright 1950, The John Day Company.

DODD, MEAD & COMPANY for quotation from *Transcience* by Sarojini Naidu, reprinted by permission of Dodd, Mead & Co. For quotation from *Star in a Well* by Nancy Byrd Turner, reprinted by permission of Dodd, Mead & Co.

DOUBLEDAY & COMPANY, INC. for quotation from *How to Live on 24 Hours a Day* by Arnold Bennett, copyright 1910 by George H. Doran Co.; permission received from Doubleday & Co., Inc. For quotations from *Adventures in Contentment* by David Grayson, copyright 1907, Hurst & Company; permission received from Doubleday & Co., Inc. For quotation from *Adventures in Friendship* by David Grayson, copyright 1910, Grosset & Dunlap; permission received from Doubleday & Co., Inc. For quotations from *Under My Elm* by David Grayson, copyright 1942, Doubleday & Co., Inc. For quotation from *We Bereaved* by Helen Keller, reprinted by permission of the author and Doubleday & Co., Inc. For quotations from *Peace in My Heart* by Archibald Rutledge, copyright 1930, Doubleday & Co., Inc. For quotation by Woodrow Wilson from *The New Freedom*, edited by William Bayard Hale, copyright 1913, 1933, Doubleday & Co., Inc.

E. P. DUTTON & COMPANY, INC. for quotations from *Marriage* by

William Lyon Phelps, copyright 1940 William Lyon Phelps, published by E. P. Dutton & Co., Inc. For quotation from *Happiness* by William Lyon Phelps, courtesy of E. P. Dutton & Co., Inc., N. Y.; copyright 1927, The Curtis Publishing Company.

FARRAR, STRAUS & YOUNG for quotations by Dwight D. Eisenhower, in *Eisenhower Speaks*, edited by Rudolph L. Treuenfels, N. Y. copyright 1948, Farrar, Straus & Young.

JAMES G. GILKEY for quotation from *When Life Gets Hard* by James Gordon Gilkey (Macmillan Co.). For quotation from *Best Sermons, 1944 Selections* (Ziff-Davis Publishing Co.).

HARCOURT, BRACE & Co., INC. for quotation by James T. Shotwell, from *Beyond Victory*, edited by Ruth Nanda Anshen, copyright 1943, by Harcourt, Brace & Co., Inc.

HARPER & BROTHERS for lines from *Light of the Years* by Grace Noll Crowell, copyright 1936, by Harper & Bros. For selection from *Collected Poems* by William H. Davies, copyright 1923, by Harper & Bros. For selections from *On Being a Real Person* by Harry E. Fosdick, copyright 1943, Harper & Bros.; permission of author. For selection from *On Being Fit to Live With* by Harry E. Fosdick, copyright 1946, Harper & Bros.; permission of author. For quotation from *Brave Enough for Life* by Bonaro W. Overstreet, copyright 1941, Harper & Bros. For selection from *This I Do Believe* by David E. Lilienthal, copyright 1949 by David E. Lilienthal. For selection from *You Can't Go Home Again* by Thomas Wolfe, copyright 1940, by Maxwell Perkins as executor.

HOUGHTON, MIFFLIN COMPANY for quotation by John Burroughs from *Literary Values*. For quotation from *What Men Live By* by Richard C. Cabot. For quotation by Ralph Waldo Emerson from his essay "Self-Reliance." For quotation from *The Chambered Nautilus* by Oliver Wendell Holmes. For quotation by John Greenleaf Whittier from *Complete Poems of John Greenleaf Whittier*. For quotations from *Walden* by Henry D. Thoreau.

GRENVILLE KLEISER for quotations from *Inspirations and Ideals* by Grenville Kleiser, copyright 1918, Funk & Wagnalls; permission of the author.

ALFRED A. KNOPF, INC. for quotations reprinted from *The Prophet* by Kahlil Gibran; by permission of Alfred A. Knopf, Inc.; copyright 1923 by Kahlil Gibran. For quotation reprinted from *Tales from the Congo* by André Gide, copyright 1939, Alfred A. Knopf, Inc.

JOSEPH LEWIS for quotation by Robert Ingersoll from *Ingersoll, a Biographical Appreciation* by Herman E. Kittridge, Dresden Publishing Co.; permission of Joseph Lewis.

LIFE MAGAZINE for quotation from "The American Destiny" by Walter Lippmann, copyright 1939, *Life* magazine.

J. B. LIPPINCOTT for quotation from *River of Years: an Autobiography*, copyright 1946 by Joseph Fort Newton, published by J. B. Lippincott Co. For quotation by Charles Francis Potter from *The Art of Being Happy*, edited by Kling & Kling, copyright 1948, J. B. Lippincott Co.

LITTLE, BROWN & Co. for quotation from "Chartless" and other material from *The Poems of Emily Dickinson*. For quotation from *Speeches* by Oliver Wendell Holmes.

EVELYN LOOMIS for quotation from *In a Chinese Garden* by Frederick Loomis; permission of Loomis Publishing Co. and Evelyn Loomis. For quotation from "The Best Medicine" by Frederick Loomis, reprinted from *This Week* magazine, copyright 1949 by The United Newspapers Magazine Corp.; permission Evelyn Loomis.

LOTHROP, LEE & SHEPARD CO. for quotation from "The House by the

Side of the Road" by Sam W. Foss in *Dreams in Homespun*, copyright 1897, Lothrop, Lee & Shepard Co.

David McKay Co. for quotation by André Gide from introduction to *Living Thoughts of Montaigne*, copyright 1939, Longmans Green; permission David McKay Co.

The Macmillan Company for quotations from *Aphorisms and Reflections* by Thomas H. Huxley, copyright 1907, The Macmillan Co.

Juanita Miller for poem *Columbus* by Joaquin Miller, G. P. Putnam's Sons; permission of Juanita Miller.

New York Herald Tribune for quotation by William G. Farrow from news item, *Herald Tribune* Bureau, copyright 1947, New York Herald Tribune, Inc.

The New York Times for quotation "Home for the Holidays" from Editorial, Dec. 25, 1948. For quotation from "The Challenge: One World or None" by Raymond B. Fosdick, *The New York Times* Magazine, copyright 1945, New York Times Co.; permission of author. For quotation from "The Art of Happiness" by William Ogden in *Topics of the Times*, copyright 1945, New York Times Co.

W. W. Norton & Company for quotation from *The Mature Mind* by H. A. Overstreet, copyright 1949, W. W. Norton & Co. For quotation from *Our Free Minds* by H. A. Overstreet.

The Philosophical Library for quotation from *Letters to My Son* by Dagobert D. Runes, copyright 1949, The Philosophical Library.

Mary Pickford for quotation from *Why Not Try God?* by Mary Pickford, copyright 1934, Mary Pickford, H. C. Kinsey & Co., Inc.

G. P. Putnam's Sons for quotations from *Alone* by Richard E. Byrd, copyright 1938 by Richard E. Byrd, permission of author. For quotation by J. B. Priestley, from *What Is Happiness?*, H. C. Kinsey & Co., Inc., and G. P. Putnam's Sons. For quotations by Sir Hugh Walpole from *What Is Happiness?*, H. C. Kinsey & Co., Inc. and G. P. Putnam's Sons.

Reader's Digest for quotation by Alexis Carrel from article, "Prayer Is Power," in *Reader's Digest*, March 1941. For quotation from "The Turning Point of My Career" by A. J. Cronin, copyright 1941, *Reader's Digest*. For quotation from "The Basic Axiom of Marital Felicity" by Donald Culross Peattie, copyright 1941, *Reader's Digest;* permission of author.

E. H. R. Revere for quotation from *A Way of Life* by Sir William Osler, given at Yale, 1913; permission of E. H. R. Revere, Trustee for Osler Estate.

Eddie Rickenbacker for quotation from pamphlet *We Prayed;* permission of author.

Rinehart & Co., Inc. for quotation from *The Selected Poems of Lizette Woodworth Reese*, copyright by Lizette Woodworth Reese, 1926, and reprinted by permission of Rinehart & Co., Inc., publishers. For quotations from *How to Be Happy Though Human* by W. Beran Wolfe, copyright 1931 by W. Beran Wolfe and reprinted by permission of Rinehart & Co., Inc., publishers.

Charles Scribner's Sons for quotations from *Thoughts for Everyday Living* by Maltbie B. Babcock, copyright 1901 by Charles Scribner's Sons, 1929 by Katharine T. Babcock; used by permission of the publishers. For quotation from *The Life of Robert Louis Stevenson* by Graham Balfour, Charles Scribner's Sons. For quotation by Edward Bok from *The Americanization of Edward Bok*, copyright 1923, Charles Scribner's Sons. For quotation from *Morning Prayer* by Robert Louis Stevenson, Charles Scribner's Sons. For quotation by Josiah G. Holland from *Bartlett's Familiar Quotations*, Charles Scribner's Sons. For quotation from *The Poems of Henry van Dyke*, copyright 1911 by

Charles Scribner's Sons, 1939 by Tertius Van Dyke; used by permission of the publishers. For quotation by Robert Falcon Scott from *Courage*, copyright 1932, Charles Scribner's Sons.

RALPH FLETCHER SEYMOUR for quotation from poem "Carpe Diem" by Anne Higginson Spicer.

SIMON AND SCHUSTER, INC. for quotations from *Wake Up and Live* by Dorothea Brande, copyright 1936, Simon & Schuster, Inc. For quotation from *Modern Arms and Free Men* by Vannevar Bush, copyright 1949 by the Trustees of the Vannevar Bush Trust. For quotation from *How to Stop Worrying and Start Living* by Dale Carnegie, copyright 1948, Simon & Schuster, Inc. For quotation from *Release from Nervous Tension* by David Harold Fink, copyright 1943, Simon & Schuster, Inc. For quotations from *Peace of Mind* by Joshua Loth Liebman, copyright 1946 by Joshua Loth Liebman. For quotation from *One World* by Wendell Willkie, copyright 1943 by Wendell Willkie.

ORA SEARLE for poem "Around the Corner" by Charles H. Towne, Appleton Century Crofts, Inc.; permission from Ora Searle.

ROBERT R. UPDEGRAFF for quotations from *Yours to Venture* by Robert R. Updegraff, copyright 1937 by Whittlesey House; permission of author.

UNITED NATIONS for Preamble of the United Nations Charter.

VIKING PRESS for quotation from *Candle in the Dark* by Irwin Edman, copyright 1939 by Irwin Edman; reprinted by permission of The Viking Press, N. Y.

RAY LYMAN WILBUR for quotations from address *Human Hopes* by Ray Lyman Wilbur at Stanford University, June 1937, Stanford University Press; permission of author.

WHITTLESEY HOUSE for quotation from *Life Begins at Forty* by Walter B. Pitkin, copyright 1932, Whittlesey House.

WILLIAM H. WISE & Co. for quotations by Elbert Hubbard from *Elbert Hubbard's Scrap Book*, by permission of William H. Wise & Co., publishers.

YALE UNIVERSITY PRESS for quotation from *A Common Faith* by John Dewey.

For
Richard and Anita

Every generation enjoys the use of a vast hoard bequeathed to it by antiquity, and transmits that hoard, augmented by fresh acquisitions, to future ages.   *Thomas Macaulay*

Nurture your mind with great thoughts. *Benjamin Disraeli*

We forfeit the chief source of dignity and sweetness in life . . . if we do not seek converse with the greater minds that have left their vestiges on the world. *James Martineau*

There are gems of thought that are ageless and eternal.
Cicero

Words are things, and a small drop of ink,
Falling like dew upon a thought, produces
That which makes thousands, perhaps millions, think.
Lord Byron

No man is wise enough by himself. *Plautus*

Most of us have collections of sayings we live by. . . . Whenever words fly up at me from the printed page as I read, I intercept them instantly, knowing they are for me. I turn them over carefully in my mind and cling to them hard. *David Grayson*

Who is a wise man? He who learns of all men. *Talmud*

It is not how much you know about life but how you live your life that counts. Those who can avoid mistakes by observing the mistakes of others are most apt to keep free from sorrow. In a world full of uncertainties, the record of what has gone before—human experience—is as sure and reliable as anything of which we know.
Ray Lyman Wilbur

The men who have gone before us have taught us how to live and how to die. We are the heirs of the ages.
Sidney Dark

"We are the heirs of the ages."

The manner in which one single ray of light, one single precious hint, will clarify and energize the whole mental life of him who receives it, is among the most wonderful and heavenly of intellectual phenomena.   *Arnold Bennett*

The glow of inspiration warms us; it is a holy rapture.
Ovid

The images of men's wits and knowledge remain in books. . . . They generate still, and cast their seeds in the minds of others, provoking and causing infinite actions and opinions in succeeding ages.   *Francis Bacon*

A word spoken in due season, how good it is.
Proverbs 15:23

Time is of no account with great thoughts. They are as fresh today as when they first passed through their authors' minds, ages ago.   *Samuel Smiles*

> Who can mistake great thoughts?
> They seize upon the mind; arrest and search,
> And shake it; bow the tall soul as by wind;
> Rush over it like a river over reeds.
> *Philip James Bailey*

If I can line up the people who, back through the ages, have gone at life in ways I greatly admire, then I can feel all their strength supporting me, all their standards and values pointing the way in which I am to go.
Bonaro W. Overstreet

TABLE OF CONTENTS

PART THREE

Courage & The Conquest of Fear 79

"The things courage can do!"
SIR JAMES M. BARRIE

PART FOUR
Confidence & Achievement

"Men were born to succeed, not to fail."
HENRY DAVID THOREAU

PART FIVE

Self-Discipline & The Development of Character 171

"A man's own character is the arbiter of his fortune."
SYRUS

PART SIX

Personality & Relationship to Others 197

"The art of pleasing requires only the desire."
LORD CHESTERFIELD

PART SEVEN
Peace of Heart and Mind 229

"Nothing can bring you peace but yourself."
RALPH WALDO EMERSON

PART EIGHT
Love & Family Life   257

*"To be happy at home is the ultimate result
of all ambition."*

SAMUEL JOHNSON

PART NINE
Contentment in Later Years   281

"It is magnificent to grow old, if one keeps young."
HARRY EMERSON FOSDICK

PART TEN
Hope for the Future   303

*"We are just at the beginning of progress
in every field of human endeavor."*
CHARLES F. KETTERING

INTRODUCTION

I

WE WHO *live today stand at the apex of a vast pyramid of
human development, slowly accumulated through the many
long struggling generations of the past. We are the heirs
of all that has ever been accomplished, all that man has
ever done to improve himself and the world in which he
lives. We are the heirs of all that man has ever dreamed,
thought out, fought and died for—all that he has eloquently written or expressed and left behind for the guidance
of future generations.*

*Today when we face what is probably the greatest chal-
lenge history has ever known—today when millions of
people are troubled, uncertain, and confused—the rich de-
posits of inspiration left by preceding generations take on
a new and vital significance. There has never been a time
when people were more desperately in need of faith and
hope, of courage and peace of mind, of standards and
ideals by which to live, and above all an abiding belief in
the future and in the progress of mankind. There has never
been a time when the tried and tested philosophies of the
past were more urgently needed to give perspective and
understanding—to give people something to cling to, something on which to build the strong, firm structure of their
own lives.*

*But where in the staggering wealth of ideas and ideals
that have come down from the past can you find exactly
the help, the guidance, and the inspiration you need today?
Where in the thousands upon thousands of books, papers,
and records which preserve and transmit the best that man
has ever written or spoken are you likely to find the words*

that can mean most to you now, that can have the greatest impact and influence on your daily life?

The purpose of Light from Many Lamps *is to help meet this need. It brings the highlights of man's enormous inspirational heritage within the compass of a single volume. Here is the winnowed best of the most brilliant and constructive thinking of all times, past and present, selected to meet the needs and problems of today. Here is a distillation of the greatest thoughts, ideas, and philosophies that have come down to us through the ages in an ever-widening stream of inspiration, from Aristotle to Emerson, from Plato to William James. Here is reading with a purpose, timely and provocative reading for these troubled times, guideposts to happier and more confident living—and to that inner peace and tranquillity for which so many are now searching.*

II

"Great men taken up in any _way_ are profitable company," says Thomas Carlyle. Light from Many Lamps *will bring you into contact with the great of every age and land, leaders in every field of human thought from ancient times to our own. You will encounter the immortals at their moments of highest inspiration. Buddha and Mohammed are here, Seneca and St. Paul, Horace and Dante. Names that will never die are here: Bacon, Goethe, Pope—Shakespeare, Voltaire—Amiel and Montaigne—Browning and Walt Whitman—all are here, the long shining caravan of the great, represented at their best.*

From the Analects *of Confucius and the* Meditations *of Marcus Aurelius; from the* Ethics *of Aristotle and the* Confessions *of St. Augustine; from the* Dialogues *of Plato and Cicero's* De Officiis; *from the sacred Bhagavad-Gita and the Upanishads, and from the Koran, Talmud, and Bible—from history, literature, biography, and scripture— have come the highlights of inspiring quotation that you will find in this book.*

But it is not from such classic sources alone that we have garnered the material which goes to make up Light from Many Lamps. *Quotations from letters and diaries are here, from articles and editorials, from sermons, speeches, and even songs. Selections were not made on the basis of literary excellence or beauty of expression, but solely on the basis of inspirational impact. Readers who wonder about the varied and diverse character of the selections, who question the proximity of such intellectual titans as Plato and Aristotle with, let us say, Elbert Hubbard and Henry Ford, should bear in mind that this is not a collection of literary masterpieces, nor is it by any means intended to be. It is, as its name signifies,* Light from Many Lamps— *inspiration from many and varied sources—a treasury of great truths and enduring ideas, reflecting the whole wide range of human thought.*

We have, of course, made every effort to maintain high literary standards throughout. We have tried, wherever possible, to make our selections from among the world's most beautiful and eloquent quotations. But we have not allowed ourselves to be unduly influenced by mere language or composition, or by the aura of fame and prestige surrounding an author's name. For as Ruskin says, "The highest thoughts are those least dependent on language." When people are profoundly moved, they do not necessarily speak with the eloquence of literature. What we have searched for, rather than mere beauty, have been "thoughts that breathe and words that burn"—words that have the power to ease the heart and lift the spirit, to encourage and sustain, to give hope, faith, and consolation. We have searched for words that "knock at the gates of the soul," that have a vital message or meaning for the reader.

Here, among the old classic favorites, you will find much that has never before appeared in any anthology. Here, among the rich grains of wisdom and philosophy that have survived through the centuries, you will find quotations from the writings and speeches of outstanding men and women of our own time. Many of the quotations are from ordinary human beings who have worked out a formula for happy, successful living, or who, at the end of a lifetime of thinking and analyzing, have expressed a single eloquent thought, ageless and compelling. In fact, some of the most helpful and inspiring passages in the book have come out of great moments in otherwise unremarkable lives.

But ancient or modern, eloquent or simple, all quotations have some bearing, in some way, on the tensions, conflicts, and anxieties of life today. All help the reader meet the challenge of the times . . . and the problems of his own personal life.

III

Samuel Johnson once said, "A man will turn over half a library to make one book." Several libraries were turned over, thousands of books and papers were searched, for the material that makes up Light from Many Lamps. *The search could go on endlessly, of course; sometimes words of rare inspirational value turn up in the most unexpected places . . . in the diaries of people long gone and forgotten, in old letters, moldering scrapbooks, even last wills and testaments! The research on so fascinating a subject as this could go on for a lifetime; but one must call a halt sometime, however regretfully.*

Obviously no book of this kind can ever be complete; nor can it be expected to please everyone. There may be selections you do not like, or with which you do not agree. Favorite quotations of your own may be missing, or there may be some you think more inspiring than those we have included. This cannot be helped. It would naturally be impossible to include everyone's favorites, or to use only material that is to every reader's liking and every reader's taste.

"All my life I have been building up my anthology," says David Grayson in Under My Elm. *"Whenever words fly up at me from the printed page as I read, I intercept them instantly, knowing they are for me. I turn them over carefully in my mind and cling to them hard."*

Here, too, you must intercept the words that "fly up" at you from the printed page. You must intercept what is meant for you and for your particular needs. If sometimes quotations appear contradictory, bear in mind that one viewpoint may help some people—another viewpoint may help others. All quotations stem from the highest moral and ethical values, or they would not be included; and each has something to offer someone. Light from Many Lamps *is not intended for any one special age group. There are selections to meet the needs of every age, just as there are selections to meet the needs of every mood and circumstance. It is a book of guidance and inspiration for the entire family.*

IV

Light from Many Lamps *is not a book to read through in one or two sittings. It is a book to keep at the bedside, or on the living-room table—a book to dip into as needed, to browse in now and then, to enjoy in small stimulating portions. It is a book for the hour, and for the years; a book to turn to over and over again, as to a friend; a book of moral, spiritual, and ethical guidance—an unfailing source of comfort and inspiration.*

The contents of Light from Many Lamps *"speak to your condition," as the Quakers say. You will find something here for every mood, every need. There are selections for the worried, the ailing, the bereaved—for the physically handicapped and emotionally disturbed—for those who have lost courage or faith—for those who have lost hope.*

The book has been planned for readers who need specific help along certain lines, and who want it when they need it, without searching for it. Every effort has been made to arrange the material in such form that the reader can find what he needs or wants at once. Arrangement is by sections, according to subject. For example, all quotations on courage are in one section. This section is divided into chapters on the different kinds of courage: courage to rise above the trials of life, courage to accept loss or defeat, courage to meet illness or disaster, courage to face danger or death, and so on. You should be able to find what you want as easily as looking up a word in a dictionary or thesaurus.

V

What makes this anthology different from others is the biographical data that give the origins of famous quotations, and tell what their influence has been on the lives and careers of others.

Light from Many Lamps *is therefore not only a treasury of the world's most inspiring thoughts and ideas but a collection of brief, stimulating biographies as well. This makes for what we hope you will find interesting reading throughout.*

VI

Here, then, is a treasury of inspiration from many sources and on many subjects . . . Light from Many Lamps.

We have, of course, like Montaigne, made "only a nosegay of culled flowers"—though we have brought to it much of our own in the interpretive biographical material. Our sincere hope is that you will enjoy reading and using this book as much as we have enjoyed preparing it.

We conclude wistfully with the words of Martin Luther: "Only a little of the first fruits of wisdom, only a few fragments of the boundless heights, breadths, and depths of truth, have I been able to gather."

Lillian Eichler Watson

PART ONE

HAPPINESS

&

The Enjoyment of Living

"Most folks are about as happy as they
make up their minds to be."

ABRAHAM LINCOLN

DOWN THROUGH THE CENTURIES men have sought to explain the meaning and the art of happiness. Millions upon millions of words have been written on the subject. Poets and priests, philosophers and scientists, teachers, preachers, and leaders of every age have sought to work out a simple formula for what Sir Philip Gibbs called "the eternal quest of mankind"—a happy and contented life.

For in the end happiness is what all people want, regardless of the many ways they may seek it. To be happy is the ultimate goal of all ambition, all endeavor, all hopes and plans. "Happiness is the meaning and the purpose of life, the whole aim and end of human existence," declared Aristotle, supreme philosopher of the ancient world.

But what is happiness? Clearly, it means vastly different things to different people. Since earliest times men have sought and found their happiness along amazingly divergent paths—in work, achievement, success, in love and family ties, in the affection of friends, in religion.

There is one point, however, on which philosophers in every age agree: true happiness stems from a quality within ourselves, from a way of thinking of life. Of all the millions of words written on happiness, this is the oldest and most enduring truth. If the principles of contentment are not within us, no material success, no pleasures or possessions, can make us happy.

This philosophy has been expounded by writers and thinkers since civilization began; but never more beautifully and effectively than in Maeterlinck's famous play, *The Blue Bird*. Tyltyl and Mytyl, the woodcutter's children, search far and wide for happiness, only to find it on their

3

return home. ("We went so far, and it was here all the time!") It isn't necessary to search for happiness in far places, says Maeterlinck in *The Blue Bird*. It is everywhere around you and about you. The quest for happiness is always in vain unless you can find it within yourself, within your own heart and soul.

"Very little is needed to make a happy life," wrote Marcus Aurelius in his immortal *Meditations*. "It is all within yourself, in your way of thinking."

Following are selections from what leading thinkers of all ages, from ancient times to the present, have said on the subject of happiness.

1. JOHN BURROUGHS

THE SECRET OF HAPPINESS IS
SOMETHING TO DO

THE POET stood at his window and watched a neighbor walk by. He walked—not as a man should, in joy and triumph—but with slow step and sagging shoulders, like a man with a great burden on his soul.

John Burroughs knew why. The man had no work he loved, nothing to keep him busy and content, to give his days purpose and direction.

"An idle man is a wretched man," he thought, listening to the shrill cacophony of the birds, to the soft whispering of the trees. Surely no one knew better than he the blessedness of work, of life-giving and life-sustaining work!

Had he not been idle himself once, and one of the most utterly dejected of God's creatures? Life had lost its savor for him, had become empty and stagnant; he couldn't eat or sleep, couldn't think or dream.

Work had saved him. Good hard work on a farm, with his hands, raking and hoeing, plowing and planting, feeling the good earth between his fingers . . . feeling his oneness with the universe.

The plow had done its perfect work on him, as on his fields. The bitterness and boredom had been plowed under, the stagnant pools of discontent drained off. The planting and pruning had shaped his life as surely as they had shaped his fruit trees. For seeing the rivers shine and dimple in the spring, watching the birds arrive and hearing their shrill, excited laughter, looking up from his work and seeing the skies and distant hills bathed in the magic of sudden beauty, he had found renewal and inspiration. He had found his life's work.

John Burroughs turned from the window, walked slowly to his desk. *Wake-Robin* had been the first of a series of books about birds, flowers, and rural scenes that had brought him world-wide recognition. But far more important, his poems and essays on out-of-door life had brought him joy and contentment.

If only he could make others realize that happiness was no elusive will-o'-the-wisp, that real happiness was the simplest thing in the world—and within reach of all! People all about him were reaching for happiness in hopeless ways, or, like the neighbor who had just walked by, were letting their lives empty into stagnant pools. He must try to make them realize that the secret of happiness was in work, congenial work, *something to do*. He picked up his pen and began to write:

There is a condition or circumstance that has a greater bearing upon the happiness of life than any other. What is it? . . . . It is one of the simplest things in the world and within reach of all. If this secret were something I could put up at auction, what a throng of bidders I should have, and what high ones! Only the wise ones can guess what it is. Some might say it is health, or money, or friends, or this or that possession, but you may have all these things and not be happy. You may have fame and power, and not be happy. I maintain there is one thing more necessary to a happy life than any other, though health and money and friends and home are all important. That one thing is—what? The sick man will say health; the poor man, wealth; the ambitious man, power; the scholar, knowledge; the overworked man, rest.

Without the one thing I have in mind, none of these things would long help their possessors to be happy. We could not long be happy without food or drink or clothes or shelter, but we may have all these things to perfection and still want the prime condition of happiness. It is often said that a contented mind is the first condition of happiness, but what is the first condition of a contented mind? You will be disappointed when I tell you what this all-important thing is—it is so common, so near at hand, and so many people have so much of it and yet are not happy. They have too much of it, or else the kind that is not best suited to them. What is the best thing for a stream? It is to keep moving. If it stops, it stagnates. So the best thing for man is that which keeps the currents going—the physical, the moral, and the intellectual currents. Hence the secret of happiness is—something to do; some congenial work. Take away the occupation of all men, and what a wretched world it would be!

Few persons realize how much of their happiness is dependent upon their work, upon the fact that they are kept busy and not left to feed upon themselves. Happiness comes most to persons who seek her least, and think least about it. It is not an object to be sought; it is a state to be induced. It must follow and not lead. It must overtake you, and not you overtake it. How important is health to happiness, yet the best promoter of health is *something to do.*

Blessed is the man who has some congenial work, some occupation in which he can put his heart, and which affords a complete outlet to all the forces there are in him.

It was out of the richness and fullness of his own life that John Burroughs wrote the above words.

Wake-Robin had awakened him to his own destiny, had shown him what he wished most to do in life. It was followed by *Birds and Poets, Locusts and Wild Honey, Signs and Seasons, The Ways of Nature*—books that made him the successor of Henry David Thoreau as America's most popular essayist on birds, plants, and animals.

Like so many others who lived the good life, Burroughs felt in later years the need to share his philosophy with others, to pass on his secret of happiness. "Keep the currents moving," he urged. "Don't let your life stagnate."

Today he is perhaps as well remembered for his reflections on happiness as he is for his poems and essays. The selection given here has been quoted so many times it would be impossible to calculate its influence—an influence that increases with every reprinting.

> The grand essentials to happiness in this life are something to do, something to love, and something to hope for.   *Joseph Addison*

> Work and thou canst not escape the reward; whether thy work be fine or coarse, planting corn or writing epics, so only it be honest work, done to thine own approbation, it shall earn a reward to the senses as well as to the thought. No matter how often defeated, you are born to victory. The reward of a thing well done is to have done it.   *Ralph Waldo Emerson*

> Happiness, I have discovered, is nearly always a rebound from hard work. It is one of the follies of men to imagine that they can enjoy mere thought, or emotion, or sentiment. As well try to eat beauty! For happiness must be tricked! She loves to see men at work. She loves sweat, weariness, self-sacrifice. She will be found not in palaces but lurking in cornfields and factories and hovering over littered desks; she crowns the unconscious head of the busy child. If you look up suddenly from hard work you will see her, but if you look too long she fades sorrowfully away.
> There is something fine in hard physical labor. . . . One actually stops thinking. I often work long without any thought whatever, so far as I know, save that connected with the monotonous repetition of the labor itself—down with the spade, out with it, up with it, over with it—and repeat.
> And yet sometimes—mostly in the forenoon when I am not at all tired—I will suddenly have a sense as of the world opening around me—a sense of its beauty and its meanings—giving me a peculiar deep happiness, that is near complete content.   *David Grayson*

The mintage of wisdom is to know that rest is rust, and that real life is in love, laughter, and work.

Elbert Hubbard

To awaken each morning with a smile brightening my face; to greet the day with reverence for the opportunities it contains; to approach my work with a clean mind; to hold ever before me, even in the doing of little things, the Ultimate Purpose toward which I am working; to meet men and women with laughter on my lips and love in my heart; to be gentle, kind, and courteous through all the hours; to approach the night with weariness that ever woos sleep and the joy that comes from work well done—this is how I desire to waste wisely my days.   *Thomas Dekker*

Thank God every morning when you get up that you have something to do which must be done, whether you like it or not. Being forced to work, and forced to do your best, will breed in you temperance, self-control, diligence, strength of will, content, and a hundred other virtues which the idle never know.

Charles Kingsley

2. SENECA

TRUE HAPPINESS IS TO REST
SATISFIED WITH WHAT WE HAVE

LUCIUS ANNAEUS SENECA was a man of many talents. He was a poet, dramatist, orator, statesman, and one of the greatest of the Stoic philosophers. He was also one of the best-read men in Rome.

At the moment he was thoroughly enjoying the fables of a Greek slave named Aesop who was said to have lived at the court of Croesus six centuries ago. They were quaint little stories, about animals mostly—but each with a moral truth concealed in its penetrating nonsense. A pity more people couldn't read, he thought. There were some good lessons to be learned here.

Suddenly his attention was caught by a single phrase: "Be content with your lot; one cannot be first in everything." Why, that was almost exactly what *he* had written yesterday in his essay on happiness! He got it out and found the sentence: *A wise man is content with his lot, whatever it be.* Without realizing it, he had paraphrased the Greek storyteller!

But many others had said the same thing in almost the same way, he reflected. Cicero, for example, had said, "To be content with what we possess is the greatest and most secure of riches." And before Cicero, Epicurus had said it in still another way: "If thou wilt make a man happy, add not unto his riches but take away from his desires."

He read over what he had written the day before and found it good. It was what he wanted to say.

> True happiness is to understand our duties toward God and man; to enjoy the present, without anxious dependence upon the future; not to amuse ourselves

with either hopes or fears, but to rest satisfied with what we have, which is abundantly sufficient; for he that is so wants nothing. The great blessings of mankind are within us, and within our reach; but we shut our eyes and, like people in the dark, fall foul of the very thing we search for without finding it. Tranquillity is a certain equality of mind which no condition of fortune can either exalt or depress.

There must be sound mind to make a happy man; there must be constancy in all conditions, a care for the things of this world but without anxiety; and such an indifference to the bounties of fortune that either with them or without them we may live content. True joy is serene. . . . The seat of it is within, and there is no cheerfulness like the resolution of a brave mind that has fortune under its feet. It is an invincible greatness of mind not to be elevated or dejected with good or ill fortune. A wise man is content with his lot, whatever it be—without wishing for what he has not.

The times in which Seneca lived were turbulent and exciting, as are all periods of change and transition. It was the first century of a great new era, a time rich in hope and promise. But it was also a time of moral laxity, of political corruption, of cruelty and greed.

Seneca preached against the errors and evils of his day, against selfishness, greed, and pride. He stressed the more enduring values of life: courage, moderation, self-control—above all, the peace of a contented mind.

In the end his death, like that of Socrates, was an inspiring testament to his own integrity. Falsely accused by Nero of conspiracy and ordered to take his own life, he turned to his weeping family and friends and gently reminded them they must accept with courage that which it was not in their power to control. Refused the right to make a will, he said he would leave them the best thing he had: the pattern of his life.

Seneca wrote for his own uneasy times; but his voice has been heard in all the centuries since. Even now, nineteen hundred years after he lived and wrote, troubled minds find

comfort in his philosophy: *"Do the best you can . . . enjoy
the present . . . rest satisfied with what you have."*

I have learned, in whatsoever state I am in, therewith
to be content.   *Philippians 4:11*

He is a wise man who does not grieve for the things
which he has not, but rejoices for those which he has.
                                                Epictetus

Let not your mind run on what you lack as much as
on what you have already. Of the things you have,
select the best; and then reflect how eagerly they
would have been sought if you did not have them.
                                            Marcus Aurelius

Before we set our hearts too much upon anything, let
us examine how happy they are who already possess
it.   *François de La Rochefoucauld*

Joy of life seems to me to arise from a sense of being
where one belongs . . . of being four-square with the
life we have chosen. All the discontented people I
know are trying sedulously to be something they are
not, to do something they cannot do. . . .
Contentment, and indeed usefulness, comes as the in-
fallible result of great acceptances, great humilities—
of not trying to make ourselves this or that (to con-
form to some dramatized version of ourselves), but of
surrendering ourselves to the fullness of life—of letting life flow through us.   *David Grayson*

The secret of contentment is the discovery by every
man of his own powers and limitations, finding satisfaction in a line of activity which he can do well, plus
the wisdom to know that his place, no matter how
important or successful he is, never counts very much
in the universe. A man may very well be so successful
in carving a name for himself in his field that he begins to imagine himself indispensable or omnipotent.

He is eaten up by some secret ambition, and then good-bye to all contentment. Sometimes it is more important to discover what one cannot do than what one can do. So much restlessness is due to the fact that a man does not know what he wants, or he wants too many things, or perhaps he wants to be somebody else, to be anybody except himself. The courage of being one's genuine self, of standing alone and of not wanting to be somebody else!   *Lin Yutang*

3. W. BERAN WOLFE

TO FIND HAPPINESS WE MUST SEEK FOR IT IN A FOCUS OUTSIDE OURSELVES

THE ROOM was empty, except for the man who sat writing. But for him it was filled with people and with voices.

"Help me or I'll commit suicide!" ... *"What's the use of it all?"* ... *"I'm lonely, doctor"* ... *"I hate my job!"* ... *"I have no time for friends."*

W. Beran Wolfe had just passed his thirtieth birthday. He was young, as psychiatrists go; but he was old with the agonies of other people. He thought of the men and women who had come to him for help—the bitter and frightened, the anguished and confused—all of them desperately unhappy, and all of them seeking some tranquil adjustment to life.

His mind turned to Epictetus, a humble Greek slave in Nero's Rome, lame and poor but serenely content. "If a man is unhappy," wrote Epictetus, "remember that his unhappiness is his own fault; for God has made all men to be happy."

How true that is, the young psychiatrist reflected. People are unhappy because they look inward instead of outward. They think too much about themselves instead of things outside themselves. They worry too much about what they lack—about circumstances they cannot change—about things they feel they must *have* or must *be* before they can lead full and satisfying lives.

But happiness is not in having or being; it is in *doing*. That was a point he must emphasize and make clear in this book he was writing. Almost every human being could be happier at once if he realized this basic truth and accepted it.

He thought again of those ghostly malcontents, crowding

14

the corners of his room. Most of them had one trait in common: a selfish concept of life. Absorbed in their own interests and desires, they failed in their human relationships, and so created their own unhappiness. He must make them realize that the only ambition consistent with happiness is the ambition to do things with and for others—that the only way to find happiness is to look for it in a focus outside themselves.

He glanced again at the last three words he had written: *"What is happiness?"* There was no hesitation now; he knew what he wanted to say. The words came swiftly as he began to write.

If we want to know what happiness is we must seek it, not as if it were a pot of gold at the end of the rainbow, but among human beings who are living richly and fully the good life. If you observe a really happy man you will find him building a boat, writing a symphony, educating his son, growing double dahlias in his garden. He will not be searching for happiness as if it were a collar button that has rolled under the radiator. He will have become aware that he is happy in the course of living twenty-four crowded hours of the day.

Just as no one can be happy in work which is centered entirely about his own person and deals exclusively with the satisfaction of his own immediate needs, so no one can be entirely happy in social relations which focus only in himself and his immediate and narrow sphere of influence. To find happiness we must seek for it in a focus outside ourselves. . . .

If you live only for yourself you are always in immediate danger of being bored to death with the repetition of your own views and interests. It matters little, for psychological purposes, whether you interest yourself in making your town cleaner, or enlist in a campaign to rid your city of illicit narcotics, or whether you go in for boys' clubs. Choose a movement that presents a distinct trend toward greater human happiness and align yourself with it. No one has learned the meaning of living until he has surrendered his ego to the service of his fellow men.

If you pride yourself on your ambition, take a mental inventory of its ends, and ask yourself whether you desire to attain those personal ends and forgo the opportunities of being happy, or whether you prefer to be happy and forgo some of the prestige that your unfulfilled inferiority complex seems to demand. If your ambition has the momentum of an express train at full speed, if you can no longer stop your mad rush for glory, power, or intellectual supremacy, try to divert your energies into socially useful channels before it is too late. ...

For those who seek the larger happiness and the greater effectiveness open to human beings there can be but one philosophy of life, the philosophy of constructive altruism. The truly happy man is always a fighting optimist. Optimism includes not only altruism but also social responsibility, social courage and objectivity. Men and women who are compensating for their feelings of inferiority in terms of social service, men and women who are vigorously affirming life, facing realities like adults, meeting difficulties with stoicism, men and women who combine knowledge with kindliness, who spice their sense of humor with the zest of living—in a word, complete human beings—are to be found only in this category. The good life demands a working philosophy of active philanthropy as an orientating map of conduct. This is the golden way of life. This is the satisfying life. This is the way to be happy though human.

The career of Dr. W. Beran Wolfe was tragically short. He died at thirty-five, having in his brief lifetime helped many to a better knowledge and understanding of themselves, and to a happier way of life.

That influence continues, perpetuated by the book which grew out of his practice and is based on his experience with unhappy, maladjusted people. The paragraphs above are the most frequently quoted, for they embody his basic philosophy: that the way to find happiness is not in the possession of material things or even in personal accomplishment, but in doing things with and for others.

"Almost every human being can be happier than he is," wrote W. Beran Wolfe one evening in the quiet of his study. To those who desperately need such reassurance, his words bring the promise of hope and fulfillment. They have the same enduring quality as that famous phrase from Epictetus, as inspiring today as it ever was—"God has made all men to be happy."

Unless we think of others and do something for them, we miss one of the greatest sources of happiness.
Ray Lyman Wilbur

To me there is in happiness an element of self-forgetfulness. You lose yourself in something outside yourself when you are happy; just as when you are desperately miserable you are intensely conscious of yourself, are a solid little lump of ego weighing a ton.
J. B. Priestley

There is no happiness in having or in getting, but only in giving.
Henry Drummond

I believe the root of all happiness on this earth to lie in the realization of a spiritual life with a consciousness of something wider than materialism; in the capacity to live in a world that makes you unselfish because you are not overanxious about your personal place; that makes you tolerant because you realize your own comic fallibilities; that gives you tranquillity without complacency because you believe in something so much larger than yourself. *Sir Hugh Walpole*

Happiness is a perfume you cannot pour on others without getting a few drops on yourself.
Ralph Waldo Emerson

4. WILLIAM S. OGDON

HAPPINESS CANNOT BE BOUGHT; INDEED, MONEY HAS VERY LITTLE TO DO WITH IT

HIGH in the *Times* Building, which towers like a beacon above one of the busiest corners in the world, a newspaperman sat at his desk. Just being in this office again, hearing the busy clack of the typewriters, feeling a part of the pulsating life of a great newspaper, was sheer bliss. *William S. Ogdon was home.* He was a civilian again, in newspaper work again ... and he was happy.

In Hawaii, in Guam, through all those lonely months in the Pacific, William Ogdon had dreamed of New York, and of the blessings and comforts of life in the United States. A man gets to know what he misses when he is away from it. Nowhere in the world were people surrounded by so many opportunities and advantages. Nowhere in the world today could people be so happy and secure.

That is how he felt, returning to America. And he had expected to find his own intense feelings of pride and contentment reflected in others. He was astonished to find anger and bitterness instead, to hear grumblings and complaints on every side. People had lost sight of their many blessings. They were uneasy and insecure, without faith in the future of the country, and apparently without confidence in themselves. The whole emphasis seemed to be on material things, on money and the things money can buy, on higher wages and shorter working hours, on personal gain instead of personal qualities and achievements.

The sounds of street traffic came to him, muted and gentle, reminding him of the great city below. All about him were the sharper overtones of typing and talking, the shrill ringing of the telephone.

He thought of the phrases that were being bandied about. "What's the country coming to?" . . . "No such thing as security any more!" . . . "Why doesn't the government do something about it?"

Didn't they realize, these cynical disgruntled ones, that happiness was not something that could be arranged officially—that it was not something people could hand them, or that they could buy for themselves? Didn't they realize they must hew out their own destiny and fulfillment, *make their own happiness?*

He had a column to write for "Topics of the Times." Why not make this his subject? If there were ever a time to remind people of their blessings and urge them to stand on their own feet, this was it!

He took out a sheet of paper and put it into his typewriter.

There was never a time when so much official effort was being expended to produce happiness, and probably never a time when so little attention was paid by the individual to creating the personal qualities that make for it. What one misses most today is the evidence of widespread personal determination to develop a character that will in itself, given any reasonable odds, make for happiness. Our whole emphasis is on the reform of living conditions, of increased wages, of controls on the economic structure —the government approach—and so little on man improving himself.

The ingredients of happiness are so simple that they can be counted on one hand. Happiness comes from within, and rests most securely on simple goodness and clear conscience. Religion may not be essential to it, but no one is known to have gained it without a philosophy resting on ethical principles. Selfishness is its enemy; to make another happy is to be happy one's self. It is quiet, seldom found for long in crowds, most easily won in moments of solitude and reflection. It cannot be bought; indeed, money has very little to do with it.

No one is happy unless he is reasonably well satisfied with himself, so that the quest for tranquillity must of necessity begin with self-examination. We shall not often be content with what we discover in this scrutiny. There is so much to do, and so little done. Upon this searching self-analysis, however, depends the discovery of those qualities that make each man unique, and whose development alone can bring satisfaction.

Of all those who have tried, down the ages, to outline a program for happiness, few have succeeded so well as William Henry Channing, chaplain of the House of Representatives in the middle of the last century:

"To live content with small means; to seek elegance rather than luxury, and refinement rather than fashion; to be worthy . . . to study hard, think quietly, talk gently, act frankly; listen to the stars and birds, to babes and sages, with open heart; to bear all cheerfully, do all bravely, await occasions, hurry never; in a word to let the spiritual, unbidden and unconscious, grow up through the common."

It will be noted that no government can do this for you; you must do it for yourself.

William Ogdon's column appeared on the editorial page of *The New York Times* on December 30, 1945, under the title "The Art of Happiness." The response was immediate and unmistakable. Letters began to pour in; and it was soon apparent that readers had found something unusually helpful and stimulating in Mr. Ogdon's message.

The truth is that people *needed* a reminder like "The Art of Happiness." They needed to be told that greed and selfishness destroy peace of mind, and that those who seek happiness in material things rarely find it. It took the wholesome perspective of a newspaperman who had been away from his desk for four years, who could see through the tensions and confusions of the times to the basic and lasting values of life, to help others see straight and think clearly again.

"The Art of Happiness" has a quality of truth and sincerity that keeps it alive. It has been reprinted many times since its first appearance as a newspaper column; and it has helped many achieve a happier, more tranquil way of life.

Much happiness is overlooked because it doesn't cost anything.

What a man *is* contributes much more to his happiness than what he *has*. . . .
What a man is in himself, what accompanies him when he is alone, what no one can give him or take away, is obviously more essential to him than everything he has in the way of possessions, or even what he may be in the eyes of the world.
Arthur Schopenhauer

Money may buy the husk of things, but not the kernel. It brings you food but not appetite, medicine but not health, acquaintances but not friends, servants but not faithfulness, days of joy but not peace or happiness.
Henrik Ibsen

The greedy search for money or success will almost always lead men into unhappiness. Why? Because that kind of life makes them depend upon things outside themselves.
André Maurois

Man cannot live by bread alone. The making of money, the accumulation of material power, is not all there is to living. Life is something more than these, and the man who misses this truth misses the greatest joy and satisfaction that can come into his life—service for others.
Edward Bok

It's good to have money and the things that money can buy, but it's good, too, to check up once in a while and make sure you haven't lost the things that money can't buy.
George Horace Lorimer

5. WILLIAM LYON PHELPS

HOW ESSENTIAL IT IS . . . TO BE ABLE TO
LIVE INSIDE A MIND WITH ATTRACTIVE
AND INTERESTING PICTURES ON THE
WALLS

WILLIAM LYON PHELPS was nearing the end of a long and successful career. As writer, critic, lecturer, and for many years one of Yale's most popular professors, he had helped guide the lives and destinies of countless young people who had come under his influence. Now he had been asked to write a message for the families of America, a message of guidance and inspiration for all people, of every age and in every circumstance—a message out of the wisdom and fullness of his own rich life—to help them achieve happiness and contentment.

Professor Phelps thought back over the years. By far the best definition of happiness he had ever heard was in his senior year at college. He had never forgotten that eloquent address by President Timothy Dwight. . . . He was so young and ambitious then, and so uncertain. How eagerly he had listened to every word, hoping to find in President Dwight's message some magic talisman, some simple basic ideal by which to live and by which to guide his future!

And he had. Even now, a lifetime later, he could still see President Dwight as he had looked that day on the platform, could almost hear the timbre and reflection of his voice. One sentence stood out above all others in that long address, had burned itself indelibly on his memory: *"The happiest person is the person who thinks the most interesting thoughts."*

Through all the years that followed, that sentence had stayed with him, helping to shape his life and his ambitions —helping to keep his sights and standards high. It came to

mean more and more as time went on, and as he more
fully realized its significance. It influenced his entire career
as an educator, and through him influenced the life patterns of many others.

Real happiness is not dependent on external things, he
taught his students. *The pond is fed from within. The kind
of happiness that stays with you is the happiness that
springs from inward thoughts and emotions. You must
think of this now, while you are young. You must cultivate
your mind if you wish to achieve enduring happiness. You
must furnish your mind with interesting thoughts and ideas.
For an empty mind grows bored and cannot endure itself.
An empty mind seeks pleasure as a substitute for happiness.*

Professor Phelps thought again of the article he had
been asked to write, a message of guidance and inspiration
for the families of America. Looking back over the years,
he could think of no better message than the simple basic
philosophy by which he himself had lived and which had
served him so well—the philosophy so memorably expressed in that single sentence by Professor Dwight: "The
happiest person is the person who thinks the most interesting thoughts." He took up his pen and began to write:

No matter what may be one's nationality, sex, age,
philosophy, or religion, everyone wishes either to become or to remain happy. Hence definitions of happiness are interesting. One of the best was given in
my senior year at college by President Timothy
Dwight: "The happiest person is the person who
thinks the most interesting thoughts."

This definition places happiness where it belongs—
within and not without. The principle of happiness
should be like the principle of virtue: it should not
be dependent on things, but be a part of personality. . . .

If the happiest person is the person who thinks the
most interesting thoughts we are bound to grow
happier as we advance in years, because our minds
have more and more interesting thoughts. A well-

ordered life is like climbing a tower; the view halfway up is better than the view from the base, and it steadily becomes finer as the horizon expands.

Herein lies the real value of education. Advanced education may or may not make men and women more efficient; but it enriches personality, increases the wealth of the mind, and hence brings happiness. It is the finest insurance against old age, against the growth of physical disability, against the lack and loss of animal delights. No matter how many there may be in our family, no matter how many friends we may have, we are in a certain sense forced to lead a lonely life, because we have all the days of our existence to live with ourselves. How essential it is, then, in youth to acquire some intellectual or artistic tastes, in order to furnish the mind, to be able to live inside a mind with attractive and interesting pictures on the walls.

William Lyon Phelps's philosophy of happiness was originally published as a magazine article (later reprinted in his book, *Happiness,* published by E. P. Dutton & Co.) and has been reprinted many times since, in many forms. It has become a classic on the art of happiness, and is one of the best known and most frequently quoted essays on the subject. Only a small part of it has been quoted here; but this familiar excerpt gives the gist of Phelps's philosophy, and is generally considered to be one of the most interesting and important parts of the essay.

Biographers tell us that the influence of Professor Phelps's personality on his students was greater even than the influence of his writings. That may have been true in his lifetime; but surely today his essay on happiness must be considered one of his most vital and far-reaching influences. For though the beloved professor's voice is stilled, this message continues to guide and inspire countless young men and women. It remains an enduring monument to the great educator who believed that the more *interesting* life is, the *happier* it is . . . and that therefore the happiest people are those who cultivate their minds and think the most interesting thoughts.

Learning is an ornament in prosperity, a refuge in adversity, and a provision in old age.   *Aristotle*

The more a man finds his sources of pleasure in himself, the happier he will be. . . .
The highest, most varied and lasting pleasures are those of the mind.   *Arthur Schopenhauer*

They are never alone that are accompanied with noble thoughts.   *Sir Philip Sidney*

When we cannot find contentment in ourselves, it is useless to seek it elsewhere.
François de La Rochefoucauld

What is without us has no connection with happiness, only so far as the preservation of our lives and health depends upon it. . . . Happiness springs immediately from the mind.   *Benjamin Franklin*

He most lives who thinks most, who feels the noblest, and who acts the best.   *Philip James Bailey*

6. FREDERIC LOOMIS

ENJOY YOURSELF—IT IS LATER
THAN YOU THINK

FOR TWENTY-ONE years Dr. Frederic Loomis had been a busy obstetrician and gynecologist. For twenty-one years he had patiently listened to worried young wives, quieted their fears, given them comfort and advice—and delivered their babies. A kindly and understanding man, he had so completely devoted himself to his patients and their problems that there had been little time for a life of his own. His world, in his own words, "revolved around sex as a pivot, with love as the motive power, and with both happiness and fear as constant companions."

In 1938 Dr. Loomis came to an important decision. The time had come to retire, and to meditate on the many things he had learned in his twenty-one years of practice. He put aside his forceps and took up his pen. And one of the first things he wrote was "In a Chinese Garden"—the story of a letter that completely changed his way of life, and which has since changed the lives of many others in all parts of the world.

I have told many times the story of a certain letter, which I received years ago, because the impression it made on me was very deep. And I have never told it, on ships in distant seas or by quiet firesides nearer home, without a reflective, thoughtful response from those around me. The letter:

Peking, China

Dear Doctor:
Please don't be too surprised in getting a letter from

me. I am signing only my first name. My surname is the same as yours.

You won't even remember me. Two years ago I was in your hospital under the care of another doctor. I lost my baby the day it was born.

That same day my doctor came in to see me, and as he left he said, "Oh, by the way, there is a doctor here with the same name as yours who noticed your name on the board, and asked me about you. He said he would like to come in to see you, because you might be a relative. I told him you had lost your baby and I didn't think you would want to see anybody, but it was all right with me."

And then in a little while you came in. You put your hand on my arm and sat down for a moment beside my bed. You didn't say much of anything but your eyes and your voice were kind and pretty soon I felt better. As you sat there I noticed that you looked tired and that the lines in your face were very deep. I never saw you again but the nurses told me you were in the hospital practically night and day.

This afternoon I was a guest in a beautiful Chinese home here in Peking. The garden was enclosed by a high wall, and on one side, surrounded by twining red and white flowers, was a brass plate about two feet long. I asked someone to translate the Chinese characters for me. They said:

ENJOY YOURSELF
IT IS LATER THAN YOU THINK

I began to think about it for myself. I had not wanted another baby because I was still grieving for the one I lost. But I decided that moment that I should not wait any longer. Perhaps it may be later than I think, too.

And then, because I was thinking of my baby, I thought of you and the tired lines in your face, and the moment of sympathy you gave me when I so needed it. I don't know how old you are but I am quite sure you are old enough to be my father; and I know that those few minutes you spent with me meant little or nothing to you of course—but they meant a great deal to a woman who was desperately unhappy.

So I am so presumptuous as to think that in turn I can do something for you too. Perhaps for you it is later than you think. Please forgive me, but when your work is over, on the day you get my letter, please sit down very quietly, all by yourself, and think about it.

Marguerite

Usually I sleep very well when I am not disturbed by the telephone, but that night I woke a dozen times seeing the brass plate in the Chinese wall. I called myself a silly old fool for being disturbed by a letter from a woman I couldn't even remember, and dismissed the thing from my mind; and before I knew it I found myself saying again to myself: "Well, maybe it *is* later than you think; why don't you do something about it?"

I went to my office next morning and told them I was going away for three months.

It is a wholesome experience for any man who thinks he is important in his own organization to step out for a few months. The first time I went away on a long trip, some years before this letter came, I felt sure that everything would go to pieces, even though I had an entirely competent associate. When I returned I found there were just as many patients as when I left, everyone had recovered just as fast or faster, and most of my patients did not even know I had been away. It is humiliating to find how quickly and completely one's place is filled, but it is a very good lesson.

I telephoned to Shorty, a retired colonel who was perhaps my closest friend, and asked him to come to my office. On his arrival I told him that I wanted him to go home and pack a grip and come on down to

South America with me. He replied that he would
like to but that he had so much to attend to in the
next few months that it was out of the question to be
away for even a week.

I read him the letter. He shook his head. "I can't
go," he said. "Of course I'd like to, but for weeks
now I've been waiting to close a deal. I'm sorry, old
man, but maybe sometime—sometime—" his words
came more slowly. "What was that thing again that
woman said? 'It is later than you think'? Well—"

He sat quietly for a moment. Neither of us spoke.
I could almost see the balance swaying as he weighed
the apparent demands of the present against the rela-
tively few years each of us still had to live, exactly as
I had the night before.

At last he spoke. "I waited three months for those
people to make up their minds. I am not going to
wait any longer. They can wait for me now. When
would you like to go?"

We went to South America. We spent day after
day at sea on a comfortable freighter, feeling our
burdens slip off with the miles and our tired bodies
being made over by the winds that swept across the
Pacific from China. In the course of time we found
ourselves in one of the great cities of South America.
By good fortune, we were entertained by one of the
prominent men of the country, a man who had built
enormous steel plants and whose industries were
growing rapidly.

During the visit Shorty asked our host if he played
golf. He replied: "Señor, I play a little, I would like
to play more. My wife is on a vacation in the United
States with our children. I would like to join her. I
have beautiful horses here which I would love to ride.
I can do none of these things because I am too busy.
I am fifty-five years old and in five years more I shall
stop. It is true I said the same thing five years ago, but
I did not know how much we should be growing. We
are building a new plant; we are making steel such
as South America has never known. I cannot let go

even for an afternoon of golf. My office boy has
better leisure."

"Señor," I said, "do you know why I am in South
America?"

"Because," he said, "because perhaps you had not
too much to do and had the necessary time and
money to permit it."

"No," I replied, "I had a great deal to do and I did
not have too much of either time or money. We are
sitting here on your lovely terrace because a few
weeks ago a girl whom I wouldn't know if I saw her
looked at a brass plate in a Chinese wall in the city
of Peking in the heart of China."

I told him the story. Like Shorty, he made me repeat the words: "Enjoy yourself, it is later than you
think." During the rest of the afternoon he seemed a
bit preoccupied.

The next morning I met him in the corridor of our
hotel. "Doctor," he said, "please wait a moment. I
have not slept well. It is strange, is it not, that a
casual acquaintance, which you would say yourself
you are, could change the current of a very busy life?
I have thought long and hard since I saw you yesterday. I have cabled my wife that I am coming."

He put his hand on my shoulder. "It was a very
long finger indeed," he said, "that wrote those words
on the garden wall in China."

Many years have been added to the average ex-
pectation of life but each individual's fate is still a
hazard. The most valuable people around us have
lived largely for others. This seems the time to remind them that they will have more years, and happier ones, to do good for others if they start right
now to do something for themselves; to go places and
to do things which they have looked forward to for
years; to give those who love them the happiness of
seeing them enjoy some of the rewards which they
have earned; to replace competition with a bit of
contemplation.

The "Shorty" in this story, strong and well a few weeks ago, has gone to his reward. I spent the last hours at his bedside. Over and over again he said, "Fred, I am so happy that we went to South America together. I thank God we did not wait too long."

This, then, is the message of the brass plate in the Chinese garden—that perhaps for each of us it is *later than we think*.

"In a Chinese Garden" is a true story. It is taken without change from a book called *The Bond Between Us*,* a collection of human-interest stories based on the experiences of Dr. Loomis in his practice.

No one was more astonished than the doctor himself at the almost instant, widespread response to this story. Apparently there were many who felt the need for just such a timely, provocative message. Letters came from all over the country telling of lives suddenly reappraised and redirected, of worries and tensions relaxed, of vacations taken for the first time in years. Requests came in a flood from clubs and societies for Dr. Loomis to appear and tell the story in person. It was reprinted in the *Reader's Digest* and dozens of other publications, and continued to give evidence of its enormous appeal to readers. Finally the demand became so great that it was published as a separate book; and foreign editions carried its vital message to all parts of the world: *"Enjoy yourself—it is later than you think."*

Many have said the same thing, in many different ways, but few with the far-reaching effect of Dr. Frederic Loomis. The story of the unexpected letter from China, how it altered his way of life and reached out to influence the lives of those about him, has become an inspirational classic. A simple, human story, charged with emotion, it has made countless men and women look to the future with suddenly altered vision, has encouraged them to put

* Dr. Loomis's two books of reminiscences, *The Bond Between Us* and *Consultation Room,* and also a separate gift edition of *In a Chinese Garden,* are published by the Loomis Book Co., Piedmont, Cal.

aside their burdens for a while and enjoy themselves . . .
before it is too late.

Men spend their lives in anticipations, in determining
to be vastly happy at some period or other, when
they have time. But the present time has one advantage over every other: it is our own.

Charles C. Colton

Engrossed late and soon in professional cares, getting
and spending, you may so lay waste your powers
that you may find, too late, with hearts given away,
that there is no place in your habit-stricken souls
for those gentler influences which make your life
worth living. *Sir William Osler*

It is the part of a little soul, buried under the weight
of business, not to be able to get clean away from it
—to lay it aside and take it up again. . . .
Make use of life while you have it. Whether you have
lived enough depends upon yourself, not on the number of your years. *Michel de Montaigne*

If we are ever to enjoy life, now is the time—not tomorrow, nor next year, nor in some future life after
we have died. The best preparation for a better life
next year is a full, complete, harmonious, joyous life
this year. Our beliefs in a rich future life are of little
importance unless we coin them into a rich present
life. Today should always be our most wonderful day.

Thomas Dreier

One important source of unhappiness is the habit of
putting off living to some fictional future date. Men
and women are constantly making themselves unhappy because in deferring their lives to the future
they lose sight of the present and its golden opportunities for rich living. *W. Beran Wolfe*

Life, we learn too late, is in the living, in the tissue of each day and hour.   *Stephen Leacock*

One of the most tragic things I know about human nature is that all of us tend to put off living. We are all dreaming of some magical rose garden over the horizon—instead of enjoying the roses that are blooming outside our windows today.   *Dale Carnegie*

PART TWO

FAITH

&

Inner Calm

"Without faith a man can do nothing; with
it all things are possible."

SIR WILLIAM OSLER

MOST OF US in our passage through life, whether we are religious or not, experience what Beatrice Webb called "a yearning for the mental security of a spiritual home." We need the inner resources that give hope, strength, and peace of soul. We need a spiritual philosophy to help us meet the problems of life, to see us through the dark hours that inevitably come to us all.

"Man must be arched and buttressed from within, else the temple wavers to the dust," wrote Marcus Aurelius eighteen hundred years ago.

With faith a man is never alone, never forsaken. In illness, trouble, danger, despair, he is not alone. Faith gives him help and guidance; faith gives him comfort and peace.

"Every sort of energy and endurance, of courage and capacity for handling life's evils, is set free in those who have religious faith," said William James.

Here you will find beautiful and inspiring expressions of faith—words of comfort, guidance, and help from men and women whose lives were invested with deep spiritual values.

1. RICHARD E. BYRD

I COULD FEEL NO DOUBT OF MAN'S
ONENESS WITH THE UNIVERSE. . . .
IT WAS A FEELING THAT TRANSCENDED
REASON; THAT WENT TO THE HEART
OF A MAN'S DESPAIR AND FOUND IT
GROUNDLESS

ALL OVER the world people were talking, laughing, dining together, sharing experiences. But here, on the vast glistening immensity of Ross Barrier, there was only one man. One man, *alone* . . . alone with the wind and snow and cold, with the silence and the emptiness.

Richard E. Byrd stood for a moment watching the great waves of snow wheeling and rolling across the Barrier, vanishing into the sky. It was so cold he could see his breath crystallize in the air. He had meant to return almost at once to the comparative warmth and comfort of his shack, buried in the icecap. But something kept him standing there—listening, watching.

It was the Antarctic winter of 1934. He had come to this bleak icy shelf between Little America and the South Pole to obtain scientific data, to observe and report on polar meteorology. But he had also wanted to be by himself for a while, to be physically and spiritually on his own. He wanted to think things out in quiet and solitude, "to sink roots into some replenishing philosophy." He felt the need and desire to *believe*.

He stood, that afternoon, looking out over the Barrier, feeling its beauty and its power. He listened to the stillness, filling that vast brooding space with mystery. He thought of the orderly swing of the planets in their orbit, the everlasting movement of the constellations across the sky, the steady rhythmic change of the seasons. And he thought

38

how all these things went together, how they showed a master's touch.

"I had never known such utter quiet," he wrote later in his diary.

And suddenly, standing there alone on the Barrier, the quiet flooded in and engulfed him . . . and for an instant he was part of it, part of the silence, the space, and the harmony. For an instant he felt his oneness with the universe.

"I am not alone," he thought, as he had many times before in the silence and solitude of his self-imposed exile. "The human race is not alone in the universe." Faith welled up within him. Warmth filled and suffused him, here where "the coldest cold on the face of the earth" was manufactured.

He returned to his shack and wrote in his diary the peaceful conclusions he had come to about the universe and man's place in it.

I paused to listen to the silence. My breath, crystallized as it passed my cheeks, drifted on a breeze gentler than a whisper. The wind vane pointed toward the South Pole. Presently the wind cups ceased their gentle turning as the cold killed the breeze. My frozen breath hung like a cloud overhead.

The day was dying, the night was being born—but with great peace. Here were the imponderable processes and forces of the cosmos, harmonious and soundless. Harmony, that was it! That was what came out of the silence—a gentle rhythm, the strain of a perfect chord, the music of the spheres, perhaps.

It was enough to catch that rhythm, momentarily to be myself a part of it. In that instant I could feel no doubt of man's oneness with the universe. The conviction came that that rhythm was too orderly, too harmonious, too perfect to be a product of blind chance—that, therefore, there must be purpose in the whole and that man was part of that whole and not an accidental offshoot. It was a feeling that transcended reason; that went to the heart of a man's despair and found it groundless. The universe was a cosmos, not a chaos; man was as rightfully a part of that cosmos as were the day and night.

The inspiring paragraphs above are from *Alone*, the record of Admiral Byrd's five lonely months in the Antarctic obtaining scientific data. It is a record also of his own personal mission, his quest for a deep and abiding faith.

Here, completely cut off from all human contact, far from the accustomed world and its security, living in a shack that was less than a pinprick on the vast expanse of the Barrier—here in the bleakness, the loneliness, and the cold—Admiral Byrd learned that man is not alone. Here he came to the peaceful conclusion that man is part of the universe and its eternal harmony.

"For those who seek it, there is inexhaustible evidence of an all-pervading intelligence."

That is what Admiral Byrd discovered in the Antarctic winter of 1934, along with his discoveries about polar meteorology. That is the heartening faith he brought back, along with his scientific data and records. And that is his inspiring message to all who feel the need and desire to believe: *Man is not alone.*

The heavens declare the glory of God; and the firmament showeth his handiwork. *Psalms 19:1*

The beauty of the world and the orderly arrangement of everything celestial makes us confess that there is an excellent and eternal nature, which ought to be worshiped and admired by all mankind. *Cicero*

When I would beget content and increase confidence in the power and wisdom and providence of Almighty God, I will walk the meadows by some gliding stream, and there contemplate the lilies that take no care, and those very many other little living creatures that are not only created, but fed by the goodness of the God of Nature—and therefore trust in Him.

Izaak Walton

I cannot conceive how a man could look up into the heavens and say there is no God. *Abraham Lincoln*

If the stars should appear one night in a thousand years, how men would believe and adore, and preserve for many generations the remembrance of the City of God which had been shown! But every night come out these envoys of beauty, and light the universe with their admonishing smile. . . .
In the woods we return to reason and faith. Standing on the bare ground—my head bathed by the blithe air, and uplifted into infinite space—all mean egotism vanishes. . . . The currents of the Universal Being circulate through me.   *Ralph Waldo Emerson*

> The year's at the spring,
> And the day's at the morn;
> Morning's at seven;
> The hillside's dew-pearled;
> The lark's on the wing;
> The snail's on the thorn:
> God's in His heaven—
> All's right with the world!
>
> *Robert Browning*

It takes solitude, under the stars, for us to be reminded of our eternal origin and our far destiny.

Archibald Rutledge

2. HENRY FRANCIS LYTE

I TRIUMPH STILL, IF THOU ABIDE
WITH ME

SLOWLY the Reverend Henry Francis Lyte walked into his study. His heart was sad and burdened. This had been another Sunday like so many other Sundays in the long years behind him. A half-empty church. Tight hard faces listening without hearing, minds far away, hearts locked against the meaning of his words.

He had accomplished so little, so very little, here in Brixham! He had tried to bring these people closer to God, had tried to teach them the meaning of love and faith, of tolerance and kindness.

But he had failed. He knew by the hatreds and cruelties, by the feuds between neighbors, the greed and petty jealousies, how bitterly he had failed.

He was an old man now, near the end of the journey. He was tired and ill. The doctor had told him he had only a few months to live. He thumbed the well-worn Bible on his desk, and it fell open at one of his favorite passages: *"Abide with us; for it is toward evening and the day is far spent."* In the quiet of his curtained study, he read and reread those familiar comforting words.

And all at once he was no longer old and tired! All at once he was no longer sad and burdened, no longer discouraged! Words sang through his mind; and he put them down on paper; and in less than an hour he had written one of the most beautiful and inspiring hymns of all time:

Abide with me; fast falls the eventide;
The darkness deepens; Lord, with me abide;
When other helpers fail, and comforts flee,
Help of the helpless, oh abide with me.

Swift to its close ebbs out life's little day;
Earth's joys grow dim, its glories pass away;
Change and decay in all around I see;
O Thou who changest not, abide with me.

I need Thy presence every passing hour;
What but Thy grace can foil the tempter's power?
Who like Thyself my guide and stay can be?
Through cloud and sunshine, Lord, abide with me.

I fear no foe with Thee at hand to bless;
Ills have no weight, and tears no bitterness;
Where is death's sting? where, grave, thy victory?
I triumph still, if Thou abide with me.

Hold then Thy cross before my closing eyes;
Shine through the gloom, and point me to the skies;
Heaven's morning breaks, and earth's vain shadows flee;
In life, in death, O Lord, abide with me.

Few people today know the name of Henry Francis
Lyte. But the soul-stirring hymn he wrote in less than an
hour, a hundred years ago, is known and loved all over the
world—has given comfort and courage to millions.

When the famous nurse, Edith Cavell, went before a
German firing squad, she whispered the words of "Abide
With Me." When the R.M.S. *Stella* was sinking with one
hundred and five victims during the Second World War, a
woman—one of the noble unidentified of the world—stood
on the bridge and sang "Abide With Me" until the others
were singing with her, and they went down bravely. Countless other such stories could be told of people all over the
world.

So out of a great heart came a great hymn. At the end
of life, in a moment of shining faith and inspiration, Henry
Francis Lyte created a sentiment that lives on and on—
words of enduring power and influence.

If God be with us, who can be against us?
                                    Romans 8:31

Where faith is there is courage, there is fortitude,
there is steadfastness and strength. . . .

Faith bestows that sublime courage that rises superior
to the troubles and disappointments of life, that ac-
knowledges no defeat except as a step to victory; that
is strong to endure, patient to wait, and energetic to
struggle. . . . Light up, then, the lamp of faith in your
heart. . . . It will lead you safely through the mists of
doubt and the black darkness of despair; along the
narrow, thorny ways of sickness and sorrow, and over
the treacherous places of temptation and uncertainty.

James Allen

Come unto me, all ye who labor and are heavy laden,
and I will give you rest.　　　　*Matthew 11:28*

I will lift up mine eyes unto the hills, from whence
　　cometh my help.
My help cometh from the Lord, which made Heaven
　　and earth.
He will not suffer thy foot to be moved: He that
　　keepeth thee will not slumber.
Behold, He that keepeth Israel shall neither slumber
　　nor sleep.
The Lord is thy keeper: the Lord is thy shade upon
　　thy right hand.
The sun shall not smite thee by day, nor the moon
　　by night.
The Lord shall preserve thee from all evil: He shall
　　preserve thy soul.
The Lord shall preserve thy going out and thy com-
　　ing in from this time forth, and even for ever-
　　more.　　　　　　　　　　　　*Psalms 121*

The person who has a firm trust in the Supreme
Being is powerful in his power, wise by his wisdom,
happy by his happiness.　　　　*Joseph Addison*

3. JOHN HENRY NEWMAN

LEAD, KINDLY LIGHT. . . . THE NIGHT
IS DARK, AND I AM FAR FROM HOME

FOR NEARLY a week now the ship had been stranded in the Strait of Bonifacio, becalmed and drifting. The passengers were weary of the delay. They tried to pass the time as agreeably as possible by organizing games and other activities.

But the pale, tired-looking young clergyman did not join in the talk or in the games. He sat by himself, reading his Bible and occasionally staring off into space. His eyes burned, as with a fever. His face was drawn and thin.

John Henry Newman was tortured in body and mind. A distinguished member of the Church of England, he had recently been strongly attracted to the Church of Rome; and though this Mediterranean tour had been ostensibly for a rest, he knew in his heart that what he had wanted most was to visit Rome, to see the Vatican, to talk with the priests.

Rome had laid her mighty spell upon him but had not soothed the anxious probings of his mind. His talks with the priests had been disappointing, in some ways even disturbing. And every possible disaster had plagued him in Italy! The tour had been a series of almost unbelievable discomforts and misfortunes. He had suffered injury, pain, sleeplessness. He had been exposed to storms, an earthquake, an epidemic. In trying to help others, he himself had fallen victim to the epidemic illness in Sicily, and had very nearly died of it. In his delirium he became convinced of the weakness and "utter hollowness" of his religious convictions. But as the fever subsided, he was overcome with feelings of guilt and remorse. He longed

for strength to return to his work, and perhaps to find
again the peace of soul he once had known.

Now, after a month's convalescence, he was returning
to England. He was still weak from his long illness, still in
a torment of doubt about the whole framework of his
faith. In spite of himself, his thoughts kept returning to the
experiences he had so recently been through. His recovery,
when people all about him were dying like flies, had
seemed a miracle.

All at once he saw meaning and purpose in the pattern
of his suffering. He had been struck down by the hand of
Providence—and by that hand had been raised up again!
He felt sure he had been saved for a purpose, that God
had work for him to do. He was filled with love and gratitude, and with a great humility.

He turned to his Bible, open at the Psalms. *"Teach me
Thy way, O Lord, and lead me in a plain path."* His lips
moved as he read the familiar words. "Lead me, O Lord!"
he prayed. "I need Your help and guidance. I cannot see
the way. . . . Lead, kindly Light!"

The words had a wonderfully soothing effect. He took
a pencil and paper from his pocket and began to write. A
breeze seemed to blow up gently out of nowhere, ruffling
the water; and passengers called each other in excitement
as the sails slowly filled. But John Henry Newman didn't
notice. Even before the ship was well on its way again,
sailing out of the Strait of Bonifacio toward England and
home, he had written this beautiful hymn:

> Lead, kindly Light, amid the encircling gloom,
>   Lead thou me on;
> The night is dark, and I am far from home;
>   Lead thou me on.
> Keep thou my feet; I do not ask to see
> The distant scene; one step enough for me.
>
> I was not ever thus, nor prayed that thou
>   Shouldst lead me on;
> I love to choose and see my path; but now
>   Lead thou me on.

I loved the garish day, and, spite of fears,
Pride ruled my will: remember not past years.

So long thy power hath blest me, sure it still
    Will lead me on
O'er moor and fen, o'er crag and torrent, till
    The night is gone,
And with the morn those angel faces smile
Which I have loved long since, and lost awhile.

John Henry Newman wrote "Lead, Kindly Light" when he was thirty-two years old. He was to live to be almost ninety—to become a distinguished Cardinal of the Catholic Church and to write the brilliant, passionate *Apologia,* one of the world's immortal classics. But it is for the simple hymn he wrote one anguished afternoon, his humble prayer for guidance when he was lost in a torment of doubt and indecision, that he is today best remembered.

"Lead, Kindly Light" has become one of the world's most famous and best-loved hymns. Sir John Lubbock has called it one of the most beautiful and inspiring hymns ever written. It is sung in thousands of churches, and is a source of comfort and guidance to countless people.

When Lincoln Ellsworth's plane broke down and his radio went dead in the Antarctic, hundreds of miles from the nearest base, he repeated the comforting lines of "Lead, Kindly Light." And faith surmounted his anxiety, helped give him comfort and strength.

After the funeral services of Franklin D. Roosevelt in Washington, just before the body was placed on a train for Hyde Park, the band played "Lead, Kindly Light"—his favorite hymn.

"Lead, Kindly Light" was also Mahatma Gandhi's favorite hymn—a hymn he so loved, and which so greatly influenced his life, that Vincent Sheean made it the title of his book about the Mahatma.

Hundreds of stories could be told of the help, the comfort, the guidance this famous hymn has given to men and women in all parts of the world. Out of his own great need, in a moment of shining insight and eloquence, John Henry Newman gave the world an inspired prayer . . . words of enduring power and influence that help light the way for others lost in darkness and confusion.

Cast thy burden upon the Lord, and He shall sustain thee. *Psalms 55:22*

Walk boldly and wisely. . . . There is a hand above that will help thee on. *Philip James Bailey*

He who, from zone to zone,
Guides through the boundless sky thy certain flight,
In the long way that I must tread alone
Will lead my steps aright.
William Cullen Bryant

Let nothing disturb thee,
Let nothing affright thee.
All things are passing.
God never changes.
Patience gains all things.
Who has God wants nothing.
God alone suffices.
St. Theresa of Ávila

Do not look forward to the changes and chances of this life in fear; rather look to them with full hope that, as they arise, God, whose you are, will deliver you out of them. He has kept you hitherto—do you but hold fast to His dear hand, and He will lead you safely through all things; and, when you cannot stand, He will bear you in His arms. Do not look forward to what may happen tomorrow; the same everlasting Father who cares for you today will take care of you tomorrow, and every day. Either He will shield you from suffering, or He will give you unfailing strength to bear it. Be at peace, then, and put aside all anxious thoughts and imaginations. *Francis de Sales*

The whole course of things goes to teach us faith. We need only obey. There is guidance for each of us, and by lowly listening we shall hear the right word. . . . Place yourself in the middle of the stream of power and wisdom which flows into you as life, place yourself in the full center of that flood, then you are without effort impelled to truth, to right, and a perfect contentment.   *Ralph Waldo Emerson*

To them that ask, Where hast thou seen the Gods, or how knowest thou certainly that there be Gods, that thou art so devout in their worship? I answer: Neither have I ever seen my own soul, and yet I respect and honor it.   *Marcus Aurelius*

Faith is the substance of things hoped for, the evidence of things not seen.   *Hebrews 11:1*

What is faith unless it is to believe what you do not see?   *St. Augustine*

> I know not where His islands lift
>   Their fronded palms in air;
> I only know I cannot drift
>   Beyond His love and care.
>   *John Greenleaf Whittier*

We shall be made truly wise if we be made content; content, too, not only with what we can understand, but content with what we do not understand—the habit of mind which theologians call, and rightly, faith in God.   *Charles Kingsley*

> I never saw a moor,
> I never saw the sea;
> Yet know I how the heather looks,
> And what a wave must be.

I never spoke with God,
Nor visited in heaven;
Yet certain am I of the spot
As if the chart were given.

Emily Dickinson

4. SARAH FLOWER ADAMS

SO BY MY WOES TO BE
NEARER, MY GOD, TO THEE,
NEARER TO THEE!

PROPPED AMONG the gay pillows on the sofa, Sarah Adams looked frail and wan, but still very attractive in spite of her long illness. It was three years now . . . three slow, dragging years since the curtain rang down on her theatrical career. She sighed, and turned back to her reading. But she was restless today, and her mind kept wandering from the page.

It was not the stubborn, nagging illness she minded. It was not the pain, the weakness, or even being alone so much of the time. It was giving up the ambition of a lifetime—seeing her cherished dream come true, only to lose it again, suddenly and irretrievably.

All her life, as long as she could remember, she had dreamed of becoming a great actress. She had worked and studied and struggled toward that goal, and at last had realized her ambition. At last she had scored a dramatic triumph as Lady Macbeth, had been hailed as a great actress, and had looked forward to a successful career on the stage.

But her triumph was brief, so brief! A sudden devastating illness had made her an invalid, had taken her from the stage and closed the door to her forever. It was a bitter disappointment. Being of a deeply religious nature, Sarah Flower Adams had turned to God for comfort and help in her trial, and these past three years had spent much of her time reading the Bible and the lives of the saints and martyrs. Recently she had turned to writing, mostly poems with a scriptural or religious background, and had

51

become a frequent contributor to magazines and church papers.

Yesterday her minister, Mr. Fox, had come to see her about some poems she had promised for a collection of *Hymns and Anthems* he was publishing. She had been silly again, feeling sorry for herself, complaining about her affliction. The minister had quietly taken the Old Testament from her bookshelves, had opened it to the story of Jacob's vision at Bethel, and had urged her to read it. She had read it many times before at his suggestion, and she knew the story almost as well as her own.

Her own! Suddenly she saw the unmistakable parallel between Jacob's story and her own illness and disappointment. She saw it so clearly now: the darkness, the dream, the awakening, the sunshine, the triumph, and the joy. She knew now why the minister kept insisting that she read it. She would do *more* than that! She would write a poem about it, showing how our very suffering and afflictions may be steps bringing us nearer to heaven . . . nearer to God.

She was inspired by the theme. She saw the closed door to her own life's ambition as "the cross that raiseth me." She saw her illness, her disappointment, her loneliness, her pain, as steps to heaven: *"So by my woes to be nearer, my God, to Thee, nearer to Thee!"*

It sang like a refrain through her heart and mind. She wrote it almost without effort, almost as though the words came to her from some powerful outside source:

> Nearer, my God, to Thee,
>   Nearer to Thee!
> E'en though it be a cross
>   That raiseth me;
> Still all my song shall be,
> Nearer, my God, to Thee,
>   Nearer to Thee!
>
> Though like the wanderer,
>   The sun gone down,

Darkness be over me,
    My rest a stone;
Yet in my dreams I'd be
Nearer, my God, to Thee,
    Nearer to Thee!

There let the way appear
    Steps unto heaven;
All that Thou send'st to me
    In mercy given;
Angels to beckon me
Nearer, my God, to Thee,
    Nearer to Thee!

Then, with my waking thoughts
    Bright with Thy praise,
Out of my stony griefs
    Bethel I'll raise;
So by my woes to be
Nearer, my God, to Thee,
    Nearer to Thee!

Or if on joyful wing
    Cleaving the sky,
Sun, moon, and stars forgot,
    Upward I fly,
Still all my song shall be,
Nearer, my God, to Thee,
    Nearer to Thee!

The poem Sarah Adams wrote that afternoon, out of her own great need and her own great faith, has become one of the world's most beloved hymns.

"Nearer, My God, To Thee" is today sung universally in homes, schools, and churches, the favorite of millions of people. It is often sung in times of death or disaster, for it is a hymn of great comfort in the crises of life—a hymn of promise and hope for the grief-stricken and the afflicted.

In the last tragic moments of the *Titanic* disaster, when

the ship was going down carrying hundreds of people to
their deaths, the band played "Nearer, My God, To Thee"
to the very last, until the surging waters closed above them.
Survivors told later how doomed passengers had knelt on
the deck to pray, and how many just stood quietly, without panic, joining in the hymn.

When gold was discovered in Alaska and hordes of
greedy men rushed to the Yukon to get their share, Evangeline Booth knew the Salvation Army would be needed
there. So she headed north with half a dozen assistants,
and arrived to find conditions even worse than she had
expected. Vice and lawlessness were the order of the day.
Men were shot down for a handful of gold dust, or for no
reason at all. Five men were killed the day Evangeline
Booth arrived. There were shortages of everything—
blankets, food, equipment, clothing—men were quick-
tempered and surly, and in no mood for sermons. But
Evangeline Booth knew what to do. That evening she had
her little band stood on the banks of the Yukon River and
sang "Nearer, My God, To Thee," and lonely men began
to gather by the hundreds—by the thousands—until nearly twenty-five thousand were lustily singing the hymn!
There was singing every day after that . . . and much less
disorder, many fewer shootings.

The hymn was a favorite of martyred President McKin-
ley. As he lay dying from an assassin's bullet, friends near
his bedside heard him whisper several lines of "Nearer,
My God, To Thee." It was a favorite also of Theodore
Roosevelt, of Harriet Beecher Stowe, of countless others.

Weaving the pattern of her own life story into a familiar
scriptural background, Sarah Flower Adams produced a
hymn of enduring beauty—a hymn of hope and faith—
an inspiring source of comfort to millions.

God is our refuge and strength, a very present help
in trouble.   *Psalms 46:1*

Have courage for the great sorrows of life and
patience for the small ones; and when you have

laboriously accomplished your daily task, go to sleep
in peace. God is awake.   *Victor Hugo*

God, make me brave for life: oh, braver than this.
Let me straighten after pain, as a tree straightens after
    the rain,
Shining and lovely again.
God, make me brave for life; much braver than this.
As the blown grass lifts, let me rise
From sorrow with quiet eyes,
Knowing Thy way is wise.
God, make me brave, life brings
Such blinding things.
Help me to keep my sight;
Help me to see aright
That out of dark comes light.

                            Author unknown

One watches people starting out in life quite adequately, handling life with active vigor, as they run, one
after another, into experiences where something
deeper than vigor is needed. Serious failure, for example. Some night in his lifetime everyone comes
home to find a new guest there—disappointment.
What he had set his heart on has gone. . . . If one is
to come through difficult experiences unembittered,
unspoiled, still a real person, one needs deep resources. . . . Not alone in such experiences as sorrow
and failure does this need arise but in man's search
for the indispensable spiritual requirements of a
satisfying life—inner peace, for example, some serenity in the soul to come home to at night and go out
from in the morning. Who does not need that? But
no one can get inner peace by pouncing on it, by
vigorously willing to have it. Peace is a margin of
power around our daily need. Peace is a consciousness of springs too deep for earthly droughts to dry
up. Peace is an awareness of reserves from beyond
ourselves, so that our power is not so much in us as
through us.   *Harry Emerson Fosdick*

5. WILLIAM G. FARROW

MY FAITH IN GOD IS COMPLETE, SO
I AM UNAFRAID

THE YOUNG Lieutenant sat in his cell writing what was to be his last letter. He wasn't thinking of himself, or of the cruel death that awaited him and the two other Doolittle fliers condemned with him. He was thinking of his mother, and of the girl he now would never marry. How could he comfort them, except to remind them of the faith that was his own great comfort in this hour of trial?

The time was getting short. He reread what he had written to his mother and, anxious to spare her as much grief as possible, added these closing words:

> Don't let this get you down. Just remember God will make everything right and that I'll see you all again in the hereafter. . . . Read "Thanatopsis" by Bryant* if you want to know how I am taking this. My faith in God is complete, so I am unafraid.

Lieutenant William G. Farrow's letter was found in the files of the War Ministry Building in Tokyo, along with the last messages of those condemned with him. The letters were used as evidence in the war crimes trials of Japanese accused of executing the Doolittle fliers, and they were widely publicized at the time.

The above brief excerpt from Farrow's letter appeared in newspapers all over the country, and stirred the hearts of millions of readers. To many who had faced tragedy and grief during the war years, it came almost as a personal message. Parents who had lost sons clipped it and

* See pages 118–120.

carried it about with them, finding unexpected consolation in the flier's last brave message to his mother. Ministers made it the subject of moving sermons on faith, and newspapers the theme of countless editorials on courage. Appearing at a time when many people were lost and confused in the bitterness of their own bereavement, Farrow's letter made an immense impression—and helped many regain the faith and peace of mind they thought they had lost forever.

Lieutenant Farrow and his companions* gave their lives in the service of their country. Their thrilling exploit will never be forgotten by a grateful nation. But young Farrow gave far more than he knew. For his simple but eloquent words of courage and faith live on; and the now-famous quotation from his last letter to his mother takes its place among the inspirational messages of mankind.

My peace I give unto you. . . . Let not your heart be troubled, neither let it be afraid.   *John 14:27*

The Lord is my shepherd; I shall not want.
He maketh me to lie down in green pastures: He
    leadeth me besides the still waters.
He restoreth my soul: He leadeth me in the paths of
    righteousness for His name's sake.
Yea, though I walk through the valley of the shadow
    of death, I will fear no evil: for Thou art with
    me; Thy rod and Thy staff they comfort me.
Thou preparest a table before me in the presence of
    mine enemies:
Thou anointest my head with oil; my cup runneth
    over.
Surely goodness and mercy shall follow me all the
    days of my life: And I will dwell in the house
    of the Lord forever.   *Psalms 23*

The Lord is my strength and my shield; my heart
    trusteth in Him, and I am helped.   *Psalms 28:7*

---

* Lieutenant Dean E. Hallmark and Sergeant Harold A. Spatz.

No coward soul is mine,
    No trembler in the world's storm-troubled sphere;
I see heaven's glories shine,
    And faith shines equal, arming me from fear.
                         Emily Brontë

Whatever happens, abide steadfast in a determination
to cling simply to God.   *Francis de Sales*

6. ALFRED TENNYSON

I HOPE TO SEE MY PILOT
FACE TO FACE
WHEN I HAVE CROSSED THE BAR

ENGLAND'S great poet laureate was nearing the end of life. His time was running out, and he knew it. But he knew it without fear, and without regret. For to him death was not an end but a beginning; death was not the final curtain but merely a change of scene, the transition to another and perhaps an infinitely better life.

Alfred Tennyson believed in immortality. He had believed in it all his life, and now more firmly than ever.

Yes, the time was short. He was an old man now, at the end of a long and happy career—a life as rich and gratifying as any man could ask. Soon a new century would be dawning in the world: *the twentieth century.* The very sound of it was full of promise. But he would not be here to see it, for he and the nineteenth century were fading together.

Let it come, he thought—let death come when it will! He was ready. There were old friends who had gone before, good friends he longed to see again.

"Death, be not proud!" he exulted, repeating in his heart the famous, triumphant lines of John Donne. *Death, be not proud! A short sleep, and I will wake again, eternally. A short voyage, and I will meet my Maker face to face. . . .*

He thought of the narrow strait that separates the Isle of Wight from England. Often, returning home across the strait, he saw the beautiful sunset, heard the evening bells and the "moaning of the bar." The end, he knew, would be like that: a brief crossing in the twilight, the moving tide, the evening star—and *home*. Almost without intention he began to write, the lines forming themselves effortlessly:

Sunset and evening star,
    And one clear call for me!
And may there be no moaning of the bar,
    When I put out to sea,

But such a tide as moving seems asleep,
    Too full for sound and foam,
When that which drew from out the boundless deep
    Turns again home.

Twilight and evening bell,
    And after that the dark!
And may there be no sadness of farewell,
    When I embark;

For though from out our bourne of Time and Place
    The flood may bear me far,
I hope to see my Pilot face to face
    When I have crossed the bar.

The day he wrote "Crossing the Bar" Tennyson showed the verses to his son, who read them with tears in his eyes. "This is the crown of your life's work!" he said.

The poem was, in a way, Tennyson's farewell to life—for he died soon afterward. A few days before his death he gave instructions to his publishers to include this poem at the end of every edition of his works.

Exquisite in its simplicity, eloquent and deeply moving in its triumphant expression of faith, "Crossing the Bar" went straight to the hearts of millions of people, and became one of Tennyson's most famous poems. Alice and Elbert Hubbard so loved it that it was read at the memorial services for them after they went down on the *Lusitania*. John Drinkwater calls it "the greatest of all hymns"; and there are many who consider it the most beautiful poem about immortality ever written.

That day which you fear as being the end of all things is the birthday of your eternity.   *Seneca*

I am quite ready to acknowledge . . . that I ought to be grieved at death, if I were not persuaded that I am going to other gods who are wise and good (of this I am as certain as I can be of any such matters), and to men departed who are better than those whom I leave behind. And therefore I do not grieve as I might have done, for I have good hope that there is yet something remaining for the dead.   *Socrates*

What is our death but a night's sleep? For as through sleep all weariness and faintness pass away and cease, and the powers of the spirit come back again, so that in the morning we rise fresh and strong and joyous; so at the Last Day we shall rise again as if we had only slept a night, and shall be fresh and strong.
                                                                        Martin Luther

For half a century I have been writing my thoughts in prose and in verse—history, philosophy, drama, romance, tradition, satire, ode, and song. I have tried all. But I feel I have not said the thousandth part of what is in me. When I go down to the grave I can say, like many others, "I have finished my day's work!" But I cannot say, "I have finished my life." My day's work will begin again the next morning. The tomb is not a blind alley; it is a thoroughfare. It closes on the twilight, it opens on the dawn.
                                                                        Victor Hugo

When you take the wires of the cage apart, you do not hurt the bird, but you help it. You let it out of its prison. How do you know that death does not help me when it takes the wires of my cage down?—that it does not release me, and put me into some better place and better condition of life?
                                                                        Bishop Randolph S. Foster

There is no death! What seems so is a transition.
Henry Wadsworth Longfellow

The universe is God's house. This world is not the
only habitat for the living. In His house are many
rooms. Death is only pushing aside the portiere and
passing from one room to another. . . .
I think of death as a glad awakening from this troubled sleep which we call life; as an emancipation from
the world which, beautiful though it be, is still a land
of captivity; as a graduation from this primary de-
partment into some higher rank in the hierarchy of
learning. I think of the dead as possessing a more
splendid equipment for a larger life of diviner service
than was possible to them on earth—a life in which I
shall in due time join them if I am counted worthy of
their fellowship in the life eternal. . . .
I neither know nor wish to know what the future life
has for me. I would not, if I could, stand at the open
window and peer into the unknown beyond. I am
sure that He whose mercies are new every morning
and fresh every evening, who brings into every epoch
of my life a new surprise, and makes in every experience a new disclosure of His love, who sweetens
gladness with gratitude, and sorrow with comfort, who
gives the lark for the morning and the nightingale
for the twilight, who makes every year better than the
year preceding, and every new experience an experience of His marvelous skill in gift-giving, has for me
some future of glad surprise which I would not fore-
cast if I could.   *Lyman Abbott*

Life is a voyage that's homeward bound.
Herman Melville

7. ROBERT BROWNING

THE JOURNEY IS DONE. . . . O THOU
SOUL OF MY SOUL! I SHALL CLASP
THEE AGAIN

ALL THROUGH the long, long night he sat by the bedside, holding her hand. Sometimes she whispered his name, and he bent close to listen. Always it was some word of hope or cheer, or a gentle smile. Then she would doze again; and he would watch, and pray.

"My loved one!" he cried, deep in his aching heart. "You *must* get well!" You cannot leave me now!"

Robert Browning had brought his wife to Italy, hoping a change of scene and climate would improve her health. And she *had* improved, so much so that he had established a home for her in Florence. Here they spent their happiest years. Here they had lived as in a dream, thinking as one and feeling as one, planning and writing their poetry. Here they had lived a life of rich contentment.

Until now . . . Now he knew the idyl was over, the dream was spent. Elizabeth was dying. Though every fiber of him cried denial, he knew the end was near. The doctor had told him what his heart already knew.

Sometime before dawn she moved and opened her eyes. "Hold me, beloved," she whispered. He lifted her in his arms and sat with her near the window, holding her close in the fleecy blanket—as though by his very warmth and texture he could keep her with him. So they sat for a long time in silence, her head against his shoulder. There was no need for words between them.

He thought of the closing lines of one of her poems, lines he had always loved. It seemed to his anguished mind that she was speaking, though her lips were still.

63

"I love thee with the breath,
Smiles, tears, of all my life!—and, if God choose,
I shall but love thee better after death."*

He bent and kissed her cheek. It felt icy to his lips. The
first wan light of the new day was just beginning to come
through the window when she sighed and said, "It is
beautiful!" Then, suddenly, she was gone.

Robert Browning was grief-stricken by his wife's death.
For some time he couldn't write; but when at last he did,
there flowed from his pen a passionate defiance of death,
an exultant challenge. Fear death? Not he! Let the archfoe
come; he would be ready. He would meet death gladly,
boldly—for in the end he would triumph! He would meet
his beloved again, and clasp her in his arms . . . and out
of the pain would come peace. . . .

He felt the release of bitter tension as he wrote, felt
strangely comforted:

Fear death?—to feel the fog in my throat,
        The mist in my face,
When the snows begin, and the blasts denote
        I am nearing the place,
The power of the night, the press of the storm,
        The post of the foe;
Where he stands, the Arch Fear in a visible form,
        Yet the strong man must go:
For the journey is done and the summit attained,
        And the barriers fall,
Though a battle's to fight ere the guerdon be gained,
        The reward of it all.
I was ever a fighter, so—one fight more,
        The best and the last!
I would hate that death bandaged my eyes, and fore-
        bore,
        And bade me creep past.

* "How Do I Love Thee?" by Elizabeth Barrett Browning.
See pages 260–261.

No! let me taste the whole of it, fare like my peers
  The heroes of old,
Bear the brunt, in a minute pay glad life's arrears
  Of pain, darkness and cold.
For sudden the worst turns the best to the brave,
  The black minute's at end,
And the elements' rage, the fiend-voices that rave,
  Shall dwindle, shall blend,
Shall change, shall become first a peace out of pain,
  Then a light, then thy breast,
O thou soul of my soul! I shall clasp thee again,
  And with God be the rest!

Elizabeth Barrett Browning died in June, 1861. It was in the autumn of the same year that Robert Browning, out of the depths of his grief and loneliness, wrote "Prospice," one of his most famous and inspiring poems.

"Prospice" . . . "Look Forward." It is at once a challenge and a promise, a magnificent blend of defiance and faith. *"I shall clasp thee again!"* cries Browning. He is not afraid of death; he looks forward to it; for in death he and Elizabeth will be reunited.

Browning's "Prospice" brought comfort to many besides himself. It gave to those bereaved as he was the hope of someday seeing their loved ones again. Letters came to him from people who had suffered keenly and questioned deeply—and had found their answer in Browning's triumphant lines.

Born of a poet's own suffering and his own undaunted faith, "Prospice" has had, and continues to have, an enduring influence. Many have heard in its passionate rhythm the echo of an older challenge, as exultant and inspiring: *"O death, where is thy sting? O grave, where is thy victory?"*

Be not grieved above measure for thy deceased friends. They are not dead, but have only finished the journey which is necessary for every one of us to take. We ourselves must go to that great place of reception in which they are all of them assembled,

and, in this general rendezvous of mankind, live together in another state of being.   *Antiphanes*

Do not grudge your brother his rest. He has at last
become free, safe and immortal, and ranges joyous
through the boundless heavens; he has left this low-
lying region and has soared upwards to that place
which receives in its happy bosom the souls set free
from the chains of matter.
Your brother has not lost the light of day, but has
obtained a more enduring light. He has not left us,
but has gone on before.   *Seneca*

Our friend and we were invited abroad on a party
of pleasure, which is to last forever. His chair was
ready first, and he is gone before us. We could not
all conveniently start together; and why should you
and I be grieved at this, since we are soon to follow,
and know where to find him.   *Benjamin Franklin*

Good-night! good-night! as we so oft have said,
   Beneath this roof at midnight, in the days
   That are no more, and shall no more return.
Thou hast but taken up thy lamp and gone to bed;
I stay a little longer, as one stays
   To cover up the embers that still burn.
         Henry Wadsworth Longfellow

As a personal experience, none of my own ever surpassed in moving power that beautiful and dramatic
scene which, though it lies years back in the moon-
lit land of the past and of memory, is vividly alive to
me now. It happened at sunrise, and it was of a sunrise.
One dearer to me than all else in life had, for days,
lain helpless, speechless. Consciousness was gone. We
knew that the mortal mists were fast gathering; that
the irremediable river must soon be crossed. The last
morning of our watching was misty; the day emerged
so wanly that we hardly knew that it had come. Sud-

denly the one we loved so dearly sat up in bed, a
strange light on her face of a happiness past all our
mortal joy. She stretched abroad her arms, crying in
the radiant abandon of spiritual certainty, "The
Dawn! The beautiful Dawn!"

Those were her dying words—glad, triumphant. And
for me they hold the eternal promise of the sunrise.
They glow with immortality. In every sense, our
mortal dawn that day was anything but beautiful; but
she saw the beginning of an immortal day. Believing
in a God of infinite love and of infinite power, I find
it natural to believe that death is not a disastrous
sundown but rather a spiritual sunrise, ushering in the
unconjectured splendors of immortality.

Archibald Rutledge

When I consider life and its few years—
A wisp of fog betwixt us and the sun;
A call to battle, and the battle done
Ere the last echo dies within our ears;
A rose choked in the grass; an hour of fears;
The gusts that past a darkening shore do beat;
The burst of music down an unlistening street—
I wonder at the idleness of tears.
Ye old, old dead, and ye of yesternight,
Chieftains and bards, and keepers of the sheep,
By every cup of sorrow that you had,
Loose me from tears, and make me see aright
How each hath back what once he stayed to weep:
Homer his sight, David his little lad!

Lizette Woodworth Reese

8. EDDIE V. RICKENBACKER

HUMBLY WE PRAYED FOR FOOD. . . .
WITHIN AN HOUR A SEA GULL CAME
AND LANDED ON MY HEAD

THE MEN in the rubber life rafts were in a pretty bad way.
Their plane, on a war mission in the Pacific, had been
forced down eight days ago; and they had been drifting
helplessly ever since, without food or water, in the scorch-
ing tropic sun. Their feet were blistered, their faces burned,
their mouths and bodies parched. For eight days they
lived on four small oranges—no other food, and no water.
The heat, the hunger, the exhaustion, had brought them
close to the breaking point.

But not Captain Eddie Rickenbacker! He had been in
tight places before, had come face to face with death
several times in the past. And he alone refused to despair;
he alone never gave up faith that they would be found
and picked up, that somehow they would be saved.

For Eddie Rickenbacker believed in prayer. He had
learned to pray as a child at his mother's knee; and in all
the crises of his life, prayer had given him comfort and
courage, prayer had helped him through his difficulties.
He firmly believed it would help him again in this emergency.

Most of the men in the rubber life rafts were young and
inexperienced, facing their first great trial. They needed the
strength and understanding he could give them out of his
own experience. They needed the example of his great
faith and trust, those unfailing resources that buttress a
man from within and give him the endurance to face what
he must. They needed the calming, comforting influence
of prayer.

One of the men in his boat had a small Bible, and they

took turns reading aloud from it every day. It was a reassurance from the very first that they were not alone,
that God knew where they were and would take care of
them.

Now, on the eighth day of hunger and thirst, the men
were desperate. There was no sign of a boat or plane anywhere—nothing but the wide, empty, shining expanse of
sea. One of the men was violently sick from drinking sea
water. Some were beginning to show the first alarming
signs of delirium. It was suggested that the following passage of Matthew be read to the men that day:

> Therefore take no thought, saying, What shall we
> eat? or, What shall we drink? or, Wherewithal shall
> we be clothed? . . . for your heavenly Father knoweth
> that ye have need of all these things.
>
> But seek ye first the kingdom of God, and His
> righteousness; and all these things shall be added
> unto you.
>
> Take therefore no thought for the morrow; for the
> morrow shall take thought for the things of itself.
> Sufficient unto the day is the evil thereof.

What happened next seemed like a miracle to the suffering men, seemed like a direct answer to their prayer. And
who can say it was not? A gull flew in out of nowhere
and landed on Rickenbacker's head. He reached up and
caught it—*and they had food*. They ran into their first rainstorm—*and they had water for drinking*. Food and water!
Their prayers had been answered! The experience filled
the men with awe and astonishment, and there were no
longer any unbelievers in the life rafts. From then on they
prayed with new confidence, with strong new faith. From
then on they believed with "Captain Eddie" that God was
with them and that they would be saved.

And they were! They drifted for nearly two weeks
longer—weak, emaciated, and in the end more nearly dead
than alive—but still believing, and still expecting to be
saved. And at last, on the twenty-first day of their ordeal,
they were located by searching planes and picked up. It

was a truly miraculous rescue, for the rafts were less than
dots on the ocean's surface and impossible to see from
a distance. The planes had to fly almost directly above
them to find them.

When news of the rescue was flashed around the world,
people everywhere were thrilled and excited, for nearly
everyone had given the men up for lost. But what moved
people most was Rickenbacker's simple, unaffected ex-
planation: *"We prayed."* The story, as told in his own
words, went straight to the hearts of millions of people:

> After we got going naturally we got to thinking
> about our food and water, but we didn't dare go back
> to the ship for fear she would sink and suck us down
> with it. Then we ran into a five-day calm, which left
> the ocean like a mirror. It was beastly hot. . . . Our
> hands, face, and feet suffered particularly. . . .
>
> We saw nothing in the way of searching planes or
> ships. The boy in my boat had an issue Bible in the
> pocket of his jumper, and the second day out we
> organized little evening and morning prayer meetings
> and took turn about reading passages from the Bible.
> Frankly and humbly we prayed for our deliverance.
> After the oranges were gone, we experienced terrific
> pangs of hunger, and we prayed for food.
>
> We had a couple of little fish lines with hooks about
> the size of the end of my little finger, but no bait.
> Were it not for the fact that I have seven witnesses,*
> I wouldn't dare tell this story because it seems so
> fantastic. Within an hour after prayer meeting on the
> eighth day, a sea gull came out of nowhere and
> landed on my head. I reached up my hand very gently
> and got him. We wrung his head, feathered him,
> carved up his carcass and ate every bit, even the little
> bones. We distributed and used his innards for bait.
>
> Captain Cherry caught a little mackerel about six or

---

* There were originally eight men in the three tiny rubber
lifeboats, which were fastened together with rope. One man died
on the thirteenth day; but the other seven came safely through
the ordeal.

eight inches long and I caught a little speckled sea bass about the same size, so we had food for a couple of days. . . .

That night we ran into our first rainstorm. Usually you try to avoid a black squall, but in this case we made it our business to get into it and catch water for drinking. . . . Later we were able to catch more water and build up our supply.

The day this story appeared in the newspapers, people everywhere were noticeably affectd by it. For it was far more than a story of courage and physical endurance, of which there were many in those tragic war years. It was an amazing demonstration of the power of prayer, one of the most thrilling sagas of faith in action to come out of World War II.

Every paper in the land picked up Rickenbacker's story. Ministers preached sermons about it. Writers wrote glowing articles and editorials about it. Public figures discussed it from the lecture platform and over the radio.

"We prayed."

There was almost a Biblical feeling to Rickenbacker's words. He and his companions were lost at sea . . . they prayed . . . they were saved. It was as simple as that, and as inspiring. People who hadn't prayed in years began to do so again. Some who had never prayed in their lives began to search their souls with a new questioning. Many who were anguished, bitter, and despairing, who had suffered profound grief during the war, felt the pain of their hearts ease and the bitterness leave them. It was as though something wonderful and fine had happened to everyone, everywhere . . . as indeed it had! Eddie Rickenbacker's story enormously increased and intensified the feeling of faith in millions of hearts, and gave people courage and hope when they needed it most.

"I consider the story of how we prayed and how our prayers were answered the most important message I ever gave to the people of this country," wrote Captain Rickenbacker in a personal communication with the author of this book.

It is far more than that. Captain Rickenbacker's famous
saga of the Pacific, revealing the power of faith to help
men endure an almost unbelievable ordeal, is one of the
truly great stories of the war . . . and one of the most
inspiring.

Ask, and it shall be given you; seek, and ye shall find;
knock, and it shall be opened unto you.   *Matthew 7:7*

All things, whatsoever ye shall ask in prayer, believing, ye shall receive.   *Matthew 21:22*

All who call on God in true faith, earnestly from the
heart, will certainly be heard, and will receive what
they have asked and desired.   *Martin Luther*

More things are wrought by prayer
Than this world dreams of. Wherefore, let thy voice
Rise like a fountain for me night and day.
For what are men better than sheep or goats
That nourish a blind life within the brain,
If, knowing God, they lift not hands of prayer
Both for themselves and those who call them friend?
                                        Alfred Tennyson

Prayer is not only worship; it is also an invisible ema-
nation of man's worshiping spirit—the most powerful
form of energy that one can generate. The influence
of prayer on the human mind and body is as demon-
strable as that of secreting glands. Its results can be
measured in terms of increased physical buoyancy,
greater intellectual vigor, moral stamina, and a deeper
understanding of the realities underlying human relationships.
If you make a habit of sincere prayer, your life will be
very noticeably and profoundly altered. Prayer stamps
with its indelible mark our actions and demeanor. A
tranquillity of bearing, a facial and bodily repose, are
observed in those whose inner lives are thus enriched.
Within the depths of consciousness a flame kindles.

And man sees himself. He discovers his selfishness, his silly pride, his fears, his greeds, his blunders. He develops a sense of moral obligation, intellectual humility. Thus begins a journey of the soul toward the realm of grace.

Prayer is a force as real as terrestrial gravity. As a physician, I have seen men, after all other therapy has failed, lifted out of disease and melancholy by the serene effort of prayer. It is the only power in the world that seems to overcome the so-called "laws of nature"; the occasions on which prayer has dramatically done this have been termed "miracles." But a constant, quieter miracle takes place hourly in the hearts of men and women who have discovered that prayer supplies them with a steady flow of sustaining power in their daily lives.

Too many people regard prayer as a formalized routine of words, a refuge for weaklings, or a childish petition for material things. We sadly undervalue prayer when we conceive it in these terms, just as we should underestimate rain by describing it as something that fills the birdbath in our garden. Properly understood, prayer is a mature activity indispensable to the fullest development of personality—the ultimate integration of man's highest faculties. Only in prayer do we achieve that complete and harmonious assembly of body, mind, and spirit which gives the frail human reed its unshakable strength.

Alexis Carrel

Oft have I seen at some cathedral door
A laborer, pausing in the dust and heat,
Lay down his burden, and with reverent feet
Enter, and cross himself, and on the floor
Kneel to repeat his paternoster o'er;
Far off the noises of the world retreat;
The loud vociferations of the street
Become an undistinguishable roar.
So, as I enter here from day to day,
And leave my burden at this minster gate,

Kneeling in prayer, and not ashamed to pray,
The tumult of the time disconsolate
To inarticulate murmurs dies away,
While the eternal ages watch and wait.
Henry Wadsworth Longfellow

The sovereign cure for worry is prayer.
William James

9. ABRAHAM LINCOLN

WITHOUT DIVINE ASSISTANCE I CANNOT SUCCEED; WITH IT I CANNOT FAIL

THE DAY dawned gray and cheerless, and rain poured down as Abraham Lincoln was driven through the muddy streets of Springfield to the railroad station. The sidewalks were lined with people who had gathered in the wet chill of the morning to see him pass. At the station many of his old friends waited to say goodbye. Soldiers lined the passageway; and as he went through the waiting room to the platform, he was greeted with cheers.

This was to have been a happy day for him, a day of triumph. But those close enough to shake his hand and wish him well in Washington saw that he was not happy. He looked tired and distraught; and there were many who wondered that morning why he was alone, why his family was not with him.

Slowly the President-Elect mounted the steps to the observation platform. Today he was saying farewell to the past, and to the place and the people he had known so long and so well. He was going to a new life, to heavy new responsibilities. The country was on edge, the nation divided, hatreds were flaring and passions running high. He was aware of the problems and difficulties ahead, and of the great trust placed in him by the people; and he was determined to serve the nation honestly and well in the high office to which he had been called.

He turned and faced the people who had come in the rain and cold to see him off—his neighbors and friends, his fellow townsmen. He stood for a long moment gazing into their faces, as though to carry their memory forever in his mind. He didn't know when he would return to

Springfield, or whether he would ever return. He owed these people much; and he was filled with a deep sense of gratitude toward them at this moment of parting.

But there was bitterness, too, in the parting. For his family was supposed to be with him on the Presidential train. Mary and the children should have been standing here right now, beside him on the platform. But she had chosen just this day for a quarrel, for one of her screaming, hysterical tantrums. He had been forced to leave her behind, and to say good-bye alone to these good friends.

When he spoke it was in sadness, and in great humility. He bade the citizens of Springfield farewell, acknowledged the great task ahead, and asked them all to pray for his success. His cheeks were wet with rain. He looked tired and worn. But his voice was warm with affection, his words were eloquent with sincerity and faith.

My friends: No one, not in my situation, can appreciate my feeling of sadness at this parting. To this place, and the kindness of these people, I owe everything. Here I have lived a quarter of a century, and have passed from a young to an old man. Here my children have been born, and one is buried. I now leave, not knowing when or whether ever I may return, with a task before me greater than that which rested upon Washington. Without the assistance of that Divine Being who ever attended him, I cannot succeed. With that assistance I cannot fail. Trusting in Him who can go with me, and remain with you, and be everywhere for good—let us confidently hope that all will yet be well. To His care commending you, as I hope in your prayers you will commend me, I bid you an affectionate farewell.

Lincoln's farewell address at Springfield, Illinois, on February 11, 1861, was brief—less than two hundred words. It was considered of no great importance at the time, had no special political significance, and newspapers gave it little space. It was just a man's affectionate good-bye to his home town, a simple farewell to his neighbors and friends, the people among whom he had lived and worked for twenty-five years.

But it was something else, something the people of Springfield clearly sensed as they stood listening in the rain that morning, something that stayed with them like a comforting beacon through the dark years that followed. It was a great man's instinctive prayer for guidance and help, a humble but eloquent expression of faith that few who heard ever forgot.

It is this expression of complete faith and trust, this firm belief that with God's help he could not fail, which sets Lincoln's words at Springfield apart . . . and gives them the unmistakable quality of inspiration, radiant and enduring.

Why art thou cast down, O my soul? and why art thou disquieted within me? Hope thou in God.
Psalms 42:5

Faith is a most precious commodity, without which we should be very badly off.   *Sir William Osler*

And have we now forgotten that powerful Friend? Or do we imagine we no longer need His assistance? I have lived a long time; and the longer I live, the more convincing proofs I see of this truth: that God governs in the affairs of men. And if a sparrow cannot fall to the ground without His notice, is it probable that an empire can rise without His aid?
Benjamin Franklin

Faith is one of the forces by which men live, and the total absence of it means collapse.   *William James*

At all costs we must re-establish faith in spiritual values. We must worship something beyond ourselves, lest we destroy ourselves.   *Philip Gibbs*

I know there is a Supreme Being who rules the affairs of men and whose goodness and mercy have always followed the American people, and I know He will not turn from us now if we humbly and reverently seek His powerful aid. *Grover Cleveland*

PART THREE

COURAGE
&
The Conquest of Fear

"The things courage can do!"

SIR JAMES M. BARRIE

WE CANNOT EXPECT to live always on a smooth and even plane. We all face problems, worries, and fears; we all have our setbacks, our sorrows and misfortunes. They are part of the substance of living, and none of us can escape them.

"You must make up your mind to the prospect of sustaining a certain measure of pain and trouble in your passage through life," said Cardinal Newman.

As John Burroughs so eloquently pointed out, "We cannot walk through life on mountain peaks." There are rivers and valleys along the way; and some are deep and treacherous, some a cruel challenge to human endurance. But courage conquers all things; and down through the centuries poets and philosophers have been telling us so in a fascinating variety of ways.

"The things courage can do!"

You will read about some of these things in the pages that follow. Here are some of the world's most inspiring sagas of courage and endurance. Here are quotations selected from all times, past and present, to give courage today to the sick, the handicapped, the discouraged, the frightened, the anguished and bereaved.

1. PAUL HAMILTON HAYNE

THIS, TOO, SHALL PASS AWAY

LONG AGO an Eastern monarch, plagued by many worries, harassed on every side, called his wise men together. He asked them to invent a motto, a few magic words that would help him in time of trial or distress. It must be brief enough to be engraved on a ring, he said, so that he could have it always before his eyes. It must be appropriate to every situation, as useful in prosperity as in adversity. It must be a motto wise and true and endlessly enduring, words by which a man could be guided all his life, in every circumstance, no matter what happened.

The wise men thought and thought, and finally came to the monarch with their magic words. They were words for every change or chance of fortune, declared the wise men ... words to fit every situation, good or bad ... words to ease the heart and mind in every circumstance. And the words they gave the monarch to engrave on his ring were:

This, too, shall pass away.

Century after century, this old legend has survived. Whether or not the motto was invented for a troubled monarch, no one really knows—nor is it in the least important. But this much is certain: *The words are wise and true and endlessly enduring.* They have proved their power over and over again through the centuries, to uncounted numbers of men and women, in every land and every conceivable situation. They have given comfort to the afflicted, courage to the frightened, hope to the worried and distressed. *This, too, shall pass away.* Poets and philosophers have stressed these five magic words over and over

again, each in his own fashion, but always with the same
inspiring influence.

One day, about a hundred years ago, an American editor
came across the legend and was impressed by its ancient
wisdom. He was Paul Hamilton Hayne, distinguished also
as a writer of light lyric verse. He was so enchanted by the
legend that he published a brief story about it, and was at
once astonished by the lively interest it created. So he
decided—as many had before, and many have since—to
write some verses about the famous phrase. By some
mysterious alchemy, his simple lines made an enormous
appeal to the public; and for years tattered copies of "This,
Too, Shall Pass Away," by Paul Hamilton Hayne, were
carried around in purse and pocket—the favorite inspirational poem of thousands of people:

> Art thou in misery, brother? Then I pray
> Be comforted. Thy grief shall pass away.
> Art thou elated? Ah, be not too gay;
> Temper thy joy: this, too, shall pass away.
> Art thou in danger? Still let reason sway,
> And cling to hope: this, too, shall pass away.
> Tempted art thou? In all thine anguish lay
> One truth to heart: this, too, shall pass away.
> Do rays of loftier glory round thee play?
> Kinglike art thou? This, too, shall pass away!
> Whate'er thou art, where'er thy footsteps stray,
> Heed these wise words: This, too, shall pass away.

Paul Hayne's poem won wide popularity in his own day;
and it has kept circulating ever since, continuing its influence on the afflicted, the distraught, the discouraged. Every
now and then it makes a tour of the newspapers, or is
featured in magazines. Sometimes it appears with a different title, or with lines changed to suit the times, or with
verses added or subtracted. Many other poets have used
the same theme, before and since; and occasionally a
hodgepodge of verses from various sources is collected
and published as "anonymous" or "author unknown." But

the philosophy is always the same, and always helpful to the troubled or despairing. *This, too, shall pass away*.

When Ray Stannard Baker was ill and in great pain,* he remembered the famous phrase and found it comforting. He wrote in his notebook: "Nothing lasts—not even pain."

When Stevenson was suffering bodily torment, weakened and wearied by the long struggle against tuberculosis, he kept reminding himself of the famous phrase, hoping each morning would find him better. It helped him to put his suffering out of his mind, helped him to keep writing. "A chapter a day I mean to do," he wrote to his friend William E. Henley—a man whose brand of courage matched his own.†

When Lincoln was forced to endure the hatred of millions because of his steadfast loyalty to purpose and principles, when he was bitterly reviled and condemned for refusing to consider an unjust peace, he reminded himself that *this, too, would pass* in time . . . and that with God's help he would weather the storm.

Countless other stories could be told of this inspiring phrase, these five magic words which legend says were engraved by wise men on a monarch's ring many centuries ago. They were comforting words for all of us to remember in times of trial or trouble, in times of hardship or affliction. When nothing else helps, it's comforting to know that no pain or grief can last forever, that whatever your burden may be—*this, too, shall pass away*.

Thou shalt forget thy misery, and remember it as waters that pass away.   *Job 11:16*

Think often of how swiftly all things pass away and are no more—the works of Nature and the works of man. The substance of the Universe, matter, is like unto a river that flows on forever. All things are not only in a constant state of change, but they are the cause of constant and infinite change in other

---

* See pages 104–07.
† See page 93.

things. Upon a narrow ledge thou standest! Behind thee, the bottomless abyss of the Past! In front of thee, the Future that will swallow up all things that are now. Over what things, then, in this present life wilt thou, O foolish man, be disquieted or exalted— making thyself wretched; seeing that they can vex thee only for a time—a brief, brief time!

Marcus Aurelius

Come what come may;
Time and the hour runs through the darkest day.
William Shakespeare

Nay, do not grieve tho' life be full of sadness,
Dawn will not veil her splendor for your grief,
Nor spring deny their bright, appointed beauty
To lotus blossom and ashoka leaf.

Nay, do not pine, tho' life be dark with trouble,
Time will not pause or tarry on his way;
Today that seems so long, so strange, so bitter,
Will soon be some forgotten yesterday.

Nay, do not weep; new hopes, new dreams, new faces,
The unspent joy of all the unborn years,
Will prove your heart a traitor to its sorrow,
And make your eyes unfaithful to their tears.
Sarojini Naidu

Beware of desperate steps; the darkest day,
Lived till tomorrow, will have passed away.
William Cowper

This, too, will pass. O heart, say it over and over,
Out of your deepest sorrow, out of your deepest grief,
No hurt can last forever—perhaps tomorrow
Will bring relief.

This, too, will pass. It will spend itself—its fury
Will die as the wind dies down with the setting sun;

Assuaged and calm, you will rest again, forgetting
A thing that is done.

Repeat it again and again, O heart, for your comfort;
This, too, will pass as surely as passed before
The old forgotten pain, and the other sorrows
That once you bore.

As certain as stars at night, or dawn after darkness,
Inherent as the lift of the blowing grass,
Whatever your despair or your frustration—
This, too, will pass.

Grace Noll Crowell

2. WILLIAM OSLER

WHAT IS PATIENCE BUT AN
EQUANIMITY WHICH ENABLES
YOU TO RISE SUPERIOR TO
THE TRIALS OF LIFE?

THE CLOCK struck two. In the soft pool of light from a reading lamp, Dr. William Osler* sat engrossed in a favorite book, *The Meditations of Marcus Aurelius*.

The calendar on his desk read April 27, 1889. On May 1st the graduating exercises would take place at the Medical School of the University of Pennsylvania; and on that same day he would sever his own connection with the University to become professor of medicine at Johns Hopkins.

As a departing member of the Faculty, and as one of the most notable speakers of his day, he had been asked to give the valedictory address. He knew he was expected to inspire the young graduate physicians and give them some useful advice to carry into their professional careers.

He read over again the paragraph he had marked in the *Meditations*. He read it aloud to hear the sound of the words, and it was as though Marcus Aurelius spoke from the shadows of the room:

"Thou must be like a promontory of the sea, against which, though the waves beat continually, yet it both itself stands, and about it are those swelling waves still and quieted."

More than most others, perhaps, young medical men needed poise and self-possession, needed calm strength to

---

* Created a baronet in 1911, and thereafter known as Sir William Osler.

withstand whatever problems or difficulties life might bring. They must indeed be like "promontories of the sea."

He thought of the group he was to address in a few days, many of whom he knew well. Eager, inexperienced young physicians, some of them anxious and unsure . . . some of them *too* sure for their own good. They would, of course, meet the inevitable trials and tribulations of professional life, the setbacks and disappointments, perhaps even failure and disillusion. It was important that they neither falter nor despair at such times, that they carry on with courage and with patience.

Thinking along these lines, his mind turned from Marcus Aurelius to Antoninus Pius, another of the old Roman rulers. Asked on his deathbed to sum up the philosophy of life, Antoninus had answered with a single dramatic word: *"Aequanimitas."*

Dr. Osler got up and stretched. He had been sitting in one position for a long time, lost in his books and thoughts. He walked slowly toward the bedroom, thinking of the address he was about to give and what he planned to say.

Aequanimitas. Equanimity. A calm patience. Strength to accept the trials of life and rise superior to them. . . .

As he lay in bed waiting for sleep, the address slowly took shape in his mind. And on May 1st, the students and Faculty of the University of Pennsylvania heard Dr. William Osler deliver the most inspiring address of his career: *Aequanimitas.*

To many the frost of custom has made even these imposing annual ceremonies cold and lifeless. To you they should have the solemnity of an ordinance—called as you are this day to a high dignity and to so weighty an office and charge.

It is my duty to say a few words of encouragement and to bid you, in the name of the Faculty, Godspeed on your journey. . . .

In the first place, in the physician or surgeon no quality takes rank with imperturbability, and I propose for a few minutes to direct your attention to this essential bodily virtue. Perhaps I may be able to give those of you, in whom it has not developed during the critical scenes of the past month, a hint or two of its importance, possibly a suggestion for its attainment. Imperturbability means coolness and presence of mind under all circumstances, calmness amid storm, clearness of judgment in moments of grave peril, immobility, impassiveness, or to use an old and expressive word, *phlegm*. It is the quality which is most appreciated by the laity though often misunderstood by them; and the physician who has the misfortune to be without it, who betrays indecision and worry, and who shows that he is flustered and flurried in ordinary emergencies, loses rapidly the confidence of his patients.

In full development, as we see it in some of our older colleagues, it has the nature of a divine gift, a blessing to the possessor, a comfort to all who come in contact with him. You should know it well, for there have been before you for years several striking illustrations, whose example has, I trust, made a deep impression. . . .

Cultivate, then, gentlemen, such a judicious measure of obtuseness as will enable you to meet the exigencies of practice with firmness and courage, without, at the same time, hardening the human heart by which we live. . . .

In the second place, there is a mental equivalent to this bodily endowment, which is as important in our pilgrimage as imperturbability. Let me recall to your minds an incident related of that best of men and wisest of rulers, Antoninus Pius, who, as he lay dying in his home at Lorium in Etruria, summed up the philosophy of life in the watchword, *Aequanimitas*. As for him, as for you, a calm equanimity is the desirable attitude. How difficult to attain, yet how necessary, in success as in failure! Natural temperament has much to do with its development, but a clear knowledge of our relation to our fellow creatures and to the work of life is also indispensable. One of the first essentials in securing a good-natured equanimity is not to expect too much of the people amongst whom you dwell. . . . There is need of infinite patience and understanding.

It is sad to think that, for some of you, there is in store disappointment, perhaps failure. You cannot hope, of course, to escape from the cares and anxieties incident to professional life. Stand up bravely, even against the worst. Your very hopes may have passed on out of sight . . . you may be left to struggle in the night alone. Well for you if you wrestle on, for in persistency lies victory, and with the morning may come the wished-for blessing. But not always; there is a struggle with defeat which some of you will have to bear, and it will be well for you in that day to have cultivated a cheerful equanimity. . . . Even with disaster ahead and ruin imminent, it is better to face them with a smile, and with the head erect, than to crouch at their approach. And if the fight is for principle and justice, even when failure seems certain, cling to your ideal. . . .

It has been said that "in patience ye shall win your souls," and what is this patience but an equanimity which enables you to rise superior to the trials of life?

Gentlemen, farewell! Take with you into the struggle the watchword of the good old Roman—*Aequanimitas*.

It is now more than sixty years since Dr. William Osler made his famous address at the University of Pennsylvania stressing the need to face life and its problems with equanimity.

Since then the word *"Aequanimitas"* has become familiar and significant to the entire medical profession. Two generations of doctors have been influenced by its vital message. Published subsequently in essay form, *Aequanimitas* can now be found on the shelves of countless doctors, along with such well-loved volumes as *Religio Medici* by Sir Thomas Browne and *Consecratio Medici* by Dr. Harvey Cushing. It has, in fact, become a treasured inspirational classic of the medical profession. Eminent physicians often give copies to young beginners, remembering the power of its influence on their own lives and careers.

Thus across the years the voice of a distinguished physician still speaks to the members of his profession, helping them to lead useful and contented lives. But his inspiring message is not for them alone. It is for all people, in every field of human endeavor: *Be calm and strong and patient. Meet failure and disappointment with courage. Rise superior to the trials of life, and never give in to hopelessness or despair. In danger, in adversity, cling to your principles and ideals. Aequanimitas!*

The gem cannot be polished without friction, nor man perfected without trials.   *Confucius*

Make the best use of what is in your power, and take the rest as it happens.   *Epictetus*

The burden becomes light which is cheerfully borne.
                                        Ovid

To struggle when hope is banished!
To live when life's salt is gone!
To dwell in a dream that's vanished—
To endure, and go calmly on!

                                        Ben Jonson

Dear God, give us strength to accept with serenity the things that cannot be changed. Give us courage to change the things than can and should be changed. And give us wisdom to distinguish one from the other.   *Admiral Thomas C. Hart*

It's not life that counts but the fortitude you bring into it.   *John Galsworthy*

Say not the struggle nought availeth,
    The labor and the wounds are vain,

The enemy faints not, nor faileth,
    And as things have been they remain.

If hopes were dupes, fears may be liars;
    It may be, in yon smoke conceal'd,
Your comrades chase e'en now the fliers,
    And, but for you, possess the field.

For while the tired waves, vainly breaking,
    Seem here no painful inch to gain,
Far back, through creeks and inlets making,
    Comes silent, flooding in, the main.

And not by eastern windows only,
    When daylight comes, comes in the light,
In front, the sun climbs slow, how slowly,
    But westward, look, the land is bright.

Arthur Hugh Clough

A serene fortitude in the face of disappointment and chagrin should be our goal. If you have evaded all unpleasantness in life your happiness is placed in unstable equilibrium by the constant dread that some unavoidable disappointment is just around the corner. If you have faced pain and disappointment, you not only value your happiness more highly, but you are prepared for unpredictable exigencies. Just as we can immunize ourselves against certain bodily diseases by stimulating our reserves to overactivity by taking graduated doses of toxin into our bodies, so we can immunize ourselves against adversity by meeting and facing the unavoidable chagrins of life, as they occur. There may be happy human vegetables who have succeeded in avoiding unhappiness and pain, but they cannot call themselves men.   *W. Beran Wolfe*

Patience and fortitude conquer all things.
Ralph Waldo Emerson

3. WILLIAM ERNEST HENLEY

I AM THE MASTER OF MY FATE:
I AM THE CAPTAIN OF MY SOUL

THE SUN cut sharply across one corner of the room. The young man on the cot gazed at the brightness for a moment, then turned and faced the wall. He had been in the Edinburgh Infirmary nearly two years now, while Dr. Lister tried desperately to save his remaining foot. He had been subjected to so many operations he had lost count—twenty at least, in the last twenty months! But he was not beaten yet.

He turned and faced the sun again, and smiled. Words rang through his mind, sang through his mind: *"In the fell clutch of circumstance I have not winced nor cried aloud."*

The man on the cot was William Ernest Henley. Few in this world are called upon to endure all he had in his brief twenty-five years. He had suffered since childhood from an agonizing tubercular infection of the bones, for which the usual Victorian remedy was amputation. One foot had already been removed, and the other was threatened. It was the hope of avoiding a second amputation that he had submitted to this long, lonely siege on a hospital cot. Dr. Joseph Lister had a new method of treating infections which he thought might save young Henley's foot, and keep him from becoming a complete cripple.

Illness, poverty, pain, and suffering . . . endless treatments and operations testing human courage to its limits: that had been William Henley's life for almost as far back as he could remember.

"But I won't give up!" he promised himself, smiling on his hospital cot. "I won't give up, no matter what happens. I thank God for my unconquerable soul!"

Out of the pain and suffering of his own personal life,

out of the courage, and faith, and fortitude with which he accepted the cruel blows of fate, came "Invictus"*—one of the most emotionally powerful and uplifting poems ever written:

Out of the night that covers me,
    Black as the pit from pole to pole,
I thank whatever gods may be
    For my unconquerable soul.

In the fell clutch of circumstance
    I have not winced nor cried aloud.
Under the bludgeonings of chance
    My head is bloody, but unbowed

Beyond this place of wrath and tears
    Looms but the Horror of the shade,
And yet the menace of the years
    Finds and shall find me unafraid.

It matters not how strait the gate,
    How charged with punishments the scroll.
I am the master of my fate:
    I am the captain of my soul.

Today in English-speaking schools all over the world, children learn to memorize and recite this inspiring poem. Though they may not entirely understand the meaning of its words, they feel the unmistakable impact of its force and power. And to countless thousands of men and women faced with sorrow, pain, or fear, it has brought the courage to accept the blows of fate, to triumph over physical handicaps, and carry on with head unbowed.

William Henley wrote many poems in his lifetime; but on the strength of "Invictus" alone he has won immortality. For born of years of struggle in the shadow of death, profoundly personal in its sources, arising literally "out of night," "Invictus" has brought new hope and the will to

---

* Latin for *invincible, unconquered.*

live to many who nearly lost their way, many who were
on the point of giving up.

"Invictus" belongs to mankind, now and for all the
ages to come. Of all the poems ever written, this one
perhaps best typifies man's rich inspirational heritage.

The spirit of a man will sustain his infirmity.
Proverbs 15:18

Just as so many rivers, so many showers of rain from
above, so many medicinal springs do not alter the
taste of the sea, so the pressure of adversity does not
affect the mind of the brave man. For it maintains
its balance, and over all that happens it throws its
own complexion, because it is more powerful than
eternal circumstances.   *Seneca*

O joy of suffering!
To struggle against great odds! to meet enemies un-
    daunted!
To be entirely alone with them! to find how much
    one can stand!
To look strife, torture, prison, popular odium, death,
    face to face!
To mount the scaffold! to advance to the muzzles of
    guns with perfect nonchalance!
To be indeed a God!
Walt Whitman

The chief pang of most trials is not so much the actual
suffering itself as our own spirit of resistance to it.
Jean Nicolas Grou

I like the man who faces what he must
    With step triumphant and a heart of cheer;
    Who fights the daily battle without fear;
Sees his hopes fail, yet keeps unfaltering trust
That God is God; that somehow, true and just
    His plans work out for mortals; not a tear
    Is shed when fortune, which the world holds dear,

Falls from his grasp; better, with love, a crust
Than living in dishonor; envies not
    Nor loses faith in man; but does his best
Nor ever mourns over his humbler lot,
    But with a smile and words of hope, gives zest
To every toiler; he alone is great
Who by a life heroic conquers fate.

Sarah K. Bolton

4. HAROLD RUSSELL

IT IS NOT WHAT YOU HAVE LOST, BUT
WHAT YOU HAVE LEFT THAT COUNTS

THE YOUNG man on the hospital bed came back to consciousness slowly and reluctantly, almost as though he knew and dreaded the shock that awaited him.

His hands were gone!

He looked up at the ends of his arms, wrapped in bandages. He looked up at the stumps at the end of his arms, and everything inside him went cold and numb. His hands were gone. He was a cripple.

"What good am I now?" he thought bitterly. "What can a man do without hands? My life is over."

But he was wrong. His life was not over. The most radiantly happy and successful years of his life were ahead of him. The loss of his hands was the turning point that led to undreamed-of triumph and success.

For the young man without hands was Harold Russell. He was to become a moving-picture star and a best-selling author; he was to marry his childhood sweetheart and achieve happiness and success far beyond the dreams of most men. But he didn't know it then, of course. He knew only that he had lost his hands, and that he was "helpless."

A sergeant paratrooper in World War II, Harold Russell lost his hands in an accident in a training camp. In the first agonizing weeks after the accident, he was overwhelmed by a sense of failure and defeat. He was terrified at the idea of going through life with steel hooks instead of hands, dreaded the thought of leaving the hospital someday and going out among people again. He didn't care much, in those days, whether he lived or died.

One day Charley McGonegal, who had lost his own hands in World War I, visited Russell in the hospital. He made the injured paratrooper see that the first and greatest obstacle he had to overcome was *himself*. He must conquer his bitterness and fear, the older man told him. He must become reconciled to his loss and adjust himself to it. There was a quotation from Emerson that had always helped him—perhaps it would help young Russell, too: *"For everything you have missed, you have gained something else."*

It *did* help. But when the Major told him he'd soon be well, soon be going home, he was filled with panic and doubt again. How could he manage—how would he get along? He was distressed at the thought of venturing "outside" and being on his own, mingling with people.

"There's one thing you ought to keep in mind, Russell," the Major said. "You are not crippled; you are merely handicapped."

What difference did it make, Russell thought. Crippled or handicapped; it was all the same. *But was it?* He went to the hospital library and looked up the two words. *Crippled* meant "disabled, incapable of proper or effective action." *Handicapped* meant "any disadvantage or hindrance making success in an undertaking more difficult."

Then he still had a chance! He could still make a success! It would be tougher to win, but he *could* win. That was the important thing. That was what he must keep thinking about . . . that, and what Charley McGonegal had told him. From then on he forced himself to keep those two thoughts uppermost in his mind. *He was not crippled; he was handicapped. And for everything he missed, he gained something else.*

It was wonderful what a difference his new mental attitude made. He stopped thinking about his loss and concentrated on what he had left. He stopped fighting his handlessness and accepted it, began thinking and planning for the future.

Slowly but surely Harold Russell fought his way back from bleak despair to radiant triumph and victory. He was selected to play a leading role in *The Best Years of Our Lives* and made a sensational success. He won two of Hollywood's prized Academy Awards. He wrote his autobiography and was as successful an author as an actor. He decided that the best way to use his new fame and influence was to help others handicapped as he was; and he went on lecture tours, spoke on the radio, utilizing talents and abilities he never dreamed he possessed—and might never have discovered had it not been for the loss of his hands. Writing about it later, he said:

I think it was Emerson who said that a man's weakness is often his greatest strength. Waking up in a hospital bed at Camp Mackall to find that I had no hands, I wasn't quite ready to believe that. But in the years since then I have discovered and rediscovered that truth over and over again.

There is nothing startlingly new in that, I know. It is a truism as old as man, nor was Emerson the first to state it, I'm sure. Yet it is a stark fact that can be, that must be, repeated constantly so long as there are human beings on this earth. In one way or another, each of us must pass through the fires at least once in his lifetime. Each of us must find out for himself that his handicaps, his failures and shortcomings must be conquered or else he must perish.

I suppose it is natural that people should demand that every story, no matter how humble and insignificant, have its moral, its lesson, its message. I don't know whether it is possible to wrap up a man's life that neatly and say: Here is what it means. But if you can, I have a deep feeling that mine might prove the deep, abiding truth of Emerson's words. My weakness—my handlessness—my sense of inferiority —has turned out to be my greatest strength. I didn't think so at the time it happened and I don't think I'd ever willingly lose my hands, if I had it to do all over again. But having lost them, I feel perhaps I have gained many fine things I might never have had with them. In a purely material sense, I know I am better off than I ever was before. But that is not the important thing. The important thing is that this seeming disaster has brought me a priceless wealth of the spirit that I am sure I could never have possessed otherwise. I have enjoyed a life that has been full and rich and rewarding, a life that has had a meaning and depth it never had before.

There is no easy formula for a happy living. Anyone who says he has one is either joking or lying. Even if I could, I have no intention or desire of putting forth any patented, neatly packaged recipe of my own. But there is one simple thought I should like to pass on, if I may. It is no sure-fire prescription for happiness; it is not guaranteed to bring any bluebirds singing in your back yard. I offer it merely because I found it can help prevent much vain regret and self-defeat. *It is not what you have lost, but what you have left that counts.* Too many of us squander precious energy, time, and courage dreaming of things that were and never can be again, instead of dedicating ourselves to realities and the heavy tasks of today.

If this story has any value or meaning at all—and I say this in all humility and sincerity—it is only because it confirms once again an ancient truth: that man's spirit is the most powerful force for good on earth.

People frequently marvel at the things I can do with my hooks. Well, perhaps it is marvelous. But the thing I never cease to marvel at is that I was able to meet the challenge of utter disaster and master it. For me, that was and is the all-important fact—that the human soul, beaten down, overwhelmed, faced by complete failure and ruin, can still rise up against unbearable odds and triumph.

Many men and women have conquered physical handicaps, have fought their way through anguish and defeat to great personal triumph. Many have achieved outstanding success in art, literature, music, science—in almost every field of human endeavor—in spite of serious handicaps, *with what they had left.*

But because Harold Russell's story is so close to our

own times, because it has met the needs of many facing the same problem in the aftermath of the war, it has been particularly inspiring. Millions of Americans saw Russell on the screen. Millions thrilled to the story of his courage and spirit, his triumph over despair, his dazzling accomplishments. Here was a handless man who lived a rich and rewarding life, a happy husband and father, a man who drove a car, played the piano, lived a completely normal existence.

"Then maybe there's hope for *me!*" breathed thousands of handicapped men and women. "Maybe someday I'll be successful and happy, too. . . ."

His story, so eloquently portrayed on the screen, so simply and humbly told in his book, touched the hearts of millions of people. It brought new hope to many who had been anguished and in despair, brought them courage and cheer.

And Harold Russell's inspiring message goes on, helping the handicapped to stand up to themselves, to triumph over their doubts and misgivings. *"It's not what you have lost, but what you have left that counts."*

The ideal man bears the accidents of life with dignity and grace, making the best of the circumstances.

Aristotle

Sickness is a hindrance to the body, but not to the will, unless the will consent. Lameness is a hindrance to the leg, but not to the will. Say this to yourself at each event that happens, for you shall find that though it hinders something else it will not hinder *you*. . . .

Remember that you are an actor in a play, and that the Playwright chooses the manner of it: If he wants you to act a poor man you must act the part with all your powers; and so if your part be a cripple or a magistrate or a plain man. For your business is to act the character that is given you and act it well. The choice of the cast is Another's.

Epictetus

Be willing to have it so. Acceptance of what has happened is the first step to overcoming the consequences of any misfortune.   *William James*

I thank God for my handicaps, for, through them, I have found myself, my work, and my God.
         Helen Keller

Nothing in this world is more inspiriting than a soul up against crippling circumstances who carries it off with courage and faith and undefeated character—nothing!

Mr. Newton Baker, Secretary of War in President Wilson's cabinet, told me that after World War I he used to visit in the Federal hospitals the worst casualties of the American Army. One of the very worst was a man with both legs gone, one arm gone, both eyes gone, his face terribly mutilated, who was wheeled around the grounds of the hospital in a perambulator by a nurse, but who still was radiant and full of spirit. Nobody expected him to live. When later Mr. Baker met somebody from the hospital he said, "Did that young man live?" And the answer was, "Did he live? I'll say he did! He married his nurse!" Marveling at the capacity of women to love, Mr. Baker put the matter by, until a few years later as trustee of Johns Hopkins University he received a letter from the president. They wished, said the president, to do an unusual thing, to hold a mid-semester convocation to bestow the degree of Doctor of Philosophy upon a young man who, though heavily handicapped, had done one of the most brilliant pieces of work ever done at the University. His name was that of the crippled veteran. Mr. Baker, quite incredulous that it could be the same man, but struck with that phrase, "heavily handicapped," made inquiries. Sure enough, it was he! Both legs gone, one arm gone, both eyes gone, but still, not part of the world's problem but part of the answer.

Not every handicapped person can win through to so conspicuous a result, but the spirit—the spirit that stays undefeated in spite of everything—is part of the solution, and those of us still strong and well who see it take another notch in our belts and go to our tasks again with fresh courage.   *Harry Emerson Fosdick*

I discovered early that the hardest thing to overcome is not a physical disability but the mental condition which it induces. The world, I found, has a way of taking a man pretty much at his own rating. If he permits his loss to make him embarrassed and apologetic, he will draw embarrassment from others. But if he gains his own respect, the respect of those around him comes easily.   *MajorAlexander P. de Seversky**

---

* Major Seversky, famous aviation expert and author of *Victory Through Air Power*, lost a leg in World War I.

5. DAVID GRAYSON

I WOULD NO LONGER RESIST AND
STRUGGLE; I WOULD ACCEPT THE
UNAVOIDABLE. . . . I BEGAN TO LET
GO, TO RELAX. . . . THE GREAT
REWARD WAS IN THE MIND. . . . I FELT
IT DID NOT MUCH MATTER WHAT
HAPPENED TO MY BODY.
NOTHING COULD TOUCH ME

RAY STANNARD BAKER lay on his hospital bed in an agony of pain, the aftermath of a serious operation. He knew the doctors were doing what they could for him. But this pain, this endless torment! How long could a man endure it?

Mr. Baker was a well-known journalist, biographer, and historian. He was also, under the pen name of "David Grayson," the writer of delightful essays about nature and the outdoors.

He wondered, as the pain relentlessly stayed with him hour after hour, whether he would ever be well enough to be either Baker or "Grayson" again, whether he would ever be well enough to resume his life and his life's work. He rang for the nurse, and she gave him something to ease the pain. He dozed for a while; but most of the long night he lay awake, suffering intensely.

Toward morning he reached for the little red-bound book on the table beside him, the beloved copy of Marcus Aurelius' *Meditations* that had given him so much comfort through the years and which went everywhere with him. He turned to a page he had marked and underscored, and that he knew almost by heart. It was comforting to read the familiar words:

In every pain let this thought be present, that there is no dishonor in it, nor does it make the governing intelligence worse.

Indeed, in the case of most pains, let this remark of Epicurus aid thee, that pain is neither intolerable nor everlasting—if thou bearest in mind that it has its limits, and if thou addest nothing to it in imagination.

Pain is either an evil to the body (then let the body say what it thinks of it!)—or to the soul. But it is in the power of the soul to maintain its own serenity and tranquillity, and not to think that pain is an evil. . . .

It will suffice thee to remember as concerning pain . . . that the mind may by stopping all manner of commerce and sympathy with the body, still retain its own tranquillity.

He turned to another part of the *Meditations* where he had underscored a favorite sentence, read and reread many times in the years gone by. The whole doctrine of Marcus Aurelius relating to misfortune and suffering was summed up in these few words: *"Nothing happens to any man which he is not formed by nature to bear."*

In the morning, remembering that W. H. Hudson wrote one of his best books, *Far Away and Long Ago,* while ill in bed—remembering that Stevenson wrote *Treasure Island* while suffering greatly from tuberculosis—Ray Baker was ashamed of his own weakness and submission. "There must be a technique for meeting pain," he told himself. "There must be a technique of endurance based on the power of the soul to maintain its own serenity, as Marcus Aurelius taught long ago."

He decided that the thing to do was to go on with his work, even here in the hospital—to write again, in spite of the pain. He rang for the nurse and asked her to bring some notebooks and pencils. Almost the first lines he wrote made him feel better; and discovering this, he continued to write most of the day—actually forgetting the pain for long periods at a time.

"Did you think you could have the good without the evil?" he wrote in his notebook. *"Did you think you could*

have the joy without the sorrow? .... I have been think-
ing much about pain. How could I help it? .... Sooner or
later, regardless of the wit of man, we have pain to face;
a reality; a final unescapable, immutable fact of life. What
poor souls, if we have then no philosophy to face it with!"

That night, when the torment seemed again unendurable,
he told himself: "This pain will not last; it never has lasted.
I'll think about what I am going to write tomorrow—not
about my body."

It helped! He had learned a technique of endurance.
Now let pain do its worst; it could not touch him where his
life really was:

> When I first came in here, I had several attacks
> which I thought I could not bear. I tried grim opposi-
> tion; obstinate and unthinking endurance; set teeth,
> muscles rigid, breath hard-held. I knew that it could
> not last; nothing in such extreme ever lasts. Thus I
> bore the fiery cycle of the paroxysms, taking some
> credit to myself for the obstinacy of what I considered
> courage, but which was really fear. I do not know
> how it may be in other cases—for pain is as various
> as life itself—but I began to reflect that if these
> seizures were inevitable, all the force of my opposi-
> tion, the sweat on my face, was a useless waste of
> strength and in the end, since failure was certain, a
> weakening of morale.
>
> *"Pain is neither intolerable nor everlasting. ... It*
> *is in the power of the soul to maintain its own*
> *serenity. ..."*
>
> Suddenly it came to me, as a kind of new light, that
> I would no longer resist and struggle; I would accept
> the unavoidable. If it was in the nature of my disease,
> what else that was wise could I do? At first the tor-
> ment, ravaging unrestrained, seemed even worse than
> before. It consumed me utterly. But I had a glimmer-
> ing sense that I was at least playing a voluntary part
> in my own destiny; that, somehow, I was substituting
> reason for blind, involuntary, fear-driven resistance.
> This effort I continued through the greater part of one

terrible night, failing often, unable to yield completely, driven by red-hot scourges into the old resistances. At dawn, in spite of the best medication the doctors knew, I was exhausted, but I began to feel that I was on the way toward what might be, for me, a new method.

This I practiced faithfully and with increasing confidence for some time. I no longer resisted the inevitable! I am not sure that there was a great decrease in the actual physical suffering; I do know that the period of the paroxysm was reduced, since resistance seemed merely to prolong it. But the great reward was in the *mind:* in my own ability to command myself in the face of such a catastrophe; to preserve my equanimity; to rest securely upon reason when panic might so easily overwhelm me. I had moments in the midst of such paroxysms during the earlier nights when I was so secure in mind, so tranquil, that I felt it did not much matter what happened to my body. *Nothing could touch me.*

Ray Stannard Baker recovered, and continued to write delightful books under the name of "David Grayson"— books about nature, friendship, happiness, and contentment. In one of these *(Under My Elm)* he included his technique for enduring pain, from which the above paragraphs are quoted.

Written on a hospital bed, to meet the challenge of his own great suffering, Mr. Baker's words have helped countless others through illness and pain . . . inspiring them with the stoicism which goes back nearly two thousand years to the philosophy of Marcus Aurelius: *"Nothing happens to any man which he is not formed by nature to bear."*

Many others have expressed this comforting philosophy, in many different ways—some more poetically, perhaps, but few more effectively. For by interpreting it in terms of his own experience, and by showing how it helped him in his own need, Ray Stannard Baker has made it timely and pertinent. He has brought the Stoic philosophy of

Marcus Aurelius up to date, for the use of those suffering pain or misfortune *today*.

Let us bear with magnanimity whatever it is needful for us to bear.   *Seneca*

Courage conquers all things; it even gives strength to the body.   *Ovid*

The powers of the Soul are commensurate with its needs.   *Ralph Waldo Emerson*

> Be steadfast as a tower that doth not bend
> Its stately summit to the tempest's shock.
>   *Dante*

For those who will fight bravely and not yield, there is triumphant victory over all the dark things of life.
                                  James Allen

Whenever evil befalls us, we ought to ask ourselves, after the first suffering, how we can turn it into good. So shall we take occasion, from one bitter root, to raise perhaps many flowers.   *Leigh Hunt*

Our minds have unbelievable power over our bodies.
                                André Maurois

6. MARY ROBERTS RINEHART

THERE IS NOTHING TO FEAR ABOUT
MOST CASES OF CANCER—NOTHING
EXCEPT DELAY!

THE INTERVIEW took place in a beautiful Park Avenue apartment in New York, late one afternoon in 1947. Both women were writers: one a feature writer for national magazines, the other a world-famous novelist. But the interview had nothing whatever to do with writing. Its purpose was to discuss a malady that millions feared, a disease whose very name filled people with dread. Those who survived it were usually silent about it, preferring to keep it their own uneasy secret; and more often than not they lived in constant fear of its recurrence.

But there was no such absurd secrecy here, no squeamish hesitancy to discuss what was clearly of vital interest and importance to many people.

"Yes, I had cancer," Mary Roberts Rinehart said—as matter-of-factly as though she were talking about a headache or a cold.

The lovely book-lined room in which she sat was the center of a rich and busy life. The desk was covered with notes and pages of typescript, for Mrs. Rinehart was just completing a new novel. The tea-table was spread with half a dozen extra cups for the unexpected guests who usually dropped in at this hour. She was beautifully gowned and coifed, a woman of great charm and poise—and of amazing vitality. She was at the height of as brilliantly successful a career as any American woman has known, and she was enjoying life to the utmost.

"Yes, I had cancer."

"And you are willing to talk about it, to tell others about it?" Gretta Palmer asked.

"I am *glad* to talk about it! This malady has been hedged about too long with the absurd belief that it is 'unmentionable.' Many cancer deaths are needless—are caused by fear, silence, delay. If my experience can be helpful to others, if it can give them the courage to meet the challenge of cancer in time, and to take up their lives again without the constant worry and fear of recurrence —well, I have no right to be silent."

Gretta Palmer's pencil was busy as Mrs. Rinehart spoke. Here was a vital message for the people of America: a warning to face danger in time. Here was living proof that cancer is not necessarily a death sentence, that it *can* be cured if caught in time, and that life *can* go on—a rich, full, busy, zestful life such as Mary Roberts Rinehart enjoyed.

Face your danger in time. That was the gist of the inspiring message Mrs. Rinehart gave her interviewer that afternoon. *Face your danger with courage and faith, and with the will to survive:*

> In days as worrisome as these, nothing belongs to us alone. Even our sorrows cannot be hoarded; even our private sufferings should not be withheld. . . .
>
> I do not know why cancer should be considered a more disgraceful malady than whooping cough or stomach ulcers. I don't know why *any* sickness should be considered shocking.
>
> But if it is disgraceful to have cancer, then I am thoroughly disgraced in the eyes of my family and friends. I had cancer. I discovered its presence early. I was completely cured of it. And I have never made the slightest secret of the fact.
>
> It was unpleasant and—yes—dramatic. This cancer business was an emergency for which I had to gather all my forces. It had in it many distressing elements; it would not be truthful to say that a cancer operation is a trivial thing. It is a serious occurrence to know that you are suffering from a disease of which many thousands of men and women die each year.

And recovery often involves for the patient a complete mental and physical re-education.

But I contrast it with other experiences and I see that my cancer operation was by no means the worst experience I have ever had. . . . It wasn't as soul-shattering as people think. Look at me: do you think my life is ruined?

No. . . . There is nothing for the modern man or woman to fear about most cases of cancer. Nothing except delay!

Mary Roberts Rinehart was operated upon for cancer in the spring of 1936. In the autumn of that same year she began writing a new mystery novel, *The Wall*. In 1937 she went to England for the coronation. She has traveled widely and written extensively ever since . . . has lectured, entertained, kept up with her old interests and launched many new ones . . . has been busier and more successful than ever before in her life. *A Light in the Window,* which she considers one of her best novels, was completed in 1947—her *fifty-eighth book!*

She has, in fact, never really been out of harness. The operation was a distressing experience, but not a devastating one. It would have been so easy for her to give up, to stop writing and rest on her laurels. It would have been so easy to slip into self-pity, to become a worried and perhaps embittered half-invalid. But her great courage, and her tremendous will to live and to carry on her work, protected her from such depressing aftereffects. She refused to think of herself as "doomed"—refused to give in to fear or despair. The cancer had been discovered in time; and when it was removed, she was ready and eager to take up where she had left off.

"Every crucial experience can be regarded as a setback —or the start of a new kind of development."

That had been her philosophy throughout life, and it had served her well in this crisis. It had helped her make a new start, and go on to even greater heights of achievement than before.

When Mrs. Rinehart's story appeared in print, it was

eagerly read and discussed all over the country. It gave courage and hope to many people . . . and helped them face their danger in time.

Today the radiantly happy and successful life of Mary Roberts Rinehart is an example to all who face a serious illness or the ordeal of an operation. *Every crucial experience can be a setback, or a new start.* These words have inspiring impact for all of us, in every distressing problem of life that calls for courage and endurance.

It is dangerous to abandon one's self to the luxury of grief; it deprives one of courage, and even of the wish for recovery.
Henri F. Amiel

If thou faint in the day of adversity, thy strength is small.
Proverbs 24:10

Never give up! If adversity presses,
Providence wisely has mingled the cup,
And the best counsel, in all your distresses,
Is the stout watchword of "Never give up."
Martin F. Tupper

Keep your fears to yourself, but share your courage with others.
Robert Louis Stevenson

7. ROBERT FALCON SCOTT

GOOD-BYE. . . . I AM NOT AT ALL
AFRAID OF THE END

THE MOVING dots on the vast shrieking wilderness of white were men. They moved slowly, very slowly—frozen, blinded, and almost completely exhausted. At last they could move no more. They pitched a tent in the howling desolation of wind and ice; and though they knew in their hearts they had little or no chance of survival, they tried to cheer each other and keep up their hopes.

Robert Falcon Scott had selected four of the hardiest men in his expedition to accompany him on the final dash to the South Pole. These five had made the trek alone, enduring months of incredible hardship and torment, but buoyed up by the hope of being the first to reach the Pole. When at last they did reach it, bitter disappointment faced them. *They were too late!* Amundsen, the Norwegian explorer, had been there before them, had beaten them to it. Crushed and heartsick, they turned back.

The story of their cruel march back toward civilization, of their heroic struggle against the forces of nature, and of their cheerful courage and unfailing devotion to each other is one of the most inspiring sagas of the twentieth century. Week after week they pushed through cold and wind. Week after week they faced weariness, hunger, and pain.

One of the five weakened; and though they did what they could to help, he soon gave up the struggle and died.

Another was injured; and unwilling to be a burden to his companions, he quietly walked out into the blizzard and disappeared.

The three who were left pushed on, tormented and exhausted, but still trying to cheer each other and still gal-

lantly pretending there was hope. At last, unable to
continue, they pitched camp—and prayed for a break in
the weather. But it got worse. A blizzard roared day and
night over the icy wastes and kept them imprisoned. Their
fuel gave out. Their food gave out. The end was near, and
they knew it.

Captain Scott faced death with the same courage with
which he had faced disappointment and hardship. Suffering terribly, his body brittle with cold, his fingers so stiff
he could hardly hold a pencil, he wrote a last message to
the world:

> I do not regret this journey. We took risks; we
> knew we took them. Therefore we have no cause for
> complaint. We bow to the will of Providence, deter-
> mined still to do our best to the last.
> Had we lived, I should have had a tale to tell of
> the hardihood, endurance, and courage of my com-
> panions which would have stirred the heart of every
> Englishman. These notes and our dead bodies must
> tell the tale. . . .

Eight months later the bodies of the three men were
found, and with them Captain Scott's notes and diary. And
they did indeed tell the tale—mutely but eloquently, and
for all time! It was a tale that stirred and saddened the
entire world, but left a shining example of courage and
devotion to duty that will endure as long as men can read.

"It seems a pity, but I do not think I can write any
more," was Captain Scott's final entry in his diary, when
every slightest movement must have been agony. And then,
thinking not of himself but of his family, and the families
of the men who lay dead beside him, he added, "For God's
sake, look after our people!" Those were his last words
before the pencil slipped forever from his frozen grasp.

But of all the brave notes Captain Scott left, the following message to his friend, Sir James M. Barrie, is the most
poignant and memorable. Remember that it was written
when all hope was gone, when Scott and his companions

were slowly starving and freezing to death in a bitter Antarctic blizzard:

> We are pegging out in a very comfortless spot. Hoping this letter may be found and sent to you, I write a word of farewell. . . .
> We are showing that Englishmen can still die with a bold spirit, fighting it out to the end. It will be known that we have accomplished our object in reaching the Pole, and that we have done everything possible. . . .
> Good-bye. I am not at all afraid of the end, but sad to miss many a humble pleasure which I had planned for the future. . . . We are in desperate state, feet frozen, etc. No fuel, and a long way from food. But it would do your heart good to be in our tent, to hear our songs and the cheery conversation.
> (Later) We are very near the end, but have not and will not lose our good cheer. We did intend to finish ourselves* when things proved like this, but have decided to die naturally. . . . I want you to think well of me and my end. . . . As a dying man, my dear friend, be good to my wife and child!

Sir James Barrie was proud of his letter from Captain Scott, and impressed by its great moral and spiritual significance. He felt that others should have an opportunity to read it, and to share in so inspiring a testament to the strength and dignity of the human spirit. So he published it in a little book called *Courage*.

At once the letter was quoted and requoted; it was read in schools and churches; it was made the subject of ringing speeches and sermons. It traveled around the world, translated into almost every language, and has today taken its place among the famous and unforgettable letters of mankind.

Robert Falcon Scott died with his task accomplished. Though too late to be first, he *did* reach the South Pole;

---

* They had a large quantity of opium with them, taken along for just such an emergency. But they decided not to use it.

and his geological observations helped to advance knowledge of the Antarctic region. But the conquest of the Pole, the tangible scientific gains of the expedition, were not his most important achievement. He gave the world something of even more vital and enduring value: a demonstration of man's courage and integrity in the face of intense suffering—in the face of death. Generations of men yet unborn will thrill to the saga of courage and endurance that Captain Scott wrote in the frozen wastes of the Antarctic, will be inspired and encouraged by his magnificent example.

Whoever is brave is a man of great soul. *Cicero*

Cowards die many times before their deaths:
The valiant never taste of death but once.
Of all the wonders that I yet have heard,
It seems to me most strange that men should fear;
Seeing that death, a necessary end,
Will come when it will come.
William Shakespeare

Death, be not proud, though some have called thee
Mighty and dreadful, for thou are not so:
For those whom thou think'st thou dost overthrow
Die not, poor Death, nor yet canst thou kill me.
From rest and sleep, which but thy pictures be,
Much pleasure, then from thee much more must flow;
And soonest our best men with thee do go—
Rest of their bones and souls' delivery!
Thou'rt slave to fate, chance, kings, and desperate men,
And dost with poison, war, and sickness dwell;
And poppy or charms can make us sleep as well,
And better than thy stroke. Why swell'st thou then?
One short sleep past, we wake eternally,
And Death shall be no more: Death, thou shalt die.
John Donne

8. WILLIAM CULLEN BRYANT

SO LIVE THAT WHEN THY SUMMONS
COMES . . . THOU GO NOT, LIKE THE
QUARRY-SLAVE AT NIGHT . . . BUT
SUSTAINED AND SOOTHED BY AN
UNFALTERING TRUST

THE YOUTH was heartsick with disappointment. He had come to this favorite spot in the woods to brood, and to think things out for himself. There was no point in letting the family see how badly he felt about it.

He had come home for the summer holiday eagerly expecting to enter Yale in the autumn. But his father had just told him he couldn't go. They were poor, and the family was large; he was sorry but he couldn't afford it.

Young Bryant had been careful not to let his father see how disappointed he was. But out here in the woods he could let himself go. With no one about but the birds and the chipmunks, he could be as gloomy as he liked.

It was cool under the trees, and the earth was fragrant with moisture. He kicked a stone and watched an insect scurry to safety. He thought of the years ahead, and what he had hoped to do with his life. It might be difficult now to accomplish all he had planned. He might even have to give up the idea of becoming a writer. He was filled with doubts and anxieties about the future.

Well, he couldn't go to Yale—and there was no use moping about it! He'd just have to accept the circumstances and make the best of them. He'd have to start thinking about some way to make a living and help the family.

Near him a bird burst suddenly into song. All about him were the whirring, trilling sounds of insects, busy in the grass and trees. Here in the woods nature was stirring, stretching, waking once again to the promise of spring.

Life's green spring—so brief, so fleeting! Less than a moment in the limitless span of eternity. A few brief months and all this eager, bursting life would be over, and it would be bleak in the woods, and silent. That was the lesson nature taught. . . .

A phrase came to his mind and stayed with him, like the tune of a haunting melody: *"Go forth under the open sky and list to Nature's teachings."*

For him, too, this was life's green spring, full of hope and promise. And for him, too, death would come one day, as it did to all things in nature. Then why torment himself about things that didn't really matter? All that counted was to live a good and useful life; and in the end approach death, not with fear, but with courage and faith.

So young William Cullen Bryant tried to rationalize his disappointment in terms of the inevitable end of life. Slowly he walked back toward the house, the woods darkening behind him. Phrases moved with stately grace and rhythm through his mind. *"Earth, that nourished thee, shall claim thy growth, to be resolved to earth again."* He said the words aloud and was fascinated by the sound they made. *"All that tread the globe are but a handful to the tribes that slumber in its bosom."*

By the time he reached the house, bitterness and disappointment were forgotten. Doubts and fears about the future were gone. His mind was filled with images and ideas, with words and singing phrases. He went at once to his room and began writing "Thanatopsis"*—destined to become one of the world's most famous poems.

To him who in the love of Nature holds
Communion with her visible forms, she speaks
A various language; for his gayer hours
She has a voice of gladness, and a smile
And eloquence of beauty, and she glides
Into his darker musings, with a mild
And healing sympathy, that steals away

---

* From two Greek words: *thanatos* (death) and *opsis* (view)—
"A View of Death."

Their sharpness, ere he is aware. When thoughts
Of the last bitter hour come like a blight
Over thy spirit, and sad images
Of the stern agony, and shroud, and pall,
And breathless darkness, and the narrow house,
Make thee to shudder and grow sick at heart;—
Go forth, under the open sky, and list
To Nature's teachings, while from all around—
Earth and her waters, and the depths of air—
Comes a still voice.—

     Yet a few days, and thee
The all-beholding sun shall see no more
In all his course; nor yet in the cold ground,
Where thy pale form was laid, with many tears,
Nor in the embrace of ocean, shall exist
Thy image. Earth, that nourished thee, shall claim
Thy growth, to be resolved to earth again,
And, lost each human trace, surrendering up
Thine individual being, shalt thou go
To mix for ever with the elements,
To be a brother to the insensible rock
And to the sluggish clod, which the rude swain
Turns with his share, and treads upon. The oak
Shall send his roots abroad, and pierce thy mould.

 Yet not to thine eternal resting-place
Shalt thou retire alone, nor couldst thou wish
Couch more magnificent. Thou shalt lie down
With patriarchs of the infant world—with kings,
The powerful of the earth—the wise, the good,
Fair forms, and hoary seers of ages past,
All in one mighty sepulchre. The hills
Rock-ribbed and ancient as the sun,—the vales
Stretching in pensive quietness between;
The venerable woods—rivers that move
In majesty, and the complaining brooks
That make the meadows green; and, poured round all,
Old Ocean's gray and melancholy waste,—

Are but the solemn decorations all
Of the great tomb of man. The golden sun,
The planets, all the infinite host of heaven,
Are shining on the sad abodes of death,
Through the still lapse of ages. All that tread
The globe are but a handful to the tribes
That slumber in its bosom.—Take the wings
Of morning, pierce the Barcan wilderness,
Or lose thyself in the continuous woods
Where rolls the Oregon, and hears no sound,
Save his own dashings—yet the dead are there:
And millions in those solitudes, since first
The flight of years began, have laid them down
In their last sleep—the dead reign there alone.
So shalt thou rest, and what if thou withdraw
In silence from the living, and no friend
Take note of thy departure? All that breathe
Will share thy destiny. The gay will laugh
When thou art gone, the solemn brood of care
Plod on, and each one as before will chase
His favorite phantom; yet all these shall leave
Their mirth and their employments, and shall come
And make their bed with thee. As the long train
Of ages glides away, the sons of men,
The youth in life's green spring, and he who goes
In the full strength of years, matron and maid,
The speechless babe, and the gray-headed man—
Shall one by one be gathered to thy side,
By those, who in their turn shall follow them.

So live, that when thy summons comes to join
The innumerable caravan, which moves
To that mysterious realm, where each shall take
His chamber in the silent halls of death,
Thou go not, like the quarry-slave at night,
Scourged to his dungeon, but, sustained and soothed
By an unfaltering trust, approach thy grave
Like one who wraps the drapery of his couch
About him, and lies down to pleasant dreams.

All that summer of his disappointment, William Cullen Bryant wandered in the woods near his home, read, dreamed, and wrote poetry. In the autumn he went away to start making a place for himself in the world. He left "Thanatopsis" in the drawer of his desk with a number of other poems and fragments of poems he hoped someday to complete. And there it remained unnoticed for six years.

Then one day Bryant's father came across the poem and began reading it. With growing excitement he realized that here was a work far superior to anything else the boy had written. He was, in fact, so overcome by its power and beauty that he took it to one of the editors of the *North American Review,* who enthusiastically confirmed his opinion. The poem was published in 1817 and created an immediate sensation.

"Thanatopsis" has been called "the first truly great poem produced in America." It has also been called "the world's most inspiring poem about death." Yet this magnificent achievement was the work of a boy still in his teens! Young Bryant's love of nature, his faith, his ideals, are inherent in every line, and reflect an amazing insight for one so young. He saw the inevitable end of life and was reconciled to it, determined to live so that in the end he could face the last and greatest adventure with serenity, "sustained and soothed by an unfaltering trust." Though he made some changes in the poem later on, the first draft was written when he was only seventeen, and most of it remains just as he originally wrote it.

"Thanatopsis" was Bryant's own favorite poem. He often turned to it in later year when he was troubled or distressed, as one turns to an old friend for comfort and understanding. It is said that when his beloved wife died, after forty years of ideal married life, he read and reread "Thanatopsis" as relief from his great sorrow.

Many others have turned to the comforting philosophy of "Thanatopsis" for strength and courage in times of trial. William G. Farrow, one of the executed Doolittle fliers, wrote in a last letter to his mother: "Read 'Thanatopsis' if you want to know how I am taking this."* The last nine lines are the most famous, and thousands of people know them by heart. In a nation-wide poll to find America's most popular poem, "Thanatopsis" came in third—an outstanding favorite.†

Spend your brief moment according to nature's law, and serenely greet the journey's end as an olive falls when it is ripe, blessing the branch that bare it, and giving thanks to the tree that gave it life.

Marcus Aurelius

Nature herself gives us courage. . . . Death is not to be feared. It is a friend. No man dies before his hour. The time you leave behind was no more yours than that which was before your birth and concerneth you no more. Make room for others as others have done for you. Like a full-fed guest, depart to rest. . . . The profit of life consists not in the space, but in the use. Some man hath lived long that has had a short life. . . .

Depart then without fear out of this world even as you came into it. The same way you came from death to life, return from life to death. Yield your torch to others as in a race. Your death is but a piece of the world's order, but a parcel of the world's life.

Michel de Montaigne

I often feel that death is not the enemy of life, but its friend, for it is the knowledge that our years are limited which makes them so precious. It is the truth that time is but lent to us which makes us, at our best, look upon our years as a trust handed into our temporary keeping. We are like children privileged to spend a day in a great park, a park filled with many gardens and playgrounds and azure-tinted lakes with white boats sailing upon the tranquil waves. True, the

---

* See page 56.

† In first place, "A Psalm of Life," by Longfellow. In second place, "The House by the Side of the Road," by Sam Walter Foss.

day allotted to each one of us is not the same in length, in light, in beauty. Some children of earth are privileged to spend a long and sunlit day in the garden of the earth. For others the day is shorter, cloudier, and dusk descends more quickly as in a winter's tale. But whether our life is a long summery day or a shorter wintry afternoon, we know that inevitably there are storms and squalls which overcast even the bluest heaven and there are sunlit rays which pierce the darkest autumn sky. The day that we are privileged to spend in the great park of life is not the same for all human beings, but there is enough beauty and joy and gaiety in the hours if we will but treasure them. Then for each one of us the moment comes when the great nurse, death, takes man, the child, by the hand and quietly says, "It is time to go home. Night is coming. It is your bedtime, child of earth. Come; you're tired. Lie down at last in the quiet nursery of nature and sleep. Sleep well. The day is gone. Stars shine in the canopy of eternity."

Joshua Loth Liebman

The truest end of life is to know that life never ends. . . . Death is no more than a turning of us over from time to eternity.   *William Penn*

How well he fell asleep!
Like some proud river, widening toward the sea;
Calmly and grandly, silently and deep,
Life joined eternity.

Samuel T. Coleridge

If this were my last day I'm almost sure
I'd spend it working in my garden. I
Would dig about my little plants, and try
To make them happy, so they would endure
Long after me. Then I would hide secure
Where my green arbor shades me from the sky,
And watch how bird and bee and butterfly
Came hovering to every flowery lure.

Then, as I rested, perhaps a friend or two,
Lovers of flowers would come, and we would walk
About my little garden paths and talk
Of peaceful times when all the world seemed true.
This may be my last day, for all I know;
What a temptation just to spend it so!

Anne Higginson Spicer

9. ROBERT INGERSOLL

I WISH TO TAKE FROM EVERY GRAVE
ITS FEAR. . . . THE DEAD DO NOT
SUFFER. . . . DEATH IS ONLY
PERFECT REST

IT WAS a cold, gray day in January, and a persistent drizzle added to the misery of the little group gathered about the open grave. A child was being buried. The mother sobbed brokenly, and beside her stood the child's father, dry-eyed and anguished.

A few feet away, his head bared, his heart filled with sympathy for the bereaved and stricken parents, stood a man whose name was known throughout the nation. He was a brilliant lawyer, a famous writer and lecturer, one of the most eloquent and dynamic orators of his day. It so happened that he was also a free-thinker in matters of religion; and he had come to be known—disdainfully by some—as "the Great Agnostic."

Robert Ingersoll moved in different circles, was on a much higher social level, than these humble folk who were burying their child today. But they had long been his friends, and their grief was his grief. He wished there were some way he could comfort them and lighten their burden.

The undertaker stepped up to him and touched his arm. "Will you say a few words?"

But he shook his head. "No. No, I couldn't do that."

Then he saw the father's face, saw his look of anguish and appeal. "Does *he* desire it?" he asked. "Does he wish me to speak?"

The undertaker nodded; and Robert Ingersoll walked at once to the edge of the grave, stood beside the little coffin. He spoke slowly, with infinite tenderness and compassion:

125

My Friends: I know how vain it is to gild a grief with words, and yet I wish to take from every grave its fear. Here in this world, where life and death are equal kings, all should be brave enough to meet what all the dead have met. The future has been filled with fear, stained and polluted by the heartless past. From the wondrous tree of life the buds and blossoms fall with ripened fruit, and in the common bed of earth, patriarchs and babes sleep side by side.

Why should we fear that which will come to all that is? We cannot tell, we do not know, which is the greater blessing—life or death. We cannot say that death is not a good. We do not know whether the grave is the end of this life, or the door of another, or whether the night here is not somewhere else a dawn. . . .

Every cradle asks us "Whence?"~and every coffin "Whither?" The poor barbarian, weeping above his dead, can answer these questions just as well as the robed priest of the most authentic creed. The tearful ignorance of the one is as consoling as the learned and unmeaning words of the other. No man, standing where the horizon of a life has touched a grave, has any right to prophesy a future filled with pain and tears.

It may be that death gives all there is of worth to life. If those we press and strain within our arms could never die, perhaps that love would wither from the earth. Maybe this common fate treads from out the paths between our hearts the weeds of selfishness and hate. And I had rather live and love where death is king, than have eternal life where love is not. Another life is nought, unless we know and love again the ones who love us here.

They who stand with breaking hearts around this little grave need have no fear. The larger and the nobler faith in all that is, and is to be, tells us that death, even at its worst, is only perfect rest. We know that through the common wants of life—the needs and duties of each hour—their grief will lessen day by day, until at last this grave will be to them a place of rest and peace—almost of joy. There is for them this consolation: The dead do not suffer. If they live again, their lives will surely be as good as ours. We have no fear. We are all children of the same mother, and the same fate awaits us all.

We, too, have our religion, and it is this: Help for the living—Hope for the dead.

Among the many eloquent speeches Robert Ingersoll made in his lifetime, these "few words" spoken at the grave of a child stand out as unusually beautiful and inspiring. They are all the more significant in view of the fact that they were spoken by a man who was called an "unbeliever," and who had done much to tear down cherished beliefs.

We cannot tell, he says. *We do not know. But whether death is an end or a beginning, we must not fear. For death is perfect rest and peace. The dead do not suffer.*

His words came spontaneously from a heart filled with sympathy for the grieving parents. His only thought was to give them comfort and consolation, to ease the burden of their pain.

If somewhere else there is another dawn, if somewhere else your child lives again, surely its life will be as good as ours. So be comforted. Take up your daily lives; help each other; hope that someday you will know and love again the child you loved here.

It was a masterpiece of delicacy and understanding. It struck a responsive chord in every heart, and none who heard his words that day ever forgot them. He was later asked to repeat the words as nearly as he could, and they were published for the comfort of other bereaved parents.

"What other orator, ancient or modern, could have planted on the grave of a child a flower as delicate as this?" asks his biographer, Herman E. Kittredge.

Robert Ingersoll's famous oration at the grave of a child is today regarded by many as a classic of inspiration. It has long been a source of comfort to people of all faiths

in the dark hour of bereavement; and it remains an enduring monument to the memory of the man they called "the
Great Agnostic."

There is no grief which time does not lessen and
soften.   *Cicero*

It is very sad to lose your child just when he was
beginning to bind himself to you, and I don't know
that it is much consolation to reflect that the longer he
had wound himself up in your heart-strings the worse
the tear would have been, which seems to have been
inevitable sooner or later. One does not weigh and
measure these things while grief is fresh, and in my
experience a deep plunge into the waters of sorrow is
the hopefullest way of getting through them on one's
daily road of life again. No one can help another very
much in these crises of life; but love and sympathy
count for something.   *Thomas H. Huxley*

It is impossible that anything so natural, so necessary,
and so universal as death should ever have been designed as an evil to mankind.   *Jonathan Swift*

> Death is only an old door
>   Set in a garden wall.
> On quiet hinges it gives at dusk,
>   When the thrushes call.
>
> Along the lintel are green leaves,
>   Beyond, the light lies still;
> Very weary and willing feet
>   Go over that sill.
>
> There is nothing to trouble any heart,
>   Nothing to hurt at all.
> Death is only an old door
>   In a garden wall.
>
> *Nancy Byrd Turner*

10. JAMES GORDON GILKEY

FACING AND ACCEPTING A LOSS IS THE
FIRST STEP OF MANAGING BEREAVEMENT.
ONLY THE LIFE WHICH DELIBERATELY
PICKS UP AND STARTS OVER AGAIN IS
VICTORIOUS

THE MINISTER sighed as he put down the letter he had
been reading. It was the second such tragic communication in a week. This one was from a girl whose fiancé, a
naval officer in the Pacific, had been killed in action; and
she was anguished and bitter, her faith shaken.

She had lost everything, she wrote. Life no longer had
any meaning for her. How could she go on when the person she loved and needed most was gone? How could she
ever have faith in anything any more?

Dr. James Gordon Gilkey, pastor of the South Con-
gregational Church in Springfield, Massachusetts, had received frantic pleas for help and guidance before. But for
some reason this letter touched him profoundly. *"Please
help me!"* the girl had begged. *"Tell me what to do. . . ."*

It was more than a call for help; it was a challenge. This
girl was facing one of life's difficult problems. She needed
more than a few comforting words to help her. She needed
something tangible, a method for managing her bereavement, for making her way through and beyond her loss
and taking up her life again.

You must stop pitying yourself, he wrote her. *Sorrow
cannot be conquered by bitterness and resentment. You
must accept your loss, turn from it as from a closed door.
You must take up your daily activities again, make new
friends, find new interests. . . .*

He realized that others were facing the same problem

129

in these tragic war years, that death was striking cruelly in every direction. In wartime, perhaps more than any other time, people needed to know how to manage bereavement, how to bear up under the burden of grief. Suddenly he remembered a clipping someone had sent him years ago: the story of a brave young woman, the wife of a lighthouse-keeper. When her husband died she was overcome by grief; but day after day she tended the light . . . and day after day she slowly conquered her bereavement.

Dr. Gilkey took the clipping from his file and read it over again. Yes, it was an inspiring story—and a very timely one! He decided to use it in next week's sermon. He sat down and began to write:

Misfortune cannot be conquered by furious and continuing resentment. It can be conquered only by quiet acquiescence. We win victory over bereavement only when we face our loss. You ask how we make our way through it and beyond it? We do so by deliberately re-entering the world of daily activity— the busy world of problems, duties, friendships, opportunities, satisfactions. An immolated, resentful, self-pitying life is a doomed life. Only the life which deliberately picks up and starts again is victorious.

In New York Harbor, between Manhattan Island and Staten Island, is a sunken shoal called Robbins Reef. A small lighthouse stands there, and for many years the keeper was an elderly widow, Mrs. Jacob Walker. One day she told her story to a reporter, who gave it to the world.

"I was a young girl living at Sandy Hook, New Jersey," she said, "when I first met my husband. He was keeper of the Sandy Hook Light, and took me there as his bride. I was happy there, for the lighthouse was on land and I could have a garden and raise flowers. Then one day we were transferred here —to Robbins Reef. As soon as we arrived I said to my husband, 'I can't stay here! The sight of water wherever I look makes me too lonesome. I won't unpack. . . .' But somehow all the trunks and boxes got unpacked.

"Four years later my husband caught cold while tending the light. The cold turned to pneumonia, and they took him to the infirmary on Staten Island.

"I stayed behind to tend the light. A few nights later I saw a rowboat coming through the darkness. Something told me the message it was bringing. The man in the boat said, 'We're sorry, Mrs. Walker, but your husband's worse. 'You mean he's dead,' I answered; and there was no reply.

"We buried my husband on a hillside on Staten Island. Every morning when the sun comes up I stand at a porthole and look across the water toward his grave. Sometimes the hill is green, sometimes it is brown, sometimes it is white with snow. But it always brings a message from him—something I heard him say more often than anything else. Just three words—'Mind the light!' "

Facing a loss, accepting a loss, then re-entering life and so moving through and beyond the loss—there is the first secret of managing bereavement. *A self-pitying life is a doomed life. Only the life which deliberately picks up and starts over again is victorious.*

The loss of a loved one is a sorrow all of us must eventually face, and never is help more urgently needed than during the first dark days of bereavement. To many facing this unhappy period, Dr. Gilkey's message has brought strength and understanding. His philosophy of "picking up and starting over again" has helped many overcome bitterness and despair, and make a new life for themselves.

Dr. Gilkey's "Victory Over Bereavement" was intended originally as a sermon, and was used for that purpose. But it was subsequently included in his book, *When Life Gets Hard,* and its influence reached far beyond his own pulpit. It has since been published in the *Reader's Digest,* and has been widely quoted elsewhere; and it has earned its place in this anthology by proving itself a help and inspiration to the bereaved.

Excess of grief for the deceased is madness; for it is an injury to the living, and the dead know it not.

Xenophon

The true way to mourn the dead is to take care of the living who belong to them.   *Edmund Burke*

We bereaved are not alone. We belong to the largest company in all the world—the company of those who have known suffering. When it seems that our sorrow is too great to be borne, let us think of the great family of the heavy-hearted into which our grief has given us entrance, and inevitably, we will feel about us their arms, their sympathy, their understanding.

Believe, when you are most unhappy, that there is something for you to do in the world. So long as you can sweeten another's pain, life is not in vain. . . .

Robbed of joy, of courage, of the very desire to live, the newly bereaved frequently avoids companionship, feeling himself so limp with misery and so empty of vitality that he is ill-suited for human contacts. And yet no one is so bereaved, so miserable, that he cannot find someone else to succor, someone who needs friendship, understanding, and courage more than he. The unselfish effort to bring cheer to others will be the beginning of a happier life for ourselves. . . .

Often when the heart is torn with sorrow, spiritually we wander like a traveler lost in a deep wood. We grow frightened, lose all sense of direction, batter ourselves against trees and rocks in our attempt to find a path. All the while there is a path—a path of Faith—that leads straight out of the dense tangle of our difficulties into the open road we are seeking. Let us not weep for those who have gone away when their lives were at full bloom and beauty. Who are we that we should mourn them and wish them back?

Life at its every stage is good, but who shall say whether those who die in the splendor of their prime are not fortunate to have known no abatement, no dulling of the flame by ash, no slow fading of life's perfect flower.   *Helen Keller*

11. HENRY WADSWORTH LONGFELLOW

LET US, THEN, BE UP AND DOING,
WITH A HEART FOR ANY FATE;
STILL ACHIEVING, STILL PURSUING,
LEARN TO LABOR AND TO WAIT

IT WAS early morning. The bright sun streamed through the windows of the Craigie house in Cambridge where George Washington had once had his headquarters, and where a young Harvard professor now lived. He lived, in fact, in the very room that Washington had occupied. And as he stood gazing out of the window at the sloping lawn and the elms, he wondered if Washington might not have stood here once feeling perhaps as he did—unutterably lonely and dejected.

The young man's wife had died three years ago, but he longed for her still. Time had not softened his grief nor eased the torment of his memories. He turned restlessly from the window and wondered how to spend the time before breakfast.

He was a poet too, this young professor; but he had no heart for poetry these days. He had no heart for anything, it seemed. Life had become an empty dream.

But this could not go on, he told himself! He was letting the days slip by, nursing his despondency. Life was *not* an empty dream! He must be up and doing. Let the dead past bury its dead. . . .

Suddenly Henry Wadsworth Longfellow was writing in a surge of inspiration, the lines coming almost too quickly for his racing pen:

Tell me not, in mournful numbers,
Life is but an empty dream!—

For the soul is dead that slumbers,
    And things are not what they seem.

Life is real! Life is earnest!
    And the grave is not its goal;
Dust thou art, to dust returnest,
    Was not spoken of the soul.

Not enjoyment, and not sorrow,
    Is our destined end or way;
But to act, that each tomorrow
    Find us farther than today.

Art is long, and Time is fleeting,
    And our hearts, though stout and brave,
Still, like muffled drums, are beating
    Funeral marches to the grave.

In the world's broad field of battle,
    In the bivouac of Life,
Be not like dumb, driven cattle!
    Be a hero in the strife!

Trust no Future, howe'er pleasant!
    Let the dead Past bury its dead!
Act,—act in the living Present!
    Heart within, and God o'erhead!

Lives of great men all remind us
    We can make our lives sublime,
And, departing, leave behind us
    Footprints on the sands of time;

Footprints, that perhaps another,
    Sailing o'er life's solemn main,
A forlorn and shipwrecked brother,
    Seeing, shall take heart again.

Let us, then, be up and doing,
    With a heart for any fate;

> Still achieving, still pursuing,
>   Learn to labor and to wait.

Longfellow called his poem "A Psalm of Life." He put it aside at first, unwilling to show it to anyone; for as he later explained, "it was a voice from my inmost heart, at a time when I was rallying from depression."

But later he allowed it to be published . . . and it went straight to the hearts of millions of people. No poem ever written became so well known so fast. It was taught in schools, recited on the stage, discussed from pulpit and lecture platform. It crossed the ocean and spread like wildfire through England. It was translated into French, German, Italian, Spanish, Portuguese, Dutch, Swedish, Danish —even Sanskrit! In China it was printed on a fan and became immensely popular.

A whole generation of school children grew up under the influence of Longfellow's "Psalm." Many prominent men later acknowledged that influence with gratitude. Henry Ford, for example, memorized it as a lad, and in later years often said that the sixth and ninth stanzas came back to him all his life, inspiring him to effort and achievement. Firestone also freely acknowledged his indebtedness to the poem, as did many other famous men. Edward Bok made a special visit to Longfellow to tell him how much the last four lines meant to him. Even Gandhi, on the other side of the world, quoted a favorite line from it just a few days before his death (". . . things are not what they seem").

The call to courage and action of a man emerging from a great sorrow, "A Psalm of Life" is one of the best-loved and most widely read poems in the world. Its lines are full of faith and hope, its message clear and unmistakable. Its appeal is as vital and timely now as it ever was; in a recent poll to determine the nation's favorite poem, it easily won the first place. For over a hundred years "A Psalm of Life" has helped the weary, unhappy, and discouraged to be "up and doing, with a heart for any fate." No poem more richly deserves its place among the inspirational classics of mankind.

Never despair. But if you do, work on in despair.
Edmund Burke

I must lose myself in action, lest I wither in despair.
Alfred Tennyson

As a physician, I have had the happiness of seeing work cure many persons who have suffered from trembling palsy of the soul which results from over-mastering doubts, hesitations, vacillation, and fear. . . . Courage given us by our work is like the self-reliance which Emerson has made forever glorious.
Richard C. Cabot

Learn to wait——life's hardest lesson
   Conned, perchance, through blinding tears;
While the heart throbs sadly echo
   To the tread of passing years.
Learn to wait——hope's slow fruition;
   Faint not, though the way seems long;
There is joy in each condition;
   Hearts through suffering may grow strong.
Thus a soul untouched by sorrow
   Aims not at a higher state;
Joy seeks not a brighter morrow;
   Only sad hearts learn to wait.
Author unknown

When the day returns, call us up with morning faces and with morning hearts, eager to labor, happy if happiness be our portion, and if the day be marked for sorrow, strong to endure.
Robert Louis Stevenson

12. FRANKLIN D. ROOSEVELT

THE ONLY THING WE HAVE TO FEAR
IS FEAR ITSELF

IT WAS March, 1933—and America was in the depths of the worst depression in its history. The economic life of the nation had slowed almost to a standstill. An estimated fifteen million men were unemployed, their families hungry and cold, many of them homeless. Hundreds of thousands of small farmers had lost their land. Banks were closing; factories were standing idle; people were in a state of anxiety verging on despair. No one knew what to expect next. Fear hung like a heavy cloud over the nation; and panic gathered like a storm, dark and foreboding.

Against this background of national depression and fear, a new President was inaugurated on the fourth of March. Eagerly the nation awaited his address, his first message to the people. Thousands of men and women jammed the space before the east steps of the Capitol where he was to speak. Millions waited beside their radios, wondering what the new President would say, wondering what he *could* say to ease the dread in people's hearts and give them hope for the future.

Franklin Delano Roosevelt faced the huge, hushed crowd. He was conscious of his role on this fateful day, of the problems he faced, and his great responsibility to the people and to the nation. He was assuming the highest office in the land, amid the throes of a crisis unprecedented in times of peace. He knew there was hardly a home in America that had not been affected by the depression to some degree; knew that fear held the nation in its demoralizing grip—and that his first task was to restore public confidence and morale.

"This is a day of national consecration."

His voice rang out, firm and clear, reaching to the far limits of the crowd. It echoed in millions of homes across the land, dynamic and compelling. This was no time for evasion, he told the people. This was a time to speak out boldly, to face the facts. There were grave problems ahead, but he asked them to meet the challenge with courage, to have faith in the nation and its future. . . .

> This great nation will endure as it has endured, will revive and will prosper. So first of all, let me assert my firm belief that the only thing we have to fear is fear itself—nameless, unreasoning, unjustified terror which paralyzes needed efforts to convert retreat into advance.

There was an electric quality to his words, to his voice. All over the country people relaxed as they listened. His vigor, his assurance, his vast optimism about the future, had their effect; and hope revived in many hearts long attuned to despair.

The only thing we have to fear is fear itself. President Roosevelt's words thrilled the nation. They were the words millions wanted to hear, words of heartening faith and courage; nothing to fear . . . no need for panic . . . the nation would endue and prosper.

"He has revived the confidence of the common man in his country and his government," was the consensus of editorial opinion.

"We listened—some doubtfully," said William O. Douglas. "People who like statistics said it was hardly a scientific plan for getting the country going again. But after a little while it turned out we were not afraid any more. And the wheels were starting to run again. President Roosevelt's confidence had sort of reached around and got into the hearts of our people."

The only thing we have to fear is fear itself. These unforgettable words spoken by Franklin D. Roosevelt at his first inauguration, giving courage to the nation when it stood at the brink of panic and disaster, are words for all of us to remember in the crises of our personal lives. For they have the power to bolster our inner resources, to keep us from giving way to terror or despair.

When the President lay dead in the White House in 1945, Mrs. Roosevelt asked that the famous phrase from his inaugural be included in the simple funeral services. She told the officiating clergyman that these ten words best expressed the message her husband would have wanted to leave with the people. *The only thing we have to fear is fear itself.* An inspired and inspiring phrase . . . an enduring testament to a great man's faith in the nation and the people he served.

The battle is not to the strong alone; it is to the vigilant, the active, the brave.   *Patrick Henry*

We shall steer safely through every storm, so long as our heart is right, our intention fervent, our courage steadfast, and our trust fixed on God. If at times we are somewhat stunned by the tempest, never fear. Let us take breath, and go on afresh.   *Francis de Sales*

Nothing in life is to be feared. It is only to be understood.   *Marie Curie*

Quiet minds cannot be perplexed or frightened, but go on in fortune or misfortune at their own private pace, like a clock during a thunderstorm.
                Robert Louis Stevenson

PART FOUR

CONFIDENCE

&

Achievement

"Men were born to succeed, not to fail."

HENRY DAVID THOREAU

LIKE HAPPINESS, success has always been one of the fundamental goals of mankind. Many have written of success, in many different ways; but the rules have never changed and never will.

"Success depends on a *plus* condition of mind and body, on power of work, on courage," wrote Emerson, whose famous essay "Self-Reliance" has been a dominating influence in the lives of countless successful men and women.

"If we want more roses, we must plant more trees!" said George Eliot, eloquently summing up one of the oldest and most priceless secrets of achievement.

Read what others have said, in the pages that follow. Here are some of the most helpful and inspiring words ever written on success and achievement, from ancient times to our own.

1. THOMAS CARLYLE

BLESSED IS HE WHO HAS FOUND HIS WORK

THE HOUSE was quiet—so quiet he could hear the ticking of the clock in the next room. Thomas Carlyle leaned his head back against the chair and thought of what he had just written. This essay, "Labor," had a special meaning for him.

"A man must get his happiness out of his work," he thought. "That's the first of his problems: to find the work he is meant to do in this world. Without work he enjoys, he can never know what happiness is."

Thomas Carlyle knew. He knew better than most men. All his life until now had been a struggle against poverty and illness, against uncertainty and despair. He had prepared for the ministry, but gave it up when he could no longer accept the bigotry of narrow creed. He had tried teaching, but gave that up when he lost patience with stupidity. He had tried other professions, briefly and without joy, though always doing his duty as he saw it.

Not until he turned to writing did he find his life's work, and his life's happiness. He described it later in his reminiscences as "an immense victory." In finding the work he loved, he found purpose and direction; he found at last the inner satisfaction for which he had searched so long.

He picked up the essay and read what he had written. *"Know thy work and do it."* He nodded. There could be no better gospel for any man!

There is a perennial nobleness, and even sacredness, in work. Were he ever so benighted, forgetful of his high calling, there is always hope in a man that actually and earnestly works. In idleness alone is there perpetual despair.

The latest gospel in this world is, *Know thy work and do it*. It has been written, "An endless significance lies in work." A man perfects himself by working. Foul jungles are cleared away, fair seed-fields rise instead, and stately cities. . . .

Blessed is he who has found his work; let him ask no other blessedness. He has a work, a life-purpose; he has found it, and will follow it. . . . *Labor is life.*

One of the bright stars in Britain's shining galaxy of nineteenth-century genius, Thomas Carlyle left a rich legacy to world literature. But perhaps nothing he has written is so well known, certainly nothing is so widely quoted, as the eight simple words that express his lifelong philosophy: *Blessed is he who has found his work*. For over a hundred years this familiar sentence has emphasized the dignity of a life's work and a life's purpose . . . and has been a source of inspiration to countless men and women.

Browning, Dickens, Tennyson, Thackeray, were only a few of the great who were attracted by Carlyle's philosophy and influenced by it. Ruskin and Darwin were ardent disciples; like Carlyle, they found the work they were meant to do—and, like him, "asked no other blessedness." Emerson met Carlyle and was matured and inspired by his influence, clearly reflecting that influence in his own writings. Sir William Osler read Carlyle as a youth, and acquired from him the way of life to which he always in later years attributed his success. Thomas H. Huxley summed up the experience of many others when he said, "The lesson I learned from Carlyle as a boy has stuck by me all my life."

Today Carlyle's words have a deeper significance than ever. *"Get your happiness out of your work or you will never know what real happiness is."* There is an inspiring message here for those who are discouraged and discontent.

No man is born into the world whose work is not
born with him.   *James Russell Lowell*

Let me but do my work from day to day,
    In field or forest, at the desk or loom,
In roaring market-place or tranquil room;
Let me but find it in my heart to say,
When vagrant wishes beckon me astray,
    "This is my work; my blessing, not my doom:
Of all who live, I am the one by whom
    This work can best be done in the right way."

Then shall I see it not too great, nor small,
    To suit my spirit and to prove my powers;
Then shall I cheerful greet the laboring hours,
    And cheerful turn, when the long shadows fall
At eventide, to play and love and rest,
Because I know for me my work is best.
                     Henry van Dyke

My program is work, for man was designed for labor.
"Thou shalt live by the sweat of thy brow" was written centuries ago and the immutable destiny of man
will never change. What each man has to do is to try
to progress in his profession, to strive for constant
improvement so as to become effective and skillful
in whatever career he has chosen and to attain su-
periority by the cultivation of his natural gifts and by
his devotion to work. That is the path I have laid out
for myself. All the rest is mere dreaming or specula-
tion.   *Jean François Millet*

The man who is born with a talent which he is meant
to use finds his greatest happiness in using it.
                     Johann von Goethe

It is only well with me when I have a chisel in my
hand.   *Michelangelo*

If you cannot work with love but only with distaste, it is better that you should leave your work and sit at the gate of the temple and take alms of those who work with joy.   *Kahlil Gibran*

In the long run it makes little difference how cleverly others are deceived; if we are not doing what we are best equipped to do, or doing well what we have undertaken as our personal contribution to the world's work, at least by way of an earnestly followed avocation, there will be a core of unhappiness in our lives which will be more and more difficult to ignore as the years pass.   *Dorothea Brande*

2. JOAQUIN MILLER

"WHAT SHALL WE DO WHEN HOPE IS
    GONE?"
THE WORDS LEAPT LIKE A LEAPING
    SWORD:
"SAIL ON! SAIL ON! SAIL ON! AND ON!"

JOAQUIN MILLER read the words which, day after day,
Columbus had written in the log of his first voyage across
the uncharted Atlantic. *"This day we sailed on."*

The poet got up and strode about the room, his eyes
shining, his imagination on fire. *"This day we sailed on."*
Storms had ravaged the ships; the *Pinta* had lost her rudder; the men were threatening mutiny. Conditions couldn't
have been any worse, and Columbus himself must have
been on the verge of despair. But he had set his course,
and nothing could turn him from it. Through danger, darkness, hunger, panic, exhaustion, *they sailed on.*

What a magnificent epic of perseverance! The words
made a litany in the poet's mind. "Sail on! sail on!" The
roar of the sea was in his ears, the sting of the spray on his
cheeks. He stood beside Columbus and peered with him
into the darkness, feeling his strength, feeling his steadfast
purpose. . . .

And Joaquin Miller wrote like a man possessed. The
poem *had* to be written; no words ever came more spontaneously from a man's heart. An inspired tribute to the
great navigator who refused to turn his course, who firmly
sailed on in the direction he knew to be right, the poet
called it simply: "Columbus."

Behind him lay the gray Azores,
Behind the Gates of Hercules;

Before him not the ghost of shores;
Before him only shoreless seas.
The good mate said: "Now must we pray,
For lo! the very stars are gone.
Brave Adm'r'l, speak; what shall I say?"
"Why, say: 'Sail on! sail on! and on!'"

"My men grow mutinous day by day;
My men grow ghastly, wan and weak."
The stout mate thought of home; a spray
Of salt wave washed his swarthy cheek.
"What shall I say, brave Adm'r'l, say,
If we sight naught but seas at dawn?"
"Why, you shall say at break of day:
'Sail on! sail on! sail on! and on!'"

They sailed and sailed, as winds might blow,
Until at last the blanched mate said:
"Why, now not even God would know
Should I and all my men fall dead.
These very winds forget their way,
For God from these dread seas is gone.
Now speak, brave Adm'r'l; speak and say—"
He said: "Sail on! sail on! and on!"

They sailed. They sailed. Then spake the mate:
"This mad sea shows his teeth tonight.
He curls his lip, he lies in wait,
With lifted teeth, as if to bite!
Brave Adm'r'l, say but one good word:
What shall we do when hope is gone?"
The words leapt like a leaping sword:
"Sail on! sail on! sail on! and on!"

Then, pale and worn, he paced his deck,
And peered through darkness, Ah, that night
Of all dark nights! And then a speck—
A light! A light! At last a light!
It grew, a starlit flag unfurled!
It grew to be Time's burst of dawn.

> He gained a world; he gave that world
> Its grandest lesson: "On! sail on!"

Joaquin Miller* was born in a covered wagon some-where between Indiana and Ohio. He grew to lusty man-hood on the plains and mountains of the West, and was variously a pony-express rider, Indian fighter, miner, editor, lawyer, and even a judge. But always at heart he was a poet; and when he finally gave up everything else to write, he stuck to his course as stubbornly as any Columbus. In the latter half of the nineteenth century he became famous for his poems of the frontier and the great westward tide of pioneer life.

"Columbus" is one of Joaquin Miller's best-known and best-loved poems, admired as much for its powerful rhythm as for its inspiring theme. It is both a challenge and a promise: *If you have the courage and the perseverance, you will reach your goal. So set your course and stay with it. No matter what happens, don't give up. Keep going, and sooner or later you will reach your goal.* That is the stimulating message of Joaquin Miller's "Columbus" . . . a message for all who seek achievement and success in some chosen field.

> This one thing I do, forgetting those things which are
> behind. . . . I press toward the mark. . . .
> *Philippians 3:13, 14*

> Courage and perseverance have a magical talisman,
> before which difficulties disappear and obstacles van-
> ish into air.   *John Quincy Adams*

> There is no road too long to the man who advances
> deliberately and without undue haste; there are no
> honors too distant to the man who prepares himself
> for them with patience.   *Jean de La Bruyère*

---

* His real name was Cincinnatus Hiner Miller. He got his nick-name through his defense of a Mexican brigand named Joaquin Murietta. The name "Joaquin" stuck, and he adopted it as his pen name.

Great works are performed not by strength but by perseverance.   *Samuel Johnson*

Did you ever hear of a man who had striven all his life faithfully and singly toward an object and in no measure obtained it? If a man constantly aspires, is he not elevated?   *Henry David Thoreau*

Perseverance is a great element of success. If you only knock long enough and loud enough at the gate, you are sure to wake up somebody.
                            Henry Wadsworth Longfellow

3. ARNOLD BENNETT

YOU WAKE UP IN THE MORNING, AND LO!
YOUR PURSE IS MAGICALLY FILLED
WITH TWENTY-FOUR HOURS—THE
MOST PRECIOUS OF POSSESSIONS

As a poverty-stricken young clerk in a London law office, Arnold Bennett dreamed of a brilliant and successful writing career . . . and wondered how he would ever achieve that goal. He took careful stock of himself and knew he possessed the essential qualities for such a career. And he came to the conclusion that *time* was his most precious commodity, *time* the most useful tissue of his life—and that he must therefore not waste any part of it. He determined to make the best possible use of his twenty-four hours a day, to make every hour count.

So Arnold Bennett budgeted his time to take care of all the necessities of life, leaving a comfortable margin of leisure for improving himself and preparing for his writing career. He worked out a stern system of self-discipline, permitting no waste of precious time, no foolish "extravagance," to interfere with his plans and keep him from making progress.

It worked. He budgeted his time so that every hour served some useful purpose—and it worked beyond his most ambitious dreams! Stories and articles from his busy pen began to pile up. His first novel was published. His writing began to attract attention. His days of struggling clerkship were behind him—a brilliant and successful writing career lay ahead.

So well did Arnold Bennett budget and use his twenty-four hours a day that he had time for many interests and hobbies apart from his writing. He had time for painting, music, the theater—time for reading and for cultivating friends. People began to ask, "How do you manage to get so much done? Where do you find the time?"

Where do you find the time? How that question irritated Arnold Bennett every time he heard it! He didn't *find* the time. He had the same amount as everyone else: exactly twenty-four hours a day—no more, no less. It was the way he used his time that made the difference—the way he *spent* it, wisely and without waste. If people realized how priceless the hours of the day, the very minutes of the day, were, they wouldn't squander them so recklessly. They would be as careful to live within the budget of their hours as they are to live within the budget of their funds.

That would make an interesting subject to write about, Arnold Bennett decided one day: How to budget the hours and spend them wisely, how to us one's daily allotment of twenty-four hours so as to get the utmost return in happiness and satisfaction. *A stimulating idea!* He was suddenly eager to get started. He would make people aware of time as a valuable commodity, urge them to spend it for the enduring values of life instead of fleeting pleasures—for improvement, achievement, success. The more he thought about it, the more fascinated he became with the idea; and before long he had it mapped out in his mind and ready to put on paper. He called it *How to Live on Twenty-Four Hours a Day;* and in the famous paragraphs that follow he explained the gist of the philosophy that had worked so well in his own life:

Time is the inexplicable raw material of everything. With it, all is possible; without it, nothing. The supply of time is truly a daily miracle, an affair genuinely astonishing when one examines it.

You wake up in the morning, and lo! your purse is magically filled with twenty-four hours of the un-manufactured tissue of the universe of your life! It is yours. It is the most precious of possessions. . . . No one can take it from you. It is unstealable. And no one receives either more or less than you receive.

In the realm of time there is no aristocracy of wealth, and no aristocracy of intellect. Genius is never rewarded by even an extra hour a day. And there is no punishment. Waste your infinitely precious commodity as much as you will, and the supply will never be withheld from you. . . . Moreover, you cannot draw on the future. Impossible to get into debt! You can only waste the passing moment. You cannot waste tomorrow; it is kept for you. You cannot waste the next hour; it is kept for you.

I have said the affair was a miracle. Is it not?

You have to live on this twenty-four hours of daily time. Out of it you have to spin health, pleasure, money, content, respect, and the evolution of your immortal soul. Its right use, its most effective use, is a matter of the highest urgency and of the most thrilling actuality. All depends on that. Your happiness—the elusive prize that you are all clutching for, my friends! —depends on that.

If one cannot arrange that an income of twenty-four hours a day shall exactly cover all proper items of expenditure, one does muddle one's whole life indefinitely. . . .

We never shall have any more time. We have, and we have always had, all the time there is.

How to Live on Twenty-Four Hours a Day accomplished exactly what Arnold Bennett had hoped it would. It made people keenly aware of the value of time, and especially the importance of using leisure time to some advantage instead of just frittering it away. It encouraged many to budget their time and spend it more wisely, to use hours they formerly wasted to advance themselves, to improve their minds, their personalities, their careers, and their lives—*to add to their happiness*.

The little book was an immediate success. It made thousands of eager, enthusiastic converts to Arnold Bennett's method of self-discipline and self-direction. Letters began to pour in from people who had organized their time as he suggested, and had joyfully discovered it gave extra zest and interest to all their daily activities. The idea of budgeting time like money, and using it as carefully, was widely discussed in the press and from the lecture platform. *How to Live on Twenty-Four Hours a Day* became more than a title; it became one of the most familiar and inspiring phrases of that period.

Bennett himself was amazed at the ever-increasing interest in his idea. "I have received a large amount of correspondence concerning this small work!" he marveled in his preface to one of the later editions. He was to marvel even more in later years when it remained one of his most popular books—in spite of such famous works as *The Old Wives' Tales, Clayhanger, Riceyman Steps,* and *The Vanguard.*

How to Live on Twenty-Four Hours a Day has become a little classic on self-improvement, and is still one of Arnold Bennett's best-known books. An old-time favorite, it continues to make new friends; for it provides the inspired answer to all who complain they "haven't a minute to spare" or "just can't find the time." It proves that the time is there, twenty-four golden hours of it every day; and that all one has to do is spend it wisely and well to secure the greatest returns in happiness and contentment.

> Tomorrow's fate, though thou be wise,
> Thou canst not tell nor yet surmise;
> Pass, therefore, not today in vain,
> For it will never come again.
>
> *Omar Khayyám*

There is nothing of which we are apt to be so lavish as of time, and about which we ought to be more solicitous; since without it we can do nothing in this world.   *William Penn*

Know the true value of time! Snatch, seize, and enjoy every moment of it. No idleness, no laziness, no

procrastination. Never put off till tomorrow what you
can do today.　　　　　　　　　　　*Lord Chesterfield*

He who every morning plans the transactions of the
day, and follows out that plan, carries a thread that
will guide him through the labyrinth of the most busy
day. The orderly arrangement of his time is like a ray
of light which darts itself through all his occupations.
But where no plan is laid, where the disposal of time
is surrendered merely to the chance of incidents, all
things lie huddled together in one chaos, which ad-
mits of neither distribution nor review.　　*Victor Hugo*

Dost thou love life? Then do not squander time; for
that's the stuff life is made of.
If time be of all things the most precious, wasting
time must be the greatest prodigality; since lost time is
never found again and what we call time enough
always proves little enough. Let us then be up and
doing, and doing to the purpose; so by diligence
shall we do more with less perplexity. Sloth makes
all things difficult, but industry all easy.
Employ thy time well, if thou meanest to gain leisure.
Since thou art not sure of a minute, throw not away
an hour.　　　　　　　　　　　　*Benjamin Franklin*

Lost: Somewhere between sunrise and sunset, two
golden hours, each set with sixty diamond minutes.
No reward is offered, for they are gone forever.
　　　　　　　　　　　　　　　　　Horace Mann

Lo, here hath been dawning another blue day;
Think, wilt thou let it slip useless away?

Out of eternity this new day is born,
Into eternity at night will return.

Behold it aforetime no eye ever did;
So soon it forever from all eyes is hid.

Here hath been dawning another blue day;
Think, wilt thou let it slip useless away?

Thomas Carlyle

4. A. J. CRONIN

THE VIRTUE OF ALL ACHIEVEMENT IS
VICTORY OVER ONESELF. THOSE WHO
KNOW THIS VICTORY CAN
NEVER KNOW DEFEAT

THE MAN at the desk was a famous novelist; but what he was writing was no figment of the imagination. It was a true story. He was writing about a vital experience in his own life, revealing the lesson in perseverance that had brought victory over despair—and success beyond his wildest dreams.

A. J. Cronin had been a busy doctor in London when he was suddenly, at the age of thirty-three, obliged to drop everything and go away for his health. He went to a quiet little village in Scotland; and there, denied every other activity, he decided to try writing a novel, something he had long wanted to do.

In the beginning it was fun, as story and characters slowly took shape in his mind. He was possessed by the novelty and excitement of what he was doing. But he had never written before, and he had no knowledge of style or form, no idea of technique. He found it difficult to express himself. He struggled for hours over a paragraph. He got hopelessly lost and tangled in the plot. He began to feel wholly inadequate for the task he had undertaken.

Writing about it now, he remembered how wretched he had been, how he had gradually lost all confidence in himself and had been ready to give up. It was almost embarrassing, putting the naked agony and despair of those months down on paper. And yet, he must write about it honestly and sincerely or not at all. He must tell it exactly as it happened so that others facing the same problem might profit by his experience. He lived it over again as he wrote:

When I was halfway through, the inevitable happened. A sudden desolation struck me like an avalanche. I asked myself: "Why am I wearing myself out with this toil for which I am so preposterously ill-equipped? What is the use of it? I ought to be resting . . . conserving, not squandering my energies on this fantastic task." I threw down my pen. Feverishly, I read over the first chapters which had just arrived in typescript from my secretary in London. I was appalled. Never, never had I seen such nonsense in all my life. No one would read it. I saw, finally, that I was a presumptuous lunatic, that all that I had written, all that I could ever write was wasted effort, sheer futility. I decided to abandon the whole thing. Abruptly, furiously, I bundled up the manuscript, went out, and threw it in the ash can.

Drawing a sullen satisfaction from my surrender, or, as I preferred to phrase it, my return to sanity, I went for a walk in the drizzling rain. Halfway down the loch shore I came upon old Angus, the farmer, patiently and laboriously ditching a patch of the bogged and peaty heath which made up the bulk of his hard-won little croft. As I drew near, he gazed up at me in some surprise: he knew of my intention and, with that inborn Scottish reverence for "letters," had tacitly approved it. When I told him what I had just done, and why, his weathered face slowly changed, his keen blue eyes, beneath misted sandy brows, scanned me with disappointment and a queer contempt. He was a silent man and it was long before he spoke. Even then his words were cryptic.

"No doubt you're the one that's right, doctor, and I'm the one that's wrong: . . ." He seemed to look right to the bottom of me. "My father ditched this bog all his days and never made a pasture. I've dug it all *my* days and I've never made a pasture. But pasture or no pasture," he placed his foot dourly on the spade, "I canna help but dig. For my father knew and I know that if you only dig enough a pasture can be made here."

I understood. I watched his dogged working figure, with rising anger and resentment. I was resentful because he had what I had not: a terrible stubbornness to see the job through at all costs, an unquenchable flame of resolution brought to the simplest, the most arid duties of life. And suddenly my trivial dilemma became magnified, transmuted, until it stood as a touchstone of all human conduct. It became the timeless problem of mortality—the comfortable retreat, or the arduous advance without prospect of reward.

I tramped back to the farm, drenched, shamed, furious, and picked the soggy bundle from the ash can. I dried it in the kitchen oven. Then I flung it on the table and set to work again with a kind of frantic desperation. I lost myself in the ferociousness of my purpose. I would not be beaten, I would not give in. I wrote harder than ever. At last, toward the end of the third month, I wrote *finis*. The relief, the sense of emancipation, was unbelievable. I had kept my word. I had created a book. Whether it was good, bad, or indifferent I did not care.

I chose a publisher by the simple expedient of closing my eyes and pricking a catalogue with a pin. I dispatched the completed manuscript and promptly forgot about it.

In the days which followed I gradually regained my health, and I began to chafe at idleness. I wanted to be back in harness.

At last the date of my deliverance drew near. I went round the village saying good-bye to the simple folk who had become my friends. As I entered the post office, the postmaster presented me with a telegram— an urgent invitation to meet the publisher. I took it straight away and showed it, without a word, to John Angus.

The novel I had thrown away was chosen by the Book Society, dramatized and serialized, translated into nineteen languages, bought by Hollywood. It has sold, to date, some three million copies. It has altered my life radically, beyond my wildest dreams . . . and all because of a timely lesson in the grace of perseverance.

But that lesson goes deeper still. Today, when the air resounds with shrill defeatist cries, when half our stricken world is wailing in discouragement: "What is the use . . . to work . . . to save . . . to go on living . . . with Armageddon round the corner?" I am glad to recollect it. In this present chaos, with no shining vision to sustain us, the door is wide open to darkness and despair. The way to close that door is to stick to the job that we are doing, no matter how insignificant that job may be, to go on doing it, and to finish it.

Ignatius of Loyola was once playing a game of ball with his fellow students when someone demanded, suddenly and with due solemnity, what each of them would do if he knew he had to die in twenty minutes. All agreed that they would rush frantically to church and pray . . . all but Ignatius, who answered: "I should finish my game."

The virtue of all achievement, as known to Ignatius and my old Scots farmer, is victory over oneself. Those who know this victory can never know defeat.

The book A. J. Cronin threw away, then reclaimed and rewrote, was *Hatter's Castle*. It earned a fortune and made him famous. But far more important, it brought him the greatest triumph anyone can achieve—victory over himself. He went on to produce *The Citadel, The Keys of the Kingdom,* and many other popular books. But nothing gave him the intense satisfaction of that first great success: his conquest over doubt and despair.

Dr. Cronin's story, "The Turning Point of My Career," appeared in the *Reader's Digest* and was read by millions of people. It has since been retold many times, and it would be impossible to estimate the vast numbers of people who have been influenced by it. It has encouraged many to stick to the job, to go on doing it and complete it, no matter what the obstacles or difficulties. That was the lesson *he* had learned, and that was the lesson he generously shared with others.

Nothing Dr. Cronin has written, not even in his most famous books, is more inspiring than the story of his lesson in perseverance, so simply and humbly told. There are many today who can say with him that this experience was the turning point of their careers. For they discovered, with him, that victory over oneself is the only victory that counts—that it is "the virtue of all achievement."

All things are possible to him that believeth.
                                                    Mark 9:23

He who gains a victory over other men is strong; but he who gains a victory over himself is all powerful.
                                                    Lao-tse

Difficulties are the things that show what men are.
                                                    Epictetus

> Our doubts are traitors,
> And make us lose the good we oft might win
> By fearing to attempt.
                                                    William Shakespeare

Life affords no higher pleasure than that of surmounting difficulties, passing from one step of success to another, forming new wishes, and seeing them gratified. He that labors in any great or laudable undertaking has his fatigues first supported by hope, and afterwards rewarded by joy. . . .
To strive with difficulties, and to conquer them, is the highest human felicity.   *Samuel Johnson*

There is no finer sensation in life than that which comes with victory over one's self. It feels good to go fronting into a hard wind, winning against its power; but it feels a thousand times better to go forward to a

goal of inward achievement, brushing aside all your
old internal enemies as you advance.   *Vash Young*

When you get into a tight place and everything goes
against you, till it seems as though you could not hold
on a minute longer, never give up then, for that is just
the place and time that the tide will turn.

Harriet Beecher Stowe

The lowest ebb is the turn of the tide.

Henry Wadsworth Longfellow

Genius is only the power of making continuous efforts.
The line between failure and success is so fine that we
scarcely know when we pass it: so fine that we are
often on the line and do not know it. How many a
man has thrown up his hands at a time when a little
more effort, a little more patience, would have
achieved success. As the tide goes clear out, so it
comes clear in. In business, sometimes, prospects
may seem darkest when really they are on the turn. A
little more persistence, a little more effort, and what
seemed hopeless failure may turn to glorious success.
There is no failure except in no longer trying. There
is no defeat except from within, no really insurmountable barrier save our own inherent weakness of
purpose.   *Elbert Hubbard*

Perhaps the most valuable result of all education is
the ability to make yourself do the thing you have to
do, when it ought to be done, whether you like it or
not. It is the first lesson that ought to be learned.

Thomas H. Huxley

5. EDWARD ROWLAND SILL

WE MUST DO THE BEST WE CAN WITH
WHAT WE HAVE

LIFE HAD been neither generous nor kind to Edward Rowland Sill. It had bestowed upon him no special privileges, not even the usual advantages. He had, in fact, been handicapped from the start.

Both his parents died when he was still young. His health was poor, and he was prevented from doing many of the things he would have liked. For a long time he had difficulty finding his proper niche in life. He tried the ministry, but gave it up when he found he couldn't accept narrow dogma. He tried newspaper work but was physically and temperamentally unsuited to the grind. He finally made teaching his career; and here at last he was successful and content . . . until failing health forced him to give it up.

Most men would have been discouraged by so many setbacks and disappointments, would have given up and made excuses for themselves. But Edward Sill was no whiner. He believed in *making good,* not in making excuses. He believed in doing the best he could with what he had, in whatever condition he found himself.

That philosophy sustained him in every crisis, and helped him achieve a useful and happy life in spite of his handicaps. When he could no longer teach, he wrote poems and essays; and into most of his writings he poured the essence of the philosophy by which he had lived, and which he had always tried to teach others: *"We must do the best we can with what we have."* In "Opportunity," one of his best-known poems, this idea is beautifully and powerfully symbolized:

This I beheld, or dreamed it in a dream:
There spread a cloud of dust along a plain;
And underneath the cloud, or in it, raged
A furious battle, and men yelled, and swords
Shocked upon swords and shields. A prince's banner
Wavered, then staggered backward, hemmed by foes.
A craven hung along the battle's edge,
And thought, "Had I a sword of keener steel—
That blue blade that the king's son bears,—but this
Blunt thing—!" he snapped and flung it from his hand,
And lowering crept away and left the field.
Then came the king's son, wounded, sore bestead,
And weaponless, and saw the broken sword,
Hilt-buried in the dry and trodden sand,
And ran and snatched it, and with battle shout
Lifted afresh he hewed his enemy down,
And saved a great cause that heroic day.

In the glowing imagery of these lines is reflected the poet's own gallant life. Edward Sill knew his limitations and accepted them. Like the prince with the blunt sword, he refused to be beaten, courageously made the most of what he had, and turned his handicaps into opportunities.

Its dramatic symbolism and inspiring theme have made "Opportunity" one of America's favorite poems. Written more than seventy years ago, its message is as timely as ever: *Forget your limitations. Make the most of the opportunities and abilities you have and fulfill the promise within you.*

It is better to light one small candle than to curse the darkness.
                                                    Confucius

There is only one real failure in life, and that is not to be true to the best one knows.
                                        Canon Frederic W. Farrar

It is the greatest of all mistakes to do nothing because you can only do a little. Do what you can.
                                                Sydney Smith

It is not by regretting what is irreparable that true work is to be done, but by making the best of what we are. It is not by complaining that we have not the right tools, but by using well the tools we have. What we are, and where we are, is God's providential arrangement—God's doing, though it may be man's misdoing; and the manly and the wise way is to look your disadvantages in the face, and see what can be made of them.   *Frederick W. Robertson*

Rebellion against your handicaps gets you nowhere. Self-pity gets you nowhere. One must have the adventurous daring to accept oneself as a bundle of possibilities and undertake the most interesting game in the world—making the most of one's best.
                    Harry Emerson Fosdick

When the best things are not possible, the best may be made of those that are.   *Richard Hooker*

Greatness of soul consists not so much in soaring high and in pressing forward, as in knowing how to adapt and limit oneself.   *Michel de Montaigne*

No one of us escapes limitations. . . . Some people are gifted with their hands, some people are gifted in the realm of art or music, some people are gifted in the realm of abstract ideas. Almost no one is gifted in all three realms. We are limited, and we must accept ourselves with our limitations, recognizing that we can do what others cannot do, that we can contribute where others cannot contribute.

To accept ourselves with our limitations means also that we will recognize how variable and flexible our lives can be. The great thing about life is that as long as we live we have the privilege of growing. We can learn new skills, engage in new kinds of work, devote ourselves to new causes, make new friends, if only we will exercise a little initiative and refuse to become fixed, rigid. . . .

Let us, then, learn how to accept ourselves—accept the truth that we are capable in some directions and limited in others, that genius is rare, that mediocrity is the portion of almost all of us, but that all of us can contribute from the storehouse of our skills to the enrichment of our common life. Let us accept our emotional frailties, knowing that every person has some phobia lurking within his mind and that the normal person is he who is willing to accept life with its limitations and its opportunities joyfully and courageously.   *Joshua Loth Liebman*

6. MARY PICKFORD

THERE IS ALWAYS ANOTHER CHANCE.
. . . THIS THING THAT WE CALL
"FAILURE" IS NOT THE FALLING
DOWN, BUT THE STAYING DOWN

DINNER WAS OVER. The lovely hostess and her guests were
in the library, talking. They chatted idly for a while, of gay
and lively things; but soon the conversation took a more
serious turn. They talked of personal setbacks and misfortunes, and of the great need for courage and faith in overcoming such experiences.

"I have a philosophy that I have evolved over the years,"
the hostess told her guests. "It has helped me through
every heartbreak and discouragement, has stood by me
through every unhappy experience."

They urged her to tell them about it. And she confided
in these good friends her secret of calm serenity, of rising
above every distressing circumstance . . . of going on with
courage and hope, no matter what happened.

"What looks like the end of the road in our personal
experience," she said, "is only the turn in the road, the
beginning of a new and more beautiful journey. I have always tried to live by that philosophy, and it has kept me
happy."

The hostess was Mary Pickford. Among her guests that
evening was the editor of a national magazine, and he became more and more entranced as she talked about her
philosophy of life. Here was a world-famous personality, a
woman of great beauty and talent, who had achieved such
dazzling success as comes to few in a lifetime. She had
known wealth, fame, honor, devotion. But she had known
disappointments as well. She had faced unhappiness in her
personal life, and bitter disillusion. Yet she had come

through every experience serene and composed, radiantly sure of herself and the road ahead.

Surely the philosophy of such a woman would be interesting and helpful to others. The editor asked her to write an article for his magazine, expressing her views and beliefs. She was reluctant at first; but he finally convinced her that she had no right to withhold her philosophy if it would help even one other person.

So Mary Pickford agreed to write the article. And later, after the guests were gone, she began to think about what she would say in it. First of all, she would emphasize her faith in God, and show how faith gave her courage to meet the trials and disappointments of life. She would explain how she looked upon unhappy experiences as a turn in the road—an end, but also a beginning. Above all, she would try to make her readers see that life always held promise, that there was always another chance for everyone, no matter how hopeless things might seem. This last, she felt, was very important for those seeking a serene, confident way of life. She began to write it down. . . .

Today is a new day. You will get out of it just what you put into it. . . . If you have made mistakes, even serious mistakes, there is always another chance for you. And supposing you have tried and failed again and again, you may have a fresh start any moment you choose, for this thing that we call "failure" is not the falling down, but the staying down.

Mary Pickford's article appeared, and created something of a sensation. The way letters poured in amazed even Miss Pickford, who had once, at the height of her career, received more mail than anyone else in the world.

Two things were at once apparent: people admired Mary Pickford as much for her courage and gallant spirit as for her fabulous career in pictures. And many found in her way of life a helpful, inspiring pattern for themselves.

Because of the unusual interest in the article, it was published in the form of a little book, *Why Not Try God?*, which was widely circulated. Countless men and women, impressed by Mary Pickford's valiant way of life, adopted her philosophy and tried to live by the principles of faith and courage she outlined. The paragraph quoted seems to have particular influence; many people have written to Miss Pickford to tell her how these words helped them overcome feelings of hopelessness and defeat.

"You are never beaten unless you give up," is the gist of Mary Pickford's stimulating message. *"You may have a fresh start any moment you choose."*

For many, Mary Pickford's own words were what brought about the inspired moment of change . . . the beginning of a new and happier way of life.

Our greatest glory is not in never falling, but in rising every time we fall. *Oliver Goldsmith*

So long as one does not despair, so long as one doesn't look upon life bitterly, things work out fairly well in the end. *George Moore*

It is no disgrace to start all over. It is usually an opportunity. *George Matthew Adams*

I have lived eighty-six years. I have watched men climb up to success, hundreds of them, and of all the elements that are important for success, the most important is faith. No great thing comes to any man unless he has courage. *Cardinal James Gibbons*

No one is ever beaten unless he gives up the fight.
W. Beran Wolfe

All that is necessary to break the spell of inertia and frustration is this: *Act as if it were impossible to fail.* That is the talisman, the formula, the command of right-about-face which turns us from failure towards success. *Dorothea Brande*

PART FIVE

SELF-DISCIPLINE

&

The Development of Character

"A man's own character is the arbiter of his fortune." SYRUS

AN OLD HINDU PROVERB SAYS, "There is nothing noble in being superior to some other man. The true nobility is in being superior to your previous self."

Most of us are aware of this, and are forever striving to improve ourselves, to correct our faults, control our habits, make the most of our abilities.

But self-discipline is not easy. Self-conquest, as every philosopher from Plato to William James has emphasized, is the greatest victory of all. "I have had more trouble with myself than with any other man I have ever met!" said Dwight Moody, the famous evangelist.

The greatest test of a man's character is how he takes charge of his own life. "No man need stay the way he is," says Harry E. Fosdock. The mold of a man's fortune, the shape of his life and destiny, are in his own hands. Here are some inspiring selections on self-discipline and the development of character to help along the way.

1. OLIVER WENDELL HOLMES

BUILD THEE MORE STATELY MANSIONS,
O MY SOUL

DR. OLIVER WENDELL HOLMES examined the section of shell he held in his hand. It was from the pearly nautilus—a most interesting little creature, he decided. Inside the shell was a spiral of gradually enlarging compartments in which the mollusk lived successively as it grew larger and larger. He was fascinated by the story of developing life that the fragment revealed. As the little creature that lived inside the shell outgrew one chamber, it moved on to the next—where it could grow and develop further, and so move on to a still larger chamber.

Admiring the pearly inner layer of the shell, Dr. Holmes was fascinated by the kind of poetic analogy he always enjoyed: the similitude of the human soul and spirit to other things in nature. Like the humble mollusk that lived inside his shell, the human being must also continually move on, must grow and expand. Each man was responsible for his own development. Each man was the architect of his own character.

Here was the perfect theme for his next poem! "The Chambered Nautilus." Even the name had a poetic sound to it. Tiny growing nautilus in its ship of pearl, moving from one chambered cell to the next, stretching, expanding . . . and the soul of man, building ever more stately mansions. . . . He was carried away by his own fantasy.

This is the ship of pearl, which, poets feign,
Sails the unshadowed main,—
The venturous bark that flings
On the sweet summer wind its purpled wings

174

In gulfs enchanted, where the Siren sings,
    And coral reefs lie bare,
Where the cold sea-maids rise to sun their
    streaming hair.

Its webs of living gauze no more unfurl;
    Wrecked is the ship of pearl!
    And every chambered cell,
Where its dim dreaming life was wont to dwell,
As the frail tenant shaped his growing shell,
    Before thee lies revealed,—
Its irised ceiling rent, its sunless crypt unsealed!

Year after year beheld the silent toil
    That spread his lustrous coil;
    Still, as the spiral grew,
He left the past year's dwelling for the new,
Stole with soft step its shining archway through,
    Built up its idle door,
Stretched in his last-found home, and knew the
    old no more.

Thanks for the heavenly message brought by thee,
    Child of the wandering sea,
    Cast from her lap, forlorn!
From thy dead lips a clearer note is born
Than ever Triton blew from wreathëd horn!
    While on mine ear it rings,
Through the deep caves of thought I hear a voice
    that sings:—

Build thee more stately mansions, O my soul,
    As the swift seasons roll!
    Leave thy low-vaulted past!
Let each new temple, nobler than the last,
Shut thee from heaven with a dome more vast,
    Till thou at length art free,
Leaving thine outgrown shell by life's unresting sea.

Dr. Holmes introduced "The Chambered Nautilus" to the large circle of readers who followed his famous "breakfast-table" series in the *Atlantic Monthly.**

He explained how the poem had been suggested by looking at a section of the chambered shell; and how he saw in its widening spiral the progressive steps of man's own development. "Can you find no lesson in this?" he asked his readers.

Apparently many could. Apparently many *did,* for the poem became enormously popular almost at once. Readers clearly saw the poet's idea in the beautifully expressed analogy: that their lives were what they themselves made them—that they must continually improve themselves and promote their own steady growth and development. It was a stimulating idea, and the poem was widely read and discussed. It is said that Lincoln knew it by heart and could quote whole stanzas from it.

Today "The Chambered Nautilus" is one of America's most famous poems. It is a favorite in schools; it is included in almost every important anthology of American verse; and it is frequently quoted—especially the last stanza, with its familiar opening line, known to millions. With its beautiful imagery, and its emphasis on steady self-improvement and the development of character, "The Chambered Nautilus" is an unforgettable and truly inspiring poem.

A man's own self is his friend, a man's own self is his foe.   *Bhagavad-Gita*

The great virtue of man lies in his ability to correct his mistakes and continually to make a new man of himself.   *Wang Yang-ming*

---

* *The Autocrat of the Breakfast Table, The Professor at the Breakfast Table,* and *The Poet at the Breakfast Table.* For more than forty years, Dr. Oliver Wendell Holmes contributed poems and essays to the *Atlantic Monthly* under these series titles. He was a man of many attainments, being also a physician, philosopher, lecturer, teacher, and novelist. (Not to be confused with his son, also named Oliver Wendell Holmes—the distinguished Supreme Court Justice. See pages 331–33.)

The way to gain a good reputation is to endeavor to be what you desire to appear. *Socrates*

When you are in doubt whether an action is good or bad, abstain from it. *Zoroaster*

> Man who man would be
> Must rule the empire of himself.
> *Percy Bysshe Shelley*

When a man's fight begins within himself, he is worth something. *Robert Browning*

Better keep yourself clean and bright; you are the window through which you must see the world.
George Bernard Shaw

> There is a kind of character in thy life,
> That to the observer doth thy history
> Fully unfold.
> *William Shakespeare*

Every man is the builder of a temple called his body. . . . We are all sculptors and painters, and our material is our own flesh and blood and bones. Any nobleness begins at once to refine a man's features, any meanness or sensuality to imbrute them.
Henry David Thoreau

Upon every face is written the record of the life the man has led; the prayers, the aspirations, the disappointments, all he hoped to be and was not—all are written there; nothing is hidden, nor indeed can be.
Elbert Hubbard

2. WILLIAM SHAKESPEARE

THIS ABOVE ALL: TO THINE OWN SELF BE TRUE

WILLIAM SHAKESPEARE was writing a new play. It was a tragedy based on the life of a young Prince of Denmark, a fellow named Hamlet. He had read about him in a collection of thirteenth-century legends and chronicles, and had been carried away by the dramatic possibilities of the tale. He was making fine progress with it, had already written the first two scenes of the first act. Hamlet was shaping up as a young man of complex but noble character. This was just the sort of thing he liked best to do: to take a colorful figure out of the past, give him soul and feeling, set him among his contemporaries—and let him come to life.

Now in this next scene, Laertes—who has been in Denmark for the coronation of the new king—is about to reembark for France. He is taking leave of his father, Polonius, the wise but crafty Lord Chamberlain. Here, Shakespeare decided, was his chance to put some good strong words into the mouth of Polonius, words of advice to his son about the molding of his life and character.

He had no idea, as he wrote, that these words would one day be familiar to millions of people. . . .

> There, my blessing with thee!
> And these few precepts in thy memory
> See thou character. Give thy thoughts no tongue,
> Nor any unproportion'd thought his act.
> Be thou familiar, but by no means vulgar;
> Those friends thou hast, and their adoption tried,
> Grapple them to thy soul with hoops of steel;

But do not dull thy palm with entertainment
Of each new-hatch'd, unfledg'd comrade. Beware
Of entrance to a quarrel: but being in,
Bear't that the opposed may beware of thee.
Give every man thy ear, but few thy voice:
Take each man's censure, but reserve thy judgment.
Costly thy habit as thy purse can buy,
But not express'd in fancy: rich, not gaudy;
For the apparel oft proclaims the man.
Neither a borrower nor a lender be;
For loan oft loses both itself and friend,
And borrowing dulls the edge of husbandry.
This above all: to thine own self be true;
And it must follow, as the night the day,
Thou canst not then be false to any man.

Hamlet is one of Shakespeare's greatest plays, as we all
know, and Polonius' advice to Laertes one of the best-
known quotations from it. The father's precepts to his son
are so wise and penetrating that even when taken from the
context of the play they stand by themselves, vital and
complete. Sincerity is inherent in every line. There is almost a spiritual quality to the words.

This above all: to thine own self be true. There are few
more important injunctions in the world, few with deeper
significance for the individual.

"Look to your character," Polonius urges his son. "Be
honest, moderate, sincere." His advice to Laertes is a favorite quotation from Shakespeare, and many have found it
stimulating and helpful in their own lives.

Never esteem anything as of advantage to thee that
shall make thee break thy word or lose thy self-
respect.   *Marcus Aurelius*

The end and aim of all education is the development
of character.   *Francis W. Parker*

One of the purest and most enduring of human plea-

sures is to be found in the possession of a good name
among one's neighbors and acquaintances.

Charles W. Eliot

There is a kind of greatness which does not depend
upon fortune; it is a certain manner that distinguishes
us, and which seems to destine us for great things;
it is the value we insensibly set upon ourselves; it is by
this quality that we gain the deference of other men,
and it is this which commonly raises us more above
them than birth, rank, or even merit itself.

François de La Rochefoucauld

Be true to your own highest convictions.

William E. Channing

How happy is he born and taught
That serveth not another's will;
Whose armor is his honest thought,
And simple truth his utmost skill!

Sir Henry Wotton

3. JAMES LANE ALLEN

**THE DIVINITY THAT SHAPES OUR ENDS IS
IN OURSELVES. . . . ALL THAT A MAN
ACHIEVES OR FAILS TO ACHIEVE IS THE
DIRECT RESULT OF HIS OWN THOUGHTS**

JAMES LANE ALLEN had long been impressed by the ancient philosophy that a man becomes what he thinks, that a man's character is the outward expression of his inward thoughts. He had traced it back to the *Upanishads,* sacred literature of the Hindus: *"Man becomes that of which he thinks."* He had found it eloquently expressed in the writings of Buddha: *"The mind is everything; what you think you become"* . . . and in the *Meditations* of Marcus Aurelius: *"Your life is what your thoughts make it."* He had found the same basic idea in the writings of Confucius, Mohammed, Aristotle, Socrates, scores of others. And he knew it, of course, in its most familiar form—as millions did—from the Bible: *"As he thinketh in his heart, so is he"* (Proverbs, 23:7).

All the great teachers of every age had declared this simple truth: that a man's life and character are the result of his own inmost thoughts and ideals. It was a philosophy as old as civilization, but ever fresh and new. Surely he had proved the truth of it in his own life, James Allen reflected. He had been very poor in his youth, had known none of the advantages so many young men count essential. He had started out with nothing to build on except what was within himself. But he had known what he wanted to do and be; he had kept his dream, his ideal, everlastingly before him; he had tried to live the life he imagined—and in the end his dream had become a reality.

As a man thinketh, so is he.

It was such a simple, obvious truth, he wondered how

anyone could fail to see it. People were forever complaining about things outside themselves, blaming their condition and circumstances on everything but their own thoughts and ideas. Didn't they realize that they made their own "good fortune," that their lives were the results of their own thinking? Good thoughts bear good fruit, bad thoughts bear bad fruit—and man is his own gardener.

He became intrigued with this symbolic idea of the mind as a garden, each man cultivating the soil and seed of his own life. It was the same ancient philosophy, of course, but in new dress.

"I'll develop it in the form of an essay!" he decided.

Young people counted too much on "luck" and "chance" these days. They needed some dramatic reminder that the divinity which shapes our ends is in ourselves. Here was an effective way to show the relationship between thought and character—to show how everything depended on the kind of seeds, or thoughts, that were planted in the fertile soil of the mind.

It was to be a brief essay, as Allen originally planned it. But he had been thinking about the subject for so long, and there was so much he wanted to say, that it was soon extended to book length. He called it *As a Man Thinketh* . . . and it was to become one of the most stimulating and inspiring little books of all time. He had hoped it would be helpful; he had no idea it would become a compelling influence in the lives of countless people.

Following are the paragraphs that are most frequently quoted from *As a Man Thinketh*. They reflect the heart of the book, and the essence of James Allen's philosophy:

A man is literally *what he thinks,* his character being the complete sum of all his thoughts.

As the plant springs from, and could not be without, the seed, so every act of a man springs from the hidden seeds of thought, and could not have appeared without them. . . . Act is the blossom of thought, and joy and suffering are its fruits; thus does a man garner in the sweet and bitter fruitage of his own husbandry. . . .

A man's mind may be likened to a garden, which may be intelligently cultivated or allowed to run wild; but whether cultivated or neglected, it must, and will, *bring forth*. If no useful seeds are put into it, then an abundance of useless weed-seeds will *fall* therein; and will continue to produce their kind.

Just as the gardener cultivates his plot, keeping it free from weeds, and growing the flowers and fruits which he requires, so may a man tend the garden of his mind, weeding out all the wrong, useless, and impure thoughts, and cultivating toward perfection the flowers and fruits of right, useful, and pure thoughts. By pursuing this process, a man sooner or later discovers that he is the master-gardener of his soul, the director of his life. He also reveals, within himself, the laws of thought, and understands, with ever-increasing accuracy, how the thought forces operate in the shaping of his character and destiny. . . .

Man is buffeted by circumstances so long as he believes himself to be the creature of outside conditions, but when he realizes that he is a creative power, and that he may command the hidden soil and seeds of his being out of which circumstances grow, he then becomes the rightful master of himself. . . .

Good thoughts bear good fruit, bad thoughts bad fruit.

A man will find that as he alters his thoughts towards things and other people, things and other people will alter towards him. . . . Let a man radically alter his thoughts, and he will be astonished at the rapid transformation it will effect in the material conditions of his life. Men do not attract that which they want, but that which they are. . . . The divinity that shapes our ends is in ourselves. It is our very self. . . . All that a man achieves or fails to achieve is the direct result of his own thoughts. . . . A man can only rise, conquer, and achieve by lifting up his thoughts. He remains weak and abject and miserable by refusing to lift up his thoughts. . . .

A man should conceive of a legitimate purpose in

his heart, and set out to accomplish it. He should make this purpose the centralizing point of his thoughts. . . . He should steadily focus his thought forces upon the object which he has set before him. He should make this purpose his supreme duty, and should devote himself to its attainment, not allowing his thoughts to wander away into ephemeral fancies, longings, and imaginings. This is the royal road to self-control and true concentration of thought. Even if he fails again and again to accomplish his purpose (as he necessarily must until weakness is overcome), the *strength of character* gained will be the measure of his true success, and this will form a new starting point for future power and triumph.

Into your hands will be placed the exact results of your own thoughts; you will receive that which you earn; no more, no less. Whatever your present environment may be, you will fall, remain, or rise with your thoughts, your Vision, your Ideal. You will become as small as your controlling desire; as great as your dominant aspiration. . . .

The thoughtless, the ignorant, and the indolent, seeing only the apparent effects of things and not the things themselves, talk of luck, of fortune, and chance. Seeing a man grow rich, they say, "How lucky he is!" Observing another become intellectual, they exclaim, "How highly favored he is!" And noting the saintly character and wide influence of another, they remark, "How chance aids him at every turn!" They do not see the trials and failures and struggles which these men have voluntarily encountered in order to gain their experience; have no knowledge of the sacrifices they have made, of the undaunted efforts they have put forth, of the faith they have exercised, that they might overcome the apparently insurmountable and realize the Vision of their heart. They do not know the darkness and the heartaches; they only see the light and joy, and call it "luck"; do not see the long and arduous journey, but only behold the pleasant goal, and call it "good fortune"; do not understand the process, but only perceive the results and call it "chance."

In all human affairs there are efforts, and there are results, and the strength of effort is the measure of the result. Chance is not. "Gifts," powers, material, intellectual, and spiritual possessions are the fruits of effort; *they are thoughts completed,* objects accomplished, visions realized.

The Vision that you glorify in your mind, the Ideal that you enthrone in your heart—this you will build your life by. This you will become.

Though James Allen was for many years a professor of languages, writing had always been his interest and his goal; and it was as a poet, novelist, and short-story writer that he achieved his greatest distinction. He produced a number of important and popular books in his lifetime; but now, a brief generation after his death, he is best remembered for his famous essay, *As a Man Thinketh.* Many successful people have attributed their success in life to its influence.

And quietly that influence continues. *As a Man Thinketh* is still widely read, and selections from the famous essay are frequently quoted. James Allen's inspiring message goes on: *Thought and character are one . . . good thoughts bear good fruit . . . the higher a man lifts his thoughts, the greater his achievement . . . cherish your dreams and ideals . . . keep your goal forever in your mind . . . as a man thinketh, so is he.*

Let a man strive to purify his thoughts. What a man thinketh, that is he; this is the eternal mystery. Dwelling within his Self with thoughts serene, he will obtain imperishable happiness. Man becomes that of which he thinks.   *Upanishads*

All that we are is the result of what we have thought. The mind is everything. What we think, we become.
                    Buddha

Your disposition will be suitable to that which you most frequently think on; for the soul is, as it were, tinged with the color and complexion of its own thoughts. . . .

Your life is what your thoughts make it.

Marcus Aurelius

There is nothing either good or bad, but thinking makes it so.   *William Shakespeare*

I think, therefore I am.   *René Descartes*

All that a man does outwardly is but the expression and completion of his inward thought. To work effectively, he must think clearly; to act nobly, he must think nobly.   *William E. Channing*

Make yourselves nests of pleasant thoughts. None of us yet know, for none of us have been taught in early youth, what fairy palaces we may build of beautiful thought—proof against all adversity. Bright fancies, satisfied memories, noble histories, faithful sayings, treasure-houses of precious and restful thoughts, which care cannot disturb, nor pain make gloomy, nor poverty take away from us—houses built without hands, for our souls to live in.

John Ruskin

4. RALPH WALDO EMERSON

MY LIFE IS FOR ITSELF AND NOT FOR
A SPECTACLE. . . . WHAT I MUST DO IS
ALL THAT CONCERNS ME, NOT
WHAT THE PEOPLE THINK

IT WAS nearly dawn. The man moved carefully, so as not
to disturb his wife. But she wakened suddenly and saw
that he was dressing.

"What is it, Ralph—are you ill?" she asked.

"No," he said, smiling, "just catching a few thoughts."

And *she* smiled, too, making no attempt to stop him as
he went out of the house. For by now she recognized the
pattern of his moods. A new lecture was shaping up in his
mind. . . .

In the quiet, deserted streets, Ralph Waldo Emerson
walked slowly, thinking about the lecture he was to give the
following week; but also enjoying with every alert sense the
beauty and freshness of his beloved Concord at this hour.
He thought, as he had so many times before, how perfectly this town suited him, and how glad he was that he had
bought a house here. He loved the peace and quiet of
Concord, its charm, its illustrious history. He was content
to spend the rest of his life here, writing and lecturing.

He took his favorite walk along the green bank of the
river. Yes, he reflected, he was well content. The priva-
tions, the spiritual conflicts, the difficulties and uncertainties of his early years were behind him now. He had
found his life's work, and he was happy.

Not that these were happy times, he reminded himself.
There was much to make a man despair. There was evidence everywhere of greed and corruption, of cruelty and
exploitation. There was a growing absorption in material
things—and even worse, a growing disregard for those

basic principles and ideals on which the American way of life was founded. Conditions were discouraging; but he was not pessimistic about the future, as many of his friends were. He took the long-range view of things, and came to the conclusion that all periods have their problems—and that every time is a good time, if people know what to do with it.

His mind turned back to the job at hand: *his lecture.* With people so worried and disheartened, he must make his message as reassuring and stimulating as he could. He must stress personal values, and the importance of individual character. He must urge people to think and act for themselves, to proceed on their own best impulses, to make no compromise with duty or integrity.

"Know thyself," Socrates had said many centuries ago. Yes, *know thyself*—know what you are by nature intended to do, your work, your rightful place in the world. Know yourself, and *trust* yourself! Be true to your principles, believe in your own thoughts, be confident, self-reliant.

Self-reliance—that was the important thing! That was the core of all virtue and progress. The individual must be resolute and independent—must be resourceful and courageous—must live an honest life, without pretense or apology. Development of the theme raced through his mind. He took out the little "thought-book" he always carried with him, and began to jot down ideas for his lecture: *Trust thyself; every heart vibrates to that iron string . . . Let a man know his own worth. . . . Nothing can bring you peace but the triumph of principles. . . .*

Random notes, disconnected. . . . His best thoughts always seemed to come to him like this, in flashes of inspiration. His steps quickened. He was eager now to get back to the house, to put his lecture down on paper. The town was just beginning to stir and waken as he reached his house. He went at once to his desk and began writing.

There is a time in every man's education when he arrives at the conviction that envy is ignorance; that imitation is suicide; that he must take himself for better for worse as his portion; that though the wide universe is full of good, no kernel of nourishing corn can come to him but through his toil bestowed on that plot of ground which is given to him to till. The power which resides in him is new in nature, and none but he knows what that is which he can do, nor does he know until he has tried. . . .

Trust thyself; every heart vibrates to that iron string. Accept the place the divine providence has found for you, the society of your contemporaries, the connection of events. Great men have always done so. . . .

My life is for itself and not for a spectacle. I much prefer that it should be of a lower strain, so it be genuine and equal, than that it should be glittering and unsteady. . . . Few and mean as my gifts may be, I actually am, and do not need for my own assurance or the assurance of my fellows any secondary testimony.

What I must do is all that concerns me, not what the people think. This rule, equally arduous in actual and in intellectual life, may serve for the whole distinction between greatness and meanness. It is the harder because you will always find those who think they know what is your duty better than you know it. It is easy in the world to live after the world's opinion; it is easy in solitude to live after your own; but the great man is he who in the midst of the crowd keeps with perfect sweetness the independence of solitude.

Ralph Waldo Emerson wrote that morning until the sun was high over the housetops. One crisp saying after another went into the lecture, lines that were one day to be famous and quoted everywhere: *Do your work and I shall know you. . . . The force of character is cumulative. . . . An institution is the lengthened shadow of one man. . . . All history resolves itself into the biography of a few stout and earnest persons. . . . If we live truly, we shall see truly. . . . Insist on yourself; never imitate. . . . Nothing is at last sacred but the integrity of your own mind.*

The sentences came swiftly from his eager pen. He had

given much thought to the theory of self-reliance, and he knew exactly what he wished to say. He even knew how he would conclude the lecture—with two sentences he had written in his "thought-book" days ago: *Nothing can bring you peace but yourself. Nothing can bring you peace but the triumph of principles.*

By midmorning Ralph Waldo Emerson had completed his lecture on "Self-Reliance." It was a rousing summons to independence, to initiative and confidence. It was also an ardent declaration of his faith in man and his abilities.

As a lecture, and later as an essay, it had tremendous influence. James Freeman Clarke, who knew Emerson personally, said, "By encouraging self-reliance, he did us more good than any other writer or speaker among us." His crisp, dynamic sentences were everywhere quoted, his ideas widely discussed. His belief in the worth of man, and in a friendly destiny by which the human race is guided, was reassuring—especially to the young men of his time. Emerson's stirring message excited their ambitions and their energies; and many who later achieved notable success in their chosen fields gratefully acknowledged his influence and referred to his famous lecture as the turning point in their lives.

Thoreau, Whitman, Oliver Wendell Holmes, Matthew Arnold, Lincoln, Emily Dickinson, Elbert Hubbard, Woodrow Wilson—these are only a few of the many famous people influenced by Emerson's idealism and his sincerity, by his plea for moral courage and self-reliance.

William Allen White read Emerson's essay on "Self-Reliance" when he was seventeen. In his autobiography he says, "As I read that essay my spirit expanded as though I had heard the trumpet call of life. I was thrilled and stirred. . . . I doubt if I have ever been moved so deeply by anything else that I have read."

"Self-reliance is a quality which Emerson has made forever glorious!" declares Richard C. Cabot.

"It is one of the most important essays for a young man to read," says Albert J. Beveridge.

Emerson spoke out of the needs, problems, and aspirations of his own times, and to the people of his own generation. But he speaks just as clearly to us in our times, for his words have an enduring quality that keeps them vital and alive.

A happy life is one which is in accordance with its own nature. *Seneca*

He who knows others is clever; he who knows himself is enlightened. *Lao-tse*

Of all paths a man could strike into, there is, at any given moment, a *best path* for every man; a thing which, here and now, it were of all things *wisest* for him to do; which could he but be led or driven to do, he were then doing "like a man," as we phrase it. His success, in such case, were complete, his felicity a maximum. This path, to find this path, and walk in it, is the one thing needful for him. *Thomas Carlyle*

Whatever you are by nature, keep to it; never desert your line of talent. Be what nature intended you for, and you will succeed. *Sydney Smith*

No man can produce great things who is not thoroughly sincere in dealing with himself.
James Russell Lowell

If a man does not keep pace with his companions, perhaps it is because he hears a different drummer. Let him keep step to music which he hears, however measured or far away. *Henry David Thoreau*

You owe no one as much as you owe yourself. You owe to yourself the action that opens for you the doors to the goodness, the variety, and the excitement of effort and success, of battle and victory. Making payment on this debt to yourself is the exact opposite of selfishness. You can best pay your debt to society, that has made you what you are, by being just yourself with all your might and as a matter of course. . . .

You fulfill the promise that lies latent within you by keeping your promises to yourself.

David Harold Fink

5. HIPPOCRATES

I WILL LEAD MY LIFE AND PRACTICE
MY ART IN UPRIGHTNESS AND HONOR

THE AGED physician sat in the sunshine, reflecting on the progress which had been made in medical science in the past fifty years. Though he would have been the last to admit it, much of that progress had been due to his own efforts. For this was Hippocrates, greatest of the Greek physicians . . . the "Father of Medicine."

Hippocrates was born on the island of Cos in 460 B.C., and devoted his entire life to the advancement of medical science. He studied all known methods, drugs, instruments, treatments, and ideas, and organized them into the first rational system of medicine.

Now nearing the end of life, he reflected with pleasure that his work would go on, his disciples would carry on his teachings, his writings would be used in schools to train and prepare others for the practice of medicine. His mind turned to the young men who had come here to study in recent years. Ambitious enough, most of them—serious-minded and well-intentioned young fellows. But what about their principles and ideals? What about their ethical standards? Character and personal integrity were very important in the practice of medicine.

The white-haired old man, venerated almost as a saint by his colleagues, turned his face to the friendly warmth of the sun. He had written a whole collection of medical works for the guidance of those who followed in his profession. But there was one thing more he must do, one last important section to include in his writings.

Hippocrates realized that in a profession like medicine, the highest personal standards must be maintained. The

intimate relationship between physician and patient called
for a rigid code of ethics. Knowledge and skill were not
enough; the physician must be a man of utmost honor and
trust, if the progress of medicine were to continue.

Yes, there was still one thing more he must write: an
oath of integrity for physicians, a code of standards and
ideals to which they must swear to adhere in the practice
of their profession. He would ask all physicians, now and
forever, to live upright and honest lives, to be generous,
just, and kind. He would ask all physicians to take this
oath:

I do solemnly swear by that which I hold most
sacred:

That I will be loyal to the profession of medicine
and just and generous to its members;

That I will lead my life and practice my art in up-
rightness and honor;

That into whatsoever house I shall enter, it shall be
for the good of the sick to the utmost of my power,
I holding myself aloof from wrong, from corruption,
and from the temptation of others to vice;

That I will exercise my art solely for the cure of
my patients, and will give no drug, perform no operation for a criminal purpose, even if solicited, far less
suggest it;

That whatsoever I shall see or hear of the lives of
men which is not fitting to be spoken, I will keep in-
violably secret.

These things I do promise, and in proportion as I
am faithful to this my oath may happiness and good
repute be ever mine—the opposite if I shall be for-
sworn.*

---

* The *Hippocratic Collection*, containing the best of the ancient
Greek medical writings, was put together by Aristotle and has
survived through the centuries. The "Hippocratic Oath" is one
of the last and most inspiring passages in this *Collection*. There
are a number of versions of the famous Oath; but the form given
here is the one commonly used today; and is an adaptation of a
translation from the original Greek.

The medical profession is and always has been one of the most ethical of all professions; and this is due at least in part to the centuries-old influence of the Hippocratic Oath. This famous Oath has kept alive the high standards and ideals set by Hippocrates, and forms the basis of modern medical ethics.

Written more than twenty centuries ago, the Hippocratic Oath has inspired generations of doctors . . . and continues to do so even now. The Oath is still administered by medical schools to graduating classes; and thousands of physicians have framed copies on their walls along with their diplomas. Conscientious practitioners continue to live up to the principles and ideals set down for their profession so long ago by the "Father of Medicine."

Though it was written specifically for physicians, the Hippocratic Oath sets an enduring pattern of honor, integrity, and devotion to duty for all people, in all professions.

Dignity consists not in possessing honors, but in the consciousness that we deserve them.   *Aristotle*

Acquit me, or do not acquit me; but be sure that I shall not alter my way of life, no, not if I have to die for it many times.   *Socrates*

Good name in man and woman, dear my lord,
Is the immediate jewel of their souls:
Who steals my purse steals trash; 'tis something,
nothing;
'Twas mine, 'tis his, and has been slave to
thousands;
But he that filches from me my good name
Robs me of that which not enriches him,
And makes me poor indeed.
    William Shakespeare

I hope I shall always possess firmness and virtue enough to maintain what I consider the most enviable of all titles, the character of an "honest man."

George Washington

An honest man's the noblest work of God.

Alexander Pope

God give us men! A time like this demands
Strong minds, great hearts, true faith, and ready hands,
Men whom the lust of office does not kill;
    Men whom the spoils of office cannot buy;
Men who possess opinions and a will;
    Men who have honor; men who will not lie;
Men who can stand before a demagogue
      And damn his treacherous flatteries without
         winking;
Tall men, sun-crowned, who live above the fog
    In public duty and in private thinking;
For while the rabble with their thumb-worn creeds,
Their large profession and their little deeds
Mingle in selfish strife, lo! Freedom weeps,
Wrong rules the land, and waiting Justice sleeps.

Josiah G. Holland

No personal consideration should stand in the way of performing a public duty.   *Ulysses S. Grant*

I desire so to conduct the affairs of this administration that if at the end, when I come to lay down the reins of power, I have lost every other friend on earth, I shall at least have one friend left, and that friend shall be down inside of me.   *Abraham Lincoln*

To me the highest thing, after God, is my honor.

Ludwig van Beethoven

PART SIX

PERSONALITY

&

Relationship to Others

"The art of pleasing requires only the desire."   LORD CHESTERFIELD

THE DESIRE to be well liked, to enjoy the affection of friends, to get along easily and pleasantly with other people, is one of the fundamental instincts in human nature.

Since earliest time philosophers have taught the basic principles of human relationship, have emphasized the qualities that go to make up a well-liked, agreeable personality—the qualities that mean most in association with others. There has never been a time when kindness, unselfishness, and consideration for others were not considered essential qualities. "A person completely wrapped up in himself makes a small package," says Harry E. Fosdick.

One of the oldest and most enduring rules of human relations is to *do unto others as you would have others do unto you*. It remains now, as it has been for centuries, the most important single rule of life, the basis of all moral and ethical principles. Emerson was merely expressing it another way when he said, "The only way to have a friend is to be a friend."

Here is what others have said on personality, on making and keeping friends, on getting along with others—inspiring quotations from outstanding personalities, from ancient times to our own.

1. ST. PAUL

FAITH, HOPE, AND LOVE, THESE THREE
—AND THE GREATEST OF THESE IS
LOVE

PAUL WAS dictating a letter to be sent back to the Christian community he had established in the famous Greek city of Corinth. It was his first letter to the Corinthians, among whom he had lived and worked for eighteen months. His heart was filled with love for these loyal followers, with eagerness to guide and help them as much as he could. His feelings overflowed in eloquence.

If I speak in the language of angels and have no love for you, I am only a noisy, empty gong. If I possess all knowledge and preach all truths—if I have the faith that moves mountains, but have no real love for my fellow man —I am nothing. Even if I give away everything I own, even if I sacrifice my life and become a martyr, if I am not sincere—if I do these things in pride, and not in love— they are meaningless and profit nothing.

He got up and paced about the room, a plain and unprepossessing man—short in stature, bald, his beard gray and bushy. But the light of inspiration illumined his plain round face, and the love of God and humanity glowed in his eyes. A man of intense and consuming missionary zeal, these Epistles were the ideal vehicle for his personality—informal, spontaneous, and sincere. Through them he could express himself, not as a theologian, but as a leader and a friend.

Love, kindness, charity, doing things for others—these are the essential qualities. Love never fails. Other things fade and pass away, but love endures. I myself did not see this clearly until I became a man and put aside my childish ways.

This was a very important letter. It must be more than a message of guidance. It must be a testament of love and faith . . . it must win the confidence of the people and inspire them to live up to Christian principles and ideals. They must not slip into selfish, unkind ways. He must plead with them for faith and hope, for charity and kindness, for patience and humility—and most of all, for love. For surely if a man truly loved, he possessed all other virtues as well.

Faith, hope, and love—these three. And the greatest of these is love.

He asked that the letter be read back to him. And he nodded as he listened, for this was what he wanted to say. This was the message he wanted to send in his first letter to the Corinthians:

Though I speak with the tongues of men and of angels, and have not love, I am become as sounding brass, or a tinkling cymbal.

And though I have the gift of prophecy, and understand all mysteries, and all knowledge; and though I have all faith, so that I could remove mountains, and have not love, I am nothing.

And though I bestow all my goods to feed the poor, and though I give my body to be burned, and have not love, it profiteth me nothing.

Love suffereth long, and is kind; love envieth not; love vaunteth not itself, is not puffed up,

Doth not behave itself useemly, seeketh not her own, is not easily provoked, thinketh no evil;

Rejoiceth not in iniquity, but rejoiceth in the truth;

Beareth all things, believeth all things, hopeth all things, endureth all things.

Love never faileth: but whether there be prophecies, they shall fail; whether there be tongues, they shall cease; whether there be knowledge, it shall vanish away.

For we know in part, and we prophesy in part.

But when that which is perfect is come, then that which is in part shall be done away.

When I was a child, I spake as a child, I understood as a child, I thought as a child; but when I became a man, I put away childish things.

For now we see through a glass, darkly; but then face to face: now I know in part; but then shall I know even as also I am known.

And now abideth faith, hope, love, these three; but the greatest of these is love.*

St. Paul was born about the same time as Jesus. He started out in life as Saul, of Tarsus,† and during all of his early life was a devout Jew. A few years after the Crucifixion he was converted by a vision on the road to Damascus, and thereafter he was an ardent disciple and missionary, filled with zeal to spread the gospel and win converts to Christianity.

In his later years his missionary travels took him to far places, among strange people. He was constantly in danger on his travels: from the fury of mobs, from the raging rivers and seas he had to cross, from roving bands of robbers, from illness and tainted food—and most of all, from the outraged authorities who accused him of fomenting unrest, of exciting the people on religious matters and endangering public law and order. Scorning hardship and danger, filled only with the desire to teach the kind of goodness Christ loved and taught, he continued his travels, pressing on into new territories, sending back letters to the Christian communities he founded to remind the people of his teachings and to keep them faithful. He felt impelled to do all he could before he died or was killed and had to hand on the torch to others.

Paul's first missionary letter was probably written in the year 52 A.D. He is believed to have been executed during Nero's persecution of the Christians about 67 A.D.; therefore the ten Epistles of St. Paul in the New Testament

---

* I Corinthians 13.

† According to tradition, Saul's name was changed to Paul in honor of Sergius Paulus, whom he converted (Acts 13:6–12).

represent approximately the last twelve years of his inspired ministry. The most famous is his first letter to the Corinthians, which is known and loved by millions of people—and which is considered one of the most glorious passages in world literature.

For nearly two thousand years this letter, outlining the essential virtues for a happy and useful life, has been a tremendous spiritual and moral force in the world. It is impossible to estimate its influence on human thought and behavior.

The Thirteenth Chapter of First Corinthians was a favorite of Jefferson, Lincoln, Franklin D. Roosevelt. It was a favorite of William Allen White, was read at the funeral services of his daughter when she was tragically killed at the age of eighteen. It has been the guide, the comfort, the inspiration of countless people in all the centuries since it was written. "The ancient words of Paul have always seemed to me to hold the complete answer to all of human living," says Marjorie Kinnan Rawlings.

These words have lost none of their power and influence, and none of their timeliness. The world has, perhaps, greater need of them today than ever; for they stress what is, or should be, the most vital and characteristic of Christian virtues: *love of one's fellow men.*

Thou shalt love thy neighbor as thyself.

Leviticus 19:18

We praise those who love their fellow men.

Aristotle

To love our neighbor as ourself is such a fundamental truth for regulating human society, that by that alone one might determine all the cases in social morality.

John Locke

Those who love not their fellow beings live unfruitful lives.　　*Percy Bysshe Shelley*

Lord, make me an instrument of your peace; where there is hatred, let me sow love; where there is injury, pardon; where there is doubt, faith; where there is despair, hope; where there is darkness, light; and where there is sadness, joy.

O Divine Master, grant that I may not so much seek to be consoled as to console; to be understood as to understand; to be loved as to love; for it is in giving that we receive, it is in pardoning that we are pardoned, and it is in dying that we are born to eternal life. *Amen.*   *St. Francis of Assisi*

One of the most important phases of maturing is that of growth from self-centering to an understanding relationship to others. . . . A person is not mature until he has both an ability and a willingness to see himself as one among others and to do unto those others as he would have them do to him.   *H. A. Overstreet*

You give but little when you give of your possessions. It is when you give of yourself that you truly give.
                                             Kahlil Gibran

A person completely wrapped up in himself makes a small package. . . . The great day comes when a man begins to get himself off his hands. He has lived, let us say, in a mind like a room surrounded by mirrors. Every way he turned he saw himself. Now, however, some of the mirrors change to windows. He can see through them to objective outlooks that challenge his interests. He begins to get out of himself—no longer the prisoner of self-reflections but a free man in a world where persons, causes, truths, and values exist, worthful for their own sakes. Thus to pass from a mirror-mind to a mind with windows is an essential element in the development of a real personality. Without that experience no one ever achieves a meaningful life.   *Harry Emerson Fosdick*

2.

LET ME NOT NEGLECT ANY KINDNESS,
FOR I SHALL NOT PASS THIS WAY AGAIN

THE POWER of inspiration is mighty . . . and mysterious. For more than a century a brief quotation has been making the rounds, repeated over and over again in print, and widely spread by word of mouth.

No one knows who originally wrote or said it, though it has been variously attributed to Victor Hugo, to George Eliot, to a Quaker missionary named Stephen Grellet, and to others. No one knows when it was said, why it was said, or how it came to take such firm hold of the world's heart and mind. But take hold it did, impelling untold numbers of people to be kinder and more considerate to their fellow creatures. It remains as fresh and vital as ever, a familiar little gem of inspiration:

> I shall pass through this world but once. Any good therefore that I can do, or any kindness that I can show to any human being, let me do it now. Let me not defer nor neglect it, for I shall not pass this way again.

It is astonishing how this brief quotation, the words of some inspired unknown of a century or more ago, has endured, steadily increasing in influence and popularity. It crops up over and over again in books, magazines, newspapers; has been the subject of innumerable sermons and lectures; is frequently quoted in plays and on radio and television programs. It has proudly hung on the walls of thousands of homes and offices, and has traveled to far places of the world, translated into many different languages.

I shall pass through this world but once. It was the favorite quotation of George V of England. He copied it in his own hand and kept it framed on his writing desk.

Any kindness that I can show to any human being, let me do it now. Dale Carnegie calls it one of the basic requirements for happiness in life. "Cut out this quotation and put it where you will see it every morning!" he urges his readers.

It is a reminder to all of us that we do not live for ourselves alone, that we must do what we can to help others, to lighten a burden or soften a grief whenever the need arises . . . *for we shall not pass this way again.*

As we have therefore opportunity, let us do good unto all men.   *Galatians 6:10*

A man's true wealth is the good he does in this world.
                                        Mohammed

In nothing do men more nearly approach the gods than in doing good to their fellow men.   *Cicero*

That best portion of a good man's life,—
His little nameless, unremembered acts
Of kindness and of love.
                        William Wordsworth

If I can stop one heart from breaking,
I shall not live in vain;
If I can ease one life the aching,
Or cool one pain,
Or help one fainting robin
Unto his nest again,
I shall not live in vain.

                        Emily Dickinson

3. CONFUCIUS

WHAT YOU DO NOT WISH DONE TO
YOURSELF, DO NOT DO TO OTHERS

THE GREAT Chou Dynasty was beginning to crumble. The feudal system was breaking up in a turmoil of disorder and civil strife; and all over China the duchies and baronies that had emerged as independent states were warring with one another, struggling to hold on to their lands and their people. The power of the Emperor had dwindled to nothing at all. There were moral and political chaos, widespread confusion and unrest, cruelty, oppression. For every lord who lived in luxury there were thousands who lived on the edge of starvation, humbly enduring their servitude and their suffering. Murder, pillage, invasion, were commonplace in the outlying districts. The very civilization of China was threatened; and keen minds, sensing the danger, tried to think out ways to bring peace, order, and harmony once again to their ancient land.

In the state of Lu, in those troubled times, there lived a young man who felt keenly the suffering of his people. He felt the need for a rationalized social order, and for a system of ethics and morality to guide human relationships. Out of the needs and problems of his times this young man was to create a philosophy that was not only to light the way in China and shape the nation's destiny, but was to influence the entire world—a philosophy that remains a vital and living force even now, in our own times, twenty-five hundred years later.

The young man was Ch'iu, of the clan of K'ung. Later he came to be called K'ung Fu-tse, which means "the philosopher or master K'ung." The world knows him today as Confucius.

Though reputedly a descendant of noblemen, Confucius

was born into a poor family and grew up in humble circumstances. The early years of his life are obscure, but we know that even at fifteen he was a serious-minded scholar, his heart set on learning. As he grew up he became more and more interested in the history and literature of his country, and especially in the writings of the ancient sages. China had endured as a great nation for fifteen hundred years; he was convinced that in the rules and precepts of the sages was to be found the guidance now so desperately needed.

Confucius was, of course, too close to his own generation to realize fully what was happening. But he sensed, as others did, that China was drifting from its ancient moorings. He knew that its literature and traditions were in danger of perishing through the anarchy into which the kingdom had fallen. He felt that the best way he could help the people and the nation was to gather up and preserve the records of antiquity, bring them up to date, interpret and explain their meaning—and shape them into a practical system of ethics and morals for daily living.

It was with this purpose in mind that he established, when he was only twenty-two, a school to teach the history and literature of China, and the simple but enduring virtues on which the civilization of China was founded. Students flocked to him from every part of the province, eagerly hoping for something to live by, some replenishing philosophy. When two young scions of one of the principal houses in Lu joined the growing company of his disciples, his reputation as a teacher began to grow and spread.

Because of his wisdom, and his great skill in handling people, Confucius was about this time appointed superintendent of the ranges and herds. This gave him an opportunity to try out one of the most important precepts he had been teaching at his school: *What you do not wish done to yourself, do not do to others.* The ranges belonged to the state, and the herders paid taxes for the use of the land. There was continual strife among the owners of the sheep and cattle, endless quarreling and friction. The rival herders hated and distrusted each other, raided and robbed whenever they could, killed or confiscated any animal that strayed on, or even near, their land.

Confucius called the herders together and spoke to them earnestly, for a long time. He spoke, not as the usual official or overseer, but as a friend—with kindness and understanding. This was something new; the herders listened in amazement. And here are some of the wise things Confucius told them:

The rule of life is to be found within yourself.

Ask yourself constantly, "What is the right thing to do?"

Beware of ever doing that which you are likely, sooner or later, to repent of having done.

It is better to live in peace than in bitterness and strife.

It is better to believe in your neighbors than to fear and distrust them.

The superior man does not wrangle. He is firm but not quarrelsome. He is sociable but not clannish.

The superior man sets a good example to his neighbors. He is considerate of their feelings and their property.

Consideration for others is the basis of a good life, a good society.

Feel kindly toward everyone. Be friendly and pleasant among yourselves. Be generous and fair.

But the wisest thing he told the herders that day—the maxim he was to repeat over and over again throughout his long life, and that was to become inseparably associated with his name and his philosophy—was this:

What you do not wish done to yourself, do not do to others.

We are told that the herders listened carefully to Confucius and were greatly awed and impressed by what he said. They returned to their homes and repeated his words to their families. And the strife and turmoil ceased; and the sheep and cattle multiplied; and there was peace on the ranges for the first time in years.

It was an extraordinary demonstration of applied ethics; and Confucius was encouraged to continue and expand his teachings. His success in ending the strife among the herders enormously increased his influence, and his name and fame began to spread beyond the borders of his own state. He spent most of the remainder of his life as a scholar and teacher, wandering from state to state with his disciples, spreading his wisdom wherever he went—returning to Lu in his old age to collect the ancient traditions and philosophies of his people, and his own pithy maxims and sayings, for the guidance of future generations.

When he died in 479 B.C., at the age of seventy-two, his disciples mourned him as "the wisest and greatest of mortal men." They spread his teachings far and wide, and the entire Chinese nation began to pay him homage. Among the many posthumous titles conferred upon him were "The Sage," "The Holy One," "The Master." In time beautiful temples were erected in his memory, and "Confucianism" became one of the greatest cults in history.

Today nearly a fourth of the human race love and cherish the memory of Confucius, and look upon his words as sacred writ. Hundreds of thousands of educated Chinese know the five Confucian books by heart and can repeat them word for word. Great masses of people, even among the most illiterate, live by Confucian maxims: their only religion, their only moral and ethical influence. For twenty-five centuries the teachings of Confucius have remained one of the world's strongest moral forces. And at the vital core of his philosophy is the simple, basic rule he taught the warring herders so long ago: *What you do not wish done to yourself, do not do to others.*

Confucius was neither the first nor the last to teach this important social principle. It is one of the oldest and most enduring rules of human relationship. Zoroaster taught it in Persia several hundred years before Confucius. Jesus preached it in Judea five hundred years after Confucius, changed it from its negative form into the familiar and inspiring Golden Rule of Christianity: *Do unto others as you would have others do unto you.*

But Confucius made it the basic principle of his entire philosophy, the most important single rule of life. He preached it tirelessly; his disciples passed it on from one generation to the next; it helped shape the character and destiny of the Chinese nation. Though it may not belong to Confucius alone, it was at the root of all his teachings— and through his influence has been the guiding principle of countless millions of people since.

Tsu-kung asked, saying: Is there any one maxim which may serve as a rule of practice for the whole of one's life? The Master replied: Is not the maxim of charity such? What you do not wish done to yourself, do not do to others.*

All things whatsoever ye would that men should do to you, do ye even so to them: for this is the law and the prophets.   *Matthew 7:12*

He that does good to another does good also to himself, not only in the consequence but in the very act. For the consciousness of well-doing is in itself ample reward.   *Seneca*

This is the sum of all true righteousness: deal with others as thou wouldst thyself be dealt by. Do nothing to thy neighbor which thou wouldst not have him do to thee hereafter.   *The Mahabharata*

The duty of man is not a wilderness of turnpike gates,

---

* From *The Analects of Confucius.*

through which he is to pass by tickets from one to the other. It is plain and simple, and consists but of two points—his duty to God, which every man must feel; and, with respect to his neighbor, to do as he would be done by.   *Thomas Paine*

It is one of the most beautiful compensations of this life that no man can sincerely try to help another without helping himself.   *Ralph Waldo Emerson*

I'm going your way, so let us go hand in hand. You help me and I'll help you. We shall not be here very long, for soon death, the kind old nurse, will come back and rock us all to sleep. Let us help one another while we may.   *William Morris*

4. PHILLIPS BROOKS

**YOU WHO ARE LETTING YOUR FRIEND'S
HEART ACHE FOR A WORD OF
APPRECIATION OR SYMPATHY . . .
THE TIME IS SHORT!**

As USUAL, the great church was filled. Phillips Brooks faced the enormous, hushed congregation as he had so many times before, Sunday after Sunday—the expectant, well-dressed congregation waiting for his weekly message.

He looked into the faces of men and women he long had known, men and women who had come to him with their problems, who had asked for his help and guidance. How well he knew what seethed behind the pleasant, smiling masks of their Sunday-best respectability! How well he knew the petty spites that embittered their hearts, the animosities that set neighbor against neighbor, the silly quarrels that were kept alive, the jealousies and misunderstandings, the stubborn pride!

Today his message was for those bitter, unbending ones who refused to forgive and forget. He must make them realize that life is too short to nurse grievances, to harbor grudges and resentments. He would plead for tolerance and understanding, for sympathy and kindness. He would plead for brotherly love.

"Oh, my dear friends!" he said . . . and it was as though he spoke to each separately and alone:

You who are letting miserable misunderstandings run on from year to year, meaning to clear them up some day;

You who are keeping wretched quarrels alive because you cannot quite make up your mind that now is the day to sacrifice your pride and kill them;

213

You who are passing men sullenly upon the street, not speaking to them out of some silly spite, and yet knowing that it would fill you with shame and remorse if you heard that one of those men were dead tomorrow morning;

You who are letting your neighbor starve, till you hear that he is dying of starvation;

Or letting your friend's heart ache for a word of appreciation or sympathy, which you mean to give him someday;

If you only could know and see and feel, all of a sudden, that *"the time is short,"* how it would break the spell! How you would go instantly and do the thing which you might never have another chance to do.

As the congregation poured out of the church that Sunday morning, people who hadn't spoken in years suddenly smiled and greeted each other . . . *and discovered it was what they had been wanting to do all along.* Neighbors who had disliked and avoided each other walked home together . . . *and were astonished to find how very much they enjoyed doing it.* Many who had been grudging and unkind firmly resolved to be more generous in the future, more considerate of others . . . *and all at once felt happier and more content, felt at peace with themselves and the world.*

Phillips Brooks had found just the right combination of words to inspire his listeners, to make them want to forget their grudges and patch up their quarrels. His sermon struck a responsive chord in many hearts that day; and there were some who never afterward forgot his words, for they helped change the course of their lives, helped bring back the happiness they had so nearly destroyed.

Forgive, Phillips Brooks urged his congregation. *Forget. Bear with the faults of others as you would have them bear with yours. Be patient and understanding. Life is too short to be vengeful or malicious. Life is too short to be petty or unkind.* The sermon later appeared in print, and the arc of its influence steadily widened and increased.

Phillips Brooks was one of America's greatest preachers. As Rector of Trinity Church in Boston, and later as Bishop of Massachusetts, he delivered many eloquent and memorable sermons. "The Candle of the Lord," which he preached in Westminster Abbey on July 4, 1879, remains one of the world's most famous sermons. He was also a distinguished literary personality, a writer of essays and poems. One of his poems was set to music and has achieved immortality as the beloved hymn, "O Little Town of Bethlehem."

But of all his prodigious sermons and writings, the selection we have quoted is one of the best known and best remembered. It is so frequently quoted, in print and from the pulpit, that it is familiar to vast numbers of people; and its influence has been incalculable. That influence continues . . . reminding us that life is short, that we must forget our grudges and grievances, forget and forgive while there still is time. *Don't wait to patch up that quarrel,* says Phillips Brooks. *Don't wait to say that kind word, to do that kind deed. The time is short, and tomorrow may be too late!*

Forgive us our trespasses, as we forgive them that trespass against us.   *The Lord's Prayer*

You must forgive those who transgress against you before you can look to forgiveness from Above.

Talmud

To err is human; to forgive, divine.   *Alexander Pope*

God has been very gracious to me, for I never dwell upon anything wrong which a person has done, so as to remember it afterwards. If I do remember it, I always see some other virtue in that person.

St. Theresa of Ávila

Life is short and we have not too much time for gladdening the hearts of those who are traveling the dark

way with us. Oh, be swift to love! Make haste to be
kind!
                                          Henri F. Amiel

Do not keep the alabaster boxes of your love and
tenderness sealed up until your friends are dead. Fill
their lives with sweetness. Speak approving, cheering
words while their ears can hear them and while their
hearts can be thrilled by them.   *Henry Ward Beecher*

Life is too short to be little.   *Benjamin Disraeli*

Life appears to me to be too short to be spent in nursing animosity or in registering wrongs. We are, and
must be, one and all, burdened with faults in this
world; but the time will come when, I trust, we shall
put them off in putting off our corruptible bodies;
when debasement and sin will fall from us and only
the spark will remain. . . .
. . . With this creed, revenge never worries my heart,
degradation never too deeply disgusts me, injustice
never crushes me too low. I live in calm, looking to
the end.   *Charlotte Brontë*

In this life, if you have anything to pardon, pardon
quickly. Slow forgiveness is little better than no forgiveness.   *Sir Arthur W. Pinero*

I sometimes feel the thread of life is slender,
And soon with me the labor will be wrought;
Then grows my heart to other hearts more tender,
    The time is short.

                                        Dinah M. Craik

There are many fine things which you mean to do
some day, under what you think will be favorable
circumstances. But the only time that is surely yours
is the present, hence this is the time to speak the word
of appreciation and sympathy, to do the generous
deed, to forgive the fault of a thoughtless friend, to

sacrifice self a little more for others. Today is the day in which to express your noblest qualities of mind and heart, to do at least one worthy thing which you have long postponed, and to use your God-given abilities for the enrichment of some less fortunate fellow traveler. Today you can make your life . . . significant and worth while. The present is yours to do with it as you will.

Grenville Kleiser

Around the corner I have a friend,
In this great city that has no end;
Yet days go by, and weeks rush on,
And before I know it a year is gone,
And I never see my old friend's face,
For Life is a swift and terrible race.
He knows I like him just as well
As in the days when I rang his bell
And he rang mine. We were younger then,
And now we are busy, tired men:
Tired with playing a foolish game,
Tired with trying to make a name.
"Tomorrow," I say, "I will call on Jim,
Just to show that I'm thinking of him."
But tomorrow comes—and tomorrow goes,
And the distance between us grows and grows.

Around the corner!—yet miles away . . .
"Here's a telegram, sir. . . ."

"Jim died today."

And that's what we get, and deserve in the end:
Around the corner, a vanished friend.

Charles Hanson Towne

5. ABRAHAM LINCOLN

WITH MALICE TOWARD NONE, WITH CHARITY FOR ALL . . .

THE FOURTH of March, 1865, started out to be dull and rainy. But later in the day it cleared; and it turned out to be pleasant after all for the President's second inauguration.

The streets were filled with milling crowds of people, with cavalry patrols and police. The inauguration platform had been built on the east front of the Capitol; and here there was a vast sea of humanity, stretching as far as the eye could see, filling the great plaza and flooding out into the grounds beyond. As the President appeared and took his place on the platform, a tremendous roar swept the crowd, rolling back like thunder to the outer edges, loud and prolonged.

Abraham Lincoln had not expected such an ovation. He had not, in fact, expected to be re-elected at all. No man in American history had been so hated and reviled, so bitterly denounced, as he had been these past four years. They had been difficult years—years of great struggle and suffering, of agony and bloodshed. He had taken over the leadership of the country at a time of grave crisis, and had given his best efforts to maintaining and preserving the Union—the only thing that really mattered.

But he had been misunderstood, condemned, humiliated in public and in private, assailed alike by friend and foe. One newspaper had called him "the obscene ape of Illinois." Horace Greeley had written an editorial demanding his withdrawal in favor of another candidate, declaring: "Mr. Lincoln is already beaten. He can never be elected." His life had been threatened over and over again. Even today, though every precaution had been taken, he knew there were many who feared for his safety.

No, he had not expected to be re-elected . . . not even with the high tide of the Confederacy broken and victory at last in sight. With Grant's vise closing on Lee, and Sherman moving up from the south, it was clear the war was almost over. But he felt no elation, either at the recent victories in the war or his own unexpected victory at the polls. He saw the hand of God in both these events, and was humbly grateful for the chance now given him to complete his great task. He harbored no resentments, had no slightest wish for retaliation against those who had cruelly slandered and abused him. He had one interest only: to conciliate the rebellious states and to rebuild the Union he had sworn to preserve.

The great crowd fell silent as he stepped forward to make his address. The sun, which had been obscured all day, suddenly burst through the clouds and flooded the scene with brightness. He spoke slowly and clearly, his voice vibrant with emotion, aware of the great importance of this moment and the potential influence of his words on the nation.

"On the occasion corresponding to this four years ago, all thoughts were anxiously directed to an impending civil war. . . . All knew that slavery was, somehow, the cause of the war. . . . Neither party expected for the war the magnitude or the duration which it has already attained. . . . Each looked for an easier triumph. . . . Both read the same Bible, and pray to the same God; and each invokes His aid against the other. . . . It may seem strange that any men should dare to ask a just God's assistance in wringing their bread from the sweat of other men's faces; but let us judge not, that we be not judged. . . . The Almighty has His own purposes. . . ."

The huge crowd listened without a sound. This was not party language. This was not political phraseology. Abraham Lincoln was talking out of the fullness of his heart, to a people and nation he loved, appealing for peace and tolerance, for understanding, for an end to sectional bitterness and strife.

There was no hint of self-aggrandizement anywhere in his speech, no boasting about his re-election, no praise for the administration and what it had accomplished. The *Union* was his main theme, his main interest . . . a strong, united, unbroken nation, firm in its loyalties and ideals. He wanted no gloating, no malice—above all, no malice! The issues involved were too vast to admit of malicious dealing. His aim was to end all feelings of hatred and resentment between North and South, to bind up the nation's wounds, to prevent—in so far as possible—the unhappy aftermaths of war.

He closed with this passage, which has been called "the purest gold of human eloquence":

> With malice toward none; with charity for all; with firmness in the right, as God gives us to see the right, let us strive on to finish the work we are in; to bind up the nation's wounds; to care for him who shall have borne the battle, and for his widow and his orphan— to do all which may achieve and cherish a just and lasting peace among ourselves and with all nations.

Lincoln's second inaugural address received high contemporary praise. Many newspapers called it the most inspiring speech ever made by an American President. Others declared it raised high hopes for the future, and congratulated the President on finding words so eloquent, and so adequate to his desire.

But it was the closing paragraph of Lincoln's speech that had the greatest impact, that stirred the nation and the world. In these few words were condensed the essence of his philosophy, his abiding faith in the nation and its people, his dream of an America in which all were equally free, and in which even the most humble could find peace and happiness. They were words of infinite sympathy and compassion. Though he spoke out of the depths of his own heart, he spoke for millions of others who felt as he did, voicing their hopes and prayers for a lasting peace "with liberty and justice for all."

It was a paragraph forever memorable—and forever inspiring. The language was simple but there was a majesty to it, almost a Biblical quality. It was like a "sacred poem," wrote Carl Shurz. "No President had ever spoken words like these to the American people."

Above all else, this famous closing paragraph was an expression of Lincoln's own inherent character: his great courage and integrity, his humility, his love for his fellow man. *"With malice toward none, with charity for all . . ."* Lincoln did not believe in harboring resentments or bearing grudges. He never willingly planted a thorn in any man's bosom, never did anything through malice or spite.

"Lincoln's noble sentiment of charity for all and malice toward none was not a specific for the Civil War," declared Elihu Root. *"It is a living principle of action."*

Few words have been so widely quoted; few words have had such tremendous and enduring influence on people all over the world. The late Earl Curzon, Chancellor of Oxford University, called it "one of the truly great treasures of mankind." It has guided countless men and women in ways of greater tolerance and understanding.

"With malice toward none, with charity for all . . ."

Generations of Americans still unborn will thrill to these words of love and compassion spoken by Abraham Lincoln at one of the most crucial hours in the nation's history.

Father, forgive them, for they know not what they do.
Luke 23:34

Let all bitterness, and wrath, and anger, and clamor, and evil speaking be put away from you, with all malice.   *Ephesians 4:31*

Be ever soft and pliable like a reed, not hard and unbending like a cedar.   *Talmud*

He who has not forgiven an enemy has not yet tasted one of the most sublime enjoyments of life.
Johann K. Lavater

The more we know, the better we forgive;
Whoe'er feels deeply, feels for all who live.

Madame de Staël

If we could read the secret history of our enemies we
should find in each man's life sorrow and suffering
enough to disarm all hostility.

Henry Wadsworth Longfellow

My heart was heavy, for its trust had been
Abused, its kindness answered with foul wrong;
So turning gloomily from my fellow men,
One summer Sabbath day I strolled among
The green mounds of the village burial-place;
Where, pondering how all human love and hate
Find one sad level; and how, soon or late,
Wronged and wrongdoer, each with meekened face,
And cold hands folded over a still heart,
Pass the green threshold of our common grave,
Whither all footsteps tend, whence none depart,
Awed for myself, and pitying my race,
Our common sorrow, like a mighty wave,
Swept all my pride away, and, trembling, I forgave!

John Greenleaf Whittier

6. SAM WALTER FOSS

LET ME LIVE BY THE SIDE OF THE
ROAD AND BE A FRIEND TO MAN

SAM FOSS liked to walk. But he had wandered a bit too far today in the blazing sun, lost in his thoughts; and now suddenly he realized how hot and tired he was. The big tree at the side of the road looked tempting, and he stopped for a moment to rest in its shade.

There was a little sign on the tree, and he read it with surprise and pleasure. The sign said: *"There is a good spring inside the fence. Come and drink if you are thirsty."*

Foss climbed over the fence, found the spring, and gratefully drank his fill of the cool water. Then he noticed a bench near the spring, and tacked to the bench another sign. He went over to it and read: *"Sit down and rest awhile if you are tired."*

Now thoroughly delighted, he went to a barrel of apples near by—and saw that here, too, was a sign! *"If you like apples, just help yourself,"* he read. He accepted the invitation, picked out a plump red apple, and looked up to discover an elderly man watching him with interest.

"Hello, there!" he called. "Is this your place?"

"Yes," the old man answered. "I'm glad you stopped by." And he explained the reason for the signs. The water was going to waste; the bench was gathering dust in the attic; the apples were more than they could use. He and his wife thought it would be neighborly to offer tired, thirsty passers-by a place to rest and refresh themselves. So they had brought down the bench and put up the signs—and made themselves a host of fine new friends!

"You must like people," Foss said.

"Of course," the old man answered simply. "Don't you?"

All the way home Sam Foss kept thinking of a line from

Homer's *Iliad:* "*He was a friend of man, and lived in a house by the side of the road.*" How perfectly that described the kindly old man he had just met, living in his house by the side of the road, eagerly sharing his water and the comfort of his shady grounds, befriending every stranger who passed by!

The lines of a poem began to shape up in his mind. It would be a poem about friendship, simple and sincere as the old man himself. He would call it "The House By the Side of the Road."

There are hermit souls that live withdrawn
In the place of their self-content;
There are souls like stars, that dwell apart,
In a fellowless firmament;
There are pioneer souls that blaze their paths
Where highways never ran—
But let me live by the side of the road
And be a friend to man.

Let me live in a house by the side of the road,
Where the race of men go by—
The men who are good and the men who are bad,
As good and as bad as I.
I would not sit in the scorner's seat,
Or hurl the cynic's ban—
Let me live in a house by the side of the road
And be a friend to man.

I see from my house by the side of the road,
By the side of the highway of life,
The men who press with the ardor of hope,
The men who are faint with the strife.
But I turn not away from their smiles nor their tears,
Both parts of an infinite plan—
Let me live in a house by the side of the road
And be a friend to man.

I know there are brook-gladdened meadows ahead,
And mountains of wearisome height;

That the road passes on through the long afternoon
And stretches away to the night.
But still I rejoice when the travelers rejoice,
And weep with the strangers that moan,
Nor live in my house by the side of the road
Like a man who dwells alone.

Let me live in my house by the side of the road,
Where the race of men go by—
They are good, they are bad, they are weak, they are
     strong,
Wise, foolish—so am I;
Then why should I sit in the scorner's seat,
Or hurl the cynic's ban?
Let me live in my house by the side of the road
And be a friend to man.

Sam Walter Foss, who died in 1911, was an editor, humorist, poet . . . and a friend of man. He liked people, and he liked doing things for people. His work had an intimate, endearing quality, but not necessarily an enduring one. He might be forgotten by now, were it not for "The House By the Side of the Road." This poem, known and loved by millions, is his immortality.

"The House By the Side of the Road" is today one of the best-known and most frequently quoted poems about friendship and good-fellowship. It can be found in practically every collection of popular verse. In a national poll to determine the most popular poem in America, "The House By the Side of the Road" came in second, an outstanding favorite.*

And so, because a poet went walking one summer day— and met a kindly old man who liked people and liked doing things for people—America has one of its most cherished poems. In the hustle and bustle of life today, when so few of us take time out to think of others, it's good to stop for a moment and remember the generous,

---

* In first place, Longfellow's "Psalm of Life." See pages 134–136.

friendly old man who inspired "The House By the Side of the Road."

As to the value of other things, most men differ; concerning friendships all have the same opinion.
What sweetness is left in life, if you take away friendship? Robbing life of friendship is like robbing the world of the sun.
A true friend is more to be esteemed than kinsfolk.

Cicero

Without friends the world is but a wilderness. . . .
There is no man that imparteth his joys to his friends, but he joyeth the more; and no man that imparteth his griefs to his friend, but he grieveth the less.

Francis Bacon

If a man does not make new acquaintances as he advances through life, he will soon find himself left alone. A man should keep his friendships in constant repair. . . .
To let friendship die away by negligence and silence is certainly not wise. It is voluntarily to throw away one of the greatest comforts of this weary pilgrimage.

Samuel Johnson

Like the Stone of Wisdom, friendship may be lying right in your back yard and you may never know it. Your best friend may be a stranger to you, or you may lose him because you didn't bother to hold him.
Friends must be cultivated by sincerity, frankness, and deeds of affection. No one can remain your friend if you hide your soul from him. You needn't save face before your friend. Your friend will save it for you.
Life is a chain of little events. Close your soul to your friend, and he will lose sight of you. And if you find your friend, give of your friendship and it will return to you tenfold. Those who cannot give friendship will rarely receive it and never hold it.

Dagobert D. Runes

Go often to the house of thy friend, for weeds choke the unused path. *Ralph Waldo Emerson*

So long as we love, we serve; so long as we are loved by others, I should say that we are almost indispensable; and no man is useless while he has a friend.
Robert Louis Stevenson

PART SEVEN

PEACE

of

Heart and Mind

"Nothing can bring you peace but yourself."
RALPH WALDO EMERSON

PYTHAGORAS, who lived a little more than five hundred years before Christ, and whose genius ushered in the Golden Age of Greece, taught his disciples to live for the day only. He urged them never to worry about anything, especially what was over and done with and could never be undone. One of his most famous sayings was, "Leave not the mark of the pot upon the ashes!" In other words: wipe out the past, forget it, start the day fresh. It was the only way to achieve the peace of a contented mind.

Long before Pythagoras, and in all the centuries since, men have sought what Buddha called "equanimity" . . . what Epicurus called "tranquillity" . . . what the poet Whittier called "the harvest song of inward peace." And the verdict of the ages is that "nothing can bring you peace but yourself." No one can give you the gift of a serene mind, a calm and tranquil way of life. It is something you must develop for yourself, within yourself.

Here are some inspiring messages on peace of mind, quotations selected to help you meet the needs and problems of today.

1. SIR WILLIAM OSLER

LIVE FOR THE DAY ONLY, AND FOR THE
DAY'S WORK. . . . THE CHIEF WORRIES
OF LIFE ARISE FROM THE
FOOLISH HABIT OF LOOKING BEFORE
AND AFTER

IT WAS spring again; and again Sir William Osler was to address a group of students, this time at Yale.

He thought back over the years and the many times he had addressed groups of students, here and in Canada. Always, looking into their eager young faces, he thought of himself at twenty-two, an anxious young medical student. He remembered how worried he had been about final examinations, how fearful of the future, wondering where to go, how to get started, what to do about building up a practice. Even now, across the broad expanse of years, he could recall how desperately he had longed for a simple philosophy to guide him in his career, a way of life that had worked for others and perhaps would work for him.

Then one day, in a book by Thomas Carlyle, he had come across the sentence that had been his magic talisman ever since: *"Our main business is not to see what lies dimly at a distance, but to do what lies clearly at hand."* A single inspired sentence, it instantly answered his needs and shaped the course of his future. To do the day's work superbly well, planning for the future but not worrying about it, became the guiding principle of his life.

Now sixty-four, nearing the end of a busy and happy life, Sir William Osler knew no better philosophy than the one by which he himself had lived so successfully, for so many years. Out of a lifetime of rich and gratifying experience, he could think of no better advice for young men than to live for the day and its allotted task—"to do what lies clearly at hand" and let the future take care of itself.

That is what he would tell those young students at Yale. But merely to quote Carlyle's words and call them the secret of success was not enough. He must find some way to dramatize the basic philosophy behind them, some way to etch their meaning indelibly upon the memory.

A few months before he had crossed the Atlantic on a great ocean liner. He had been impressed by the fact that the captain, standing on the bridge, could touch a button and instantly shut off parts of the ship—shut them off into watertight compartments. That was it! He would tell them to concentrate on the day's work, to do what had to be done to the best of their ability, shutting off the past and the future, living in *day-tight compartments*. He would call his address "A Way of Life."

I have a message that may be helpful. It is not philosophical, nor is it strictly moral or religious . . . and yet in a way it is all three. It is so simple that some of you may turn away disappointed. My message is but a word, a *Way*.

The way of life that I preach is a habit to be acquired gradually by long and steady repetition. It is the practice of living for the day only, and for the day's work, living in "day-tight compartments." . . . The chief worries of life arise from the foolish habit of looking before and after.

A few months ago I stood on the bridge of a great liner, plowing the ocean at twenty-five knots. "She is alive in every plate," said the Captain, "a huge monster with brain and nerves, an immense stomach, a wonderful heart and lungs, and a splendid system of locomotion." Just at that moment a signal sounded, and all over the ship the watertight compartments were closed. "Our chief factor of safety," said the Captain.

Now each one of you is a much more marvelous organization than the great liner, and bound on a longer voyage. What I urge is that you so learn to control the machinery as to live with "day-tight compartments" as the most certain way to insure safety on the voyage. Get on the bridge, and see that at least the great bulkheads are in working order. Touch a button and hear, at every level of your life, the iron doors shutting out the Past—the dead yesterdays. Touch another and shut off, with a metal curtain, the Future—the unborn tomorrows. Then you are safe, safe for today.

The load of tomorrow, added to that of yesterday, carried today makes the strongest falter. . . . Waste of energy, mental distress, nervous worries dog the steps of a man who is anxious about the future. Shut close, then, the great fore and aft bulkheads, and prepare to cultivate the habit of a life in "day-tight compartments"!

I am simply giving you a philosophy of life that I have found helpful in my work. In this philosophy or way of life each of you may learn to drive the straight furrow, and so come to the true measure of a man.

Sir William Osler's address on "A Way of Life" was given at Yale in the spring of 1913. Few who heard him ever forgot his message, the essential part of which is here quoted. Many who heard him went on to achieve notable success in various fields; and among them were some who ever after acknowledged their indebtedness to Sir William and his advice: *Live neither in the past nor in the future, but let each day's work absorb all your interest, energy, and enthusiasm. The best preparation for tomorrow is to do today's work superbly well.*

"A Way of Life" was one of the most inspiring addresses ever heard at Yale, and interest in it was so great that it was published in essay form and widely distributed. It has since been quoted in whole or in part in so many books, articles, and lectures that its basic idea of living in "day-tight compartments" is familiar to thousands.

So in an ever-widening arc of inspiration, Sir William Osler's words reach out, touching more and more lives.

Though he himself is gone, his "way of life" remains a vital influence, helping people do their day's work in confidence, without letting the mistakes of the past paralyze the efforts of today . . . without letting needless anxieties about the future waste their energies or destroy their peace of mind.

Take therefore no thought for the morrow; for the morrow shall take thought for the things of itself. Sufficient unto the day is the evil thereof.

Matthew 6:34

Trouble not thyself by pondering life in its entirety. Strive not to comprehend in one view the nature and number of burdens that, belike, will fall to thy share. Rather, as each occasion arises in the present put this question to thyself: "Where lies the unbearable, unendurable part of this task?" Confession will put thee to the blush! Next recall to mind that neither past nor future can weigh thee down, only the present. And the present will shrink to littleness if thou but set it apart, assign it its boundaries, and then ask thy mind if it avail not to bear even this! *Marcus Aurelius*

Some there are that torment themselves afresh with the memory of what is past; others, again, afflict themselves with the apprehension of evils to come; and very ridiculously both—for the one does not now concern us, and the other not yet. . . .

One should count each day a separate life. *Seneca*

Look to this day!
For it is life, the very life of life.
In its brief course
Lie all the verities and realities of your existence:
    The bliss of growth
    The glory of action
    The splendor of achievement,
For yesterday is but a dream
And tomorrow is only a vision,

But today well lived makes every yesterday a dream
   of happiness
And tomorrow a vision of hope.
Look well, therefore, to this day!
Such is the salutation to the dawn.

                                                    Kalidasa

As I got older I became aware of the folly of this
perpetual reaching after the future, and of drawing
from tomorrow, and from tomorrow only, a reason
for the joyfulness of today. I learned, when alas! it
was almost too late, to live each moment as it passed
over my head.   *William Hale White*

The greatest gift . . . is the realization that life does
not consist either of wallowing in the past or of peer-
ing anxiously at the future; and it is appalling to contemplate the great number of often painful steps by
which one arrives at a truth so old, so obvious, and so
frequently expressed. It is good for one to appreciate
that life is now. Whatever it offers, little or much, life
is now—this day—this hour.

                                        Charles Macomb Flandrau

I saw a delicate flower had grown up two feet high,
between the horses' path and the wheeltrack. An inch
more to right or left had sealed its fate, or an inch
higher; and yet it lived to flourish as much as if it had
a thousand acres of untrodden space around it, and
never knew the danger it incurred. It did not borrow
trouble, nor invite an evil fate by apprehending it.

                                        Henry David Thoreau

Let us be of good cheer, remembering that the misfortunes hardest to bear are those which never happen.   *James Russell Lowell*

2. JAMES GORDON GILKEY

YOU WANT TO GAIN EMOTIONAL
POISE? REMEMBER THE HOURGLASS,
THE GRAINS OF SAND DROPPING ONE
BY ONE. . . . THE CROWDED HOURS
COME TO YOU ALWAYS ONE
MOMENT AT A TIME

THE door closed behind the last visitor, and Dr. James Gordon Gilkey walked slowly back to his study. The same old story, the same familiar pattern; worry, strain, nervous tension—he had heard it over and over again in the past few months! So many people seemed to be troubled and harassed these days, always in a frenzy of rush and hurry, always in a turmoil. They complained they had too much to do, too many problems. They felt driven and distraught. They let their worries about the future pile on to the needs and duties of today—until the burden became too great and they became mentally and emotionally upset. Often they required the help of a psychiatrist to straighten them out again.

It was all wrong, of course. It was no way to live. This man who had just left, and the young woman earlier in the evening, and all the others who had come to talk things over with him in the past months—they were needlessly punishing themselves, destroying their own peace of mind. The relentless drive of modern life, and the goading fears and tensions, were at the root of much of the unhappiness in the world.

Dr. Gilkey thought of his own busy life, each day returning with its round of pressing duties and concerns, each day filled with its tasks and problems—yes, and the many problems of others that he was called upon to bear. Surely if anyone carried a heavy burden of responsibility, *he* did. Yet he didn't chafe under the load, didn't feel strained or driven. He was able to make his way serenely through the busiest, most crowded schedule. He was able to stay calm and poised even when there were a hundred different things to do before nightfall. How? By refusing to let everything rush in on him at once. By living one moment at a time, doing one thing at a time, facing one problem at a time. . . .

Like an hourglass, he thought, the sand dropping through it one grain at a time. That was the way it should be with the many pressing details of a busy life: one grain at a time, one thing at a time. He decided to make that the subject of next Sunday's sermon. Perhaps it would help some of his people to a more serene and confident way of life. He began working on it that evening:

Most of us think of ourselves as standing wearily and helplessly at the center of a circle bristling with tasks, burdens, problems, annoyances, and responsibilities which are rushing in upon us. At every moment we have a dozen different things to do, a dozen problems to solve, a dozen strains to endure. We see ourselves as overdriven, overburdened, overtired.

This is a common mental picture—and it is totally false. No one of us, however crowded his life, has such an existence.

What is the true picture of your life? Imagine that there is an hourglass on your desk. Connecting the bowl at the top with the bowl at the bottom is a tube so thin that only one grain of sand can pass through it at a time.

That is the true picture of your life, even on a super-busy day. The crowded hours come to you always one moment at a time. That is the only way they *can* come. The day may bring many tasks, many problems, strains, but invariably they come in single file.

You want to gain emotional poise? Remember the hourglass, the grains of sand dropping one by one. . . .

Dr. Gilkey's sermon, which he called "Gaining Emotional Poise," apparently met an urgent and long-felt need of his congregation. Many went to him later to thank him for his message, and to tell him how much it had meant to them.

Glad that his sermon had been helpful, the minister published it in the church paper. Later it was reprinted in *Best Sermons, 1944 Selection,* and subsequently was quoted in the *Reader's Digest.* Letters began to come to Dr. Gilkey from all parts of the world; and he was astonished to discover how many people were being helped by the sermon that grew out of his own experience and philosophy, and which was originally intended only for his own congregation. He was astonished to find how far a little candle can throw its beam!

So a simple sermon lives on—not because of any special eloquence, but because of its sincere and helpful message. The inspired analogy of the hourglass, with its grains of sand dropping one by one, has shown thousands the way to greater poise and balance . . . and has helped them achieve a better, more serene way of life.

Nothing in human affairs is worth any great anxiety.

Plato

It has been well said that no man ever sank under the burden of the day. It is when tomorrow's burden is added to the burden of today that the weight is more than a man can bear. Never load yourselves so, my friends. If you find yourselves so loaded, at least remember this: it is your own doing, not God's. He begs you to leave the future to Him, and mind the present.

George MacDonald

Anyone can carry his burden, however hard, until nightfall. Anyone can do his work, however hard, for one day. Anyone can live sweetly, patiently, lovingly, purely, till the sun goes down. And this is all that life really means.

Robert Louis Stevenson

Do not let trifles disturb your tranquillity of mind. The little pinpricks of daily life when dwelt upon and magnified, may do great damage, but if ignored or dismissed from thought, will disappear from inanition. Most men have worried about things which never happened, and more men have been killed by worry than by hard work. Life is so great in its opportunities and possibilities, that you should rise confidently above the inevitable trifles incident to daily contact with the world. Life is too precious to be sacrificed for the nonessential and transient. . . . Ignore the inconsequential. *Grenville Kleiser*

Finish each day and be done with it. . . . You have done what you could; some blunders and absurdities no doubt crept in; forget them as soon as you can. Tomorrow is a new day; you shall begin it well and serenely. *Ralph Waldo Emerson*

· 3. FREDERIC LOOMIS

THE BEST MEDICINE IS TO STOP
THINKING ABOUT YOURSELF, AND
START THINKING ABOUT OTHER PEOPLE

DR. FREDERIC LOOMIS leaned back against the pillows. He was so desperately tired that even sitting up was an effort. He was a sick man, and no one knew it better than he; but he had an idea for an article called "The Best Medicine," and he was determined to write it.

He knew, as he lay propped against his pillows, that death was waiting at the bedside. There was so little time left to him now! This message might be his last . . . and it was a pity, too, for there was still so much he wanted to say, so many ideas gleaned from his long years of practice that he had hoped to put down on paper.

Well, he'd probably never get to them now. But there was no use worrying about what couldn't be helped. *"It's but little good you'll do, watering last year's crops."*

As that familiar line from George Eliot went through his mind, Dr. Loomis was suddenly no longer tired. He reached for his pen—he knew now what he wanted to say:

> *"It's but little good you'll do, watering last year's crops."* Yet that is exactly what I have seen hundreds of my patients doing in the past twenty-five years— watering with freely flowing tears things of the irrevocable past. Not the bittersweet memories of loved ones, which I could understand, but things done which should not have been done, and things left undone which should have been done.
>
> I am a doctor, not a preacher; but a doctor, too, must try to understand the joys and sorrows of those

241

who come to him. He should without preaching be able to expound the philosophy that one cannot live adequately in the present, nor effectively face the future, when one's thoughts are buried in the past.

Moaning over what cannot be helped is a confession of futility and of fear, of emotional stagnation—in fact, of selfishness and cowardice. The best way to break this vicious, morbid circle—"to snap out of it"—is to stop thinking about yourself, and start thinking about other people. You can lighten your own load by doing something for someone else. By the simple device of doing an outward, unselfish act today, you can make the past recede. The present and future will again take on their true challenge and perspective.

As a doctor I have seen it tried many, many times and nearly always it has been a far more successful prescription than anything I could have ordered from the drugstore.

Dr. Loomis's premonition came true. These words were his last, for he died soon afterward.

Published shortly after his death, "The Best Medicine" is an enduring testament to the doctor's own courage and undaunted spirit. Many who read it, along with the editorial comment explaining the circumstances in which it was written, were doubly inspired. For here, if ever, was a man who practiced what he preached! Dr. Loomis knew he was dying, but he didn't believe in "moaning over what cannot be helped." He turned his thoughts away from himself, to the needs and problems of other people and what he could do to help them.

On his deathbed, out of a lifetime of service and devotion to others, Frederic Loomis left us this inspiring message: *Stop thinking about yourself . . . lighten your own load by doing something for someone else . . . it will keep you from morbid worry and fears . . . it's the best medicine.*

There is only one way to happiness, and that is to cease worrying about things which are beyond the power of our will.   *Epictetus*

Ah, my Beloved, fill the cup that clears
Today of past Regrets and future Fears:
    Tomorrow!—Why, Tomorrow I may be
Myself with Yesterday's Sev'n thousand Years.

The Moving Finger writes; and, having writ,
Moves on: nor all your Piety nor Wit
    Shall lure it back to cancel half a Line,
Nor all your Tears wash out a Word of it.
                            Omar Khayyám

Doing good to others is not a duty. It is a joy, for it increases your own health and happiness.   *Zoroaster*

The day returns and brings us the petty rounds of irritating concerns and duties. Help us to play the man, help us to perform them with laughter and kind faces, let cheerfulness abound with industry. Give us to go blithely on our business all the day, bring us to our resting beds weary and content and undishonored, and grant us in the end the gift of sleep. Amen.
                            Robert Louis Stevenson

Build a little fence of trust
    Around today;
Fill the space with loving works,
    And therein stay;
Look not through the sheltering bars
    Upon tomorrow,
God will help thee bear what comes
    Of joy or sorrow.
                            Mary Frances Butts

When any fit of anxiety or gloominess or perversion of the mind lays hold upon you, make it a rule not to publish it by complaints but exert your whole care to hide it. By endeavoring to hide it, you will drive it away. *Samuel Johnson*

Take life too seriously, and what is it worth?
If the morning wake us to no new joys, if the evening bring us not the hopes of new pleasures, is it worth while to dress and undress? Does the sun shine on me today that I may reflect on yesterday? That I may endeavor to foresee and to control what can neither be foreseen nor controlled—the destiny of tomorrow?

Johann von Goethe

No longer forward nor behind
 I look in hope or fear;
But grateful, take the good I find,
 The best of now and here.

John Greenleaf Whittier

4. JOHN BURROUGHS

I RAVE NO MORE 'GAINST TIME OR
FATE,
FOR, LO! MY OWN SHALL COME TO
ME

THERE WAS a light burning in the dingy little back office
of the village doctor. But the doctor wasn't there. The
young man bent over the dusty books of anatomy was
John Burroughs, one of the local schoolteachers. Though
he was only twenty-five, he had been teaching for eight
years; but he had recently decided to make a change.
Teaching was not for him. He didn't like it particularly,
and he knew in his heart he would never get anywhere as
a teacher. He must try something else.

It was with this thought in mind that John Burroughs
was "reading medicine" every night in the office of the local
practitioner. Perhaps in time he could become a doctor.
His wife would like that; as a doctor he would earn enough
to support her properly. . . .

But tonight the seeds of doubt and discontent were stirring in his mind. Was this what he really wished to do,
after all? Would he be any happier in the practice of medicine than he was teaching school? Was he poring over
these volumes night after night because he honestly wished
to become a doctor—or was it just to please his wife, his
parents?

He turned back to the open book before him and tried
to concentrate. But his mind kept wandering. "I'm bored,"
he thought. There was no question about it; he was utterly
and completely bored with the study of anatomy. He might
as well face it: he was not meant to be a doctor.

And instantly, on the heels of that thought, came another—swift and sure. *I know what I want to be! I know what I want to do! I think I must always have known. I want to be a naturalist. I want to study the trees and flowers and birds. I want to know them intimately, as Henry Thoreau did. I want to write about the goodness and the beauty of nature.*

There was all at once a core of certainty within him that nothing would ever again disturb. His fears and worries about the future vanished. He was filled with a serene contentment he had never known before. He knew at last what he was meant to be, what he wanted most to do.

"There's no hurry," he thought. "I can wait. It may take a long time, but I can wait. I shall be patient and calm . . . *for someday my own shall come to me.*"

Words, phrases, began to slip through his mind. He pushed aside the book of anatomy and took some discarded envelopes from the doctor's desk. On the backs of them he wrote down these verses, a comfort to himself— an inspiration to countless people since:

> Serene, I fold my hands and wait,
> Nor care for wind, or tide, or sea;
> I rave no more 'gainst Time or Fate,
> For, lo! my own shall come to me.
>
> I stay my haste, I make delays,
> For what avails this eager pace?
> I stand amid the eternal ways,
> And what is mine shall know my face.
>
> Asleep, awake, by night or day,
> The friends I seek are seeking me,
> No wind can drive my bark astray,
> Nor change the tide of destiny.
>
> What matter if I stand alone?
> I wait with joy the coming years;
> My heart shall reap where it has sown,
> And garner up its fruits of tears.

The waters know their own and draw
The brook that springs in yonder height:
So flows the good with equal law
Unto the soul of pure delight. . . .

The stars come nightly to the sky;
The tidal wave unto the sea;
Nor time, nor space, nor deep, nor high,
Can keep my own away from me.

John Burroughs was an obscure, struggling unknown in
1862, the year he wrote "Waiting." A long and distinguished career lay ahead of him; but nothing he did in the
years that followed surpassed this simple poem in the
power and impact of its inspiration.

Written during what Burroughs himself later called "the
most gloomy period of my life," "Waiting" is full of hope
and faith. Though he was burdened by many problems and
responsibilities at the time, though the outlook for the
future was anything but promising, he did not "rave
against time or fate." He did not become bitter, impatient,
resentful. He looked within himself and found his own
tranquillity. In the midst of turmoil and uncertainty he was
able to write, *Serene, I fold my hands and wait.*

In these disquieting times, "Waiting" has a special meaning for all of us. Don't worry about the future, is its comforting message. Don't be uneasy or impatient. Be calm
and serene . . . for what is best for you will come to you
in time, as surely as the tides rise and the stars shine.

If, when you look into your own heart, you find nothing wrong there, what is there to worry about, what is
there to fear?   *Confucius*

You traverse the world in search of happiness, which
is within reach of every man: a contented mind con-
fers it on all.   *Horace*

How short a time it is that we are here! Why then not
set our hearts at rest, ceasing to trouble whether we

remain or go? What boots it to wear out the soul with anxious thoughts? I want not wealth. I want not power. Let me stroll through the bright hours as they pass, in my garden among my flowers; or I will mount the hill and sing my song, or weave my verse beside the limpid brook. Thus will I work out my allotted span, content with the appointments of Fate, my spirit free from care.   *Tao Chien*

> My crown is in my heart, not on my head;
> Not deck'd with diamonds and Indian stones,
> Nor to be seen: my crown is called content.
>   *William Shakespeare*

> Happy the man, of mortals happiest he,
> Whose quiet mind from vain desires is free;
> Whom neither hopes deceive, nor fears torment,
> But lives at peace, within himself content.
>   *George Granville*

Contentment is not satisfaction. It is the grateful, faithful, fruitful use of what we have, little or much. It is to take the cup of Providence, and call upon the name of the Lord. What the cup contains is its contents. To get all there is in the cup is the act and art of contentment. Not to drink because one has but half a cup, or because one does not like its flavor, or because someone else has silver to one's own glass, is to lose the contents; and that is the penalty, if not the meaning of discontent. No one is discontented who employs and enjoys to the utmost what he has. It is high philosophy to say, we can have just what we like if we like what we have; but this much at least can be done, and this is contentment: to have the most and best in life by making the most and best of what we have.   *Maltbie Babcock*

A contented mind is the greatest blessing a man can enjoy in this world.   *Joseph Addison*

5. HENRY DAVID THOREAU

OUR LIFE IS FRITTERED AWAY BY DETAIL. . . . SIMPLIFY, SIMPLIFY!

SOMEWHERE in the woods along the shores of Walden Pond an owl screeched, and far off another answered. The moon was bright, the water still as glass. Henry Thoreau sat in the moon-filled doorway of his shack, looking out across the stillness and brightness of the lake. "This is the spot I love above all others on earth," he thought.

Here, in the quiet and peace of Walden Woods, a man could live simply and deliberately—shearing off the unessentials and getting down to the basic truths of life. Here, in the solitude, living close to nature, a man could examine his ideas, think things through, and perhaps come to some reasonable conclusion about the meaning and purpose of life.

He turned back to the open notebook on his knees and read the last few words he had written: *"The mass of men lead lives of quiet desperation. . . ."*

A squirrel came stealthily from the woods and sat watching him, wide-eyed and friendly. All about him were the soft, gentle sounds of nature, stirring, whispering, ushering in the night.

I am convinced from experience that to maintain oneself on this earth is not a hardship but a pastime, if we will live simply and wisely. . . . Most of the luxuries, and many of the so-called comforts of life, are not only not indispensable, but positive hindrances to the elevation of mankind. . . .

A cloud obscured the moon and it was suddenly dark in the woods. He put the notebook aside and took a flute from his pocket—and laughed as the squirrel scurried in alarm up the nearest tree.

"Don't be afraid, my friend!" he called into the branches. "This isn't a gun. Come and listen to my music."

Henry David Thoreau loved nature. Every sight and sound in woods and fields had meaning for him. He knew the birds by their calls, the animals by their tracks on the ground. He could find a path through the woods at night as easily as any Indian. He was at home in Walden Woods, at home and completely happy.

In Concord young Thoreau had been stifled and wretched. A Harvard graduate, he had tried teaching for a time, and a number of other uncongenial occupations. But what he wanted most to do was study, think, and write; and for these important occupations he had no quiet in the cluttered lodginghouse where he lived, no seclusion, no opportunity at all.

Did people ever do what they really wished, he wondered—what they were by nature intended to do, and what they were best suited for? Everywhere about him he saw people squandering the precious substance of their lives in pursuit of material gains. Everywhere about him he saw people feverishly piling up property and possessions, enslaving themselves at the cost of things that really counted.

Surely there must be something more to life than the mere "laying up of treasure on earth." Being a man of original mind and great personal integrity, Thoreau abhorred the idea of being poured into a fixed mold, of being forced to do what others thought right and proper instead of what he himself wished. He did not intend to let his life slip by without ever having lived. He decided to do something about it.

The world's wisest men, he reflected, the great thinkers and philosophers of the past, had lived lives of Spartan simplicity. He would take his cue from them. He would live alone in Walden Woods away from the problems, involvements, and artifices of civilization; and in the peace and solitude of the woods, living close to nature, he would improve his soul's estate, learn to think and write clearly— and perhaps come closer to an understanding of life and to the basic but elusive truths that give it meaning.

So in March, 1845, Thoreau borrowed an ax and started building a little cabin for himself on the edge of Walden Pond, on a tract of land belonging to Ralph Waldo Emerson. On July fourth, the house completed, a vegetable garden planted—with little more than his flute, some notebooks and pens, and a copy of Homer—he went to the woods to launch his experiment in simple living.

"He chose to be rich by making his wants few," said his friend Emerson.

Thoreau was twenty-eight years old when he began his experiment. He was not a hermit by nature; he had many good friends in Concord. He merely wished to escape for a time from the complex pattern of civilization and live a free, independent life, serene and uncluttered. In Walden Woods his ideas slowly came to fruition, and he shaped the inspiring truths that now illumine his name. He remained for a little more than two years; then, having exhausted the advantages of solitude—and completely satisfied with the experiment—he returned to Concord and conventional life. From notes carefully written down day after day in the woods, he produced *Walden,* the book that made him famous, and from which these passages are selected:

I went to the woods because I wished to live deliberately, to front only the essential facts of life, and see if I could not learn what it had to teach, and not, when I came to die, to discover that I had not lived. I did not wish to live what was not a life, living is so dear; nor did I wish to practice resignation, unless it was quite necessary. I wanted to live deep and suck out all the marrow of life, to live so sturdily and Spartan-like as to put to rout all that was not life, to cut a broad swath and shave close, to drive life into a corner, and reduce it to its lowest terms, and, if it proved to be mean, why then to get the whole and genuine meanness of it, and publish its meanness to the world; or if it were sublime, to know it by experience, and be able to give a true account of it in my next excursion. . . .

Our life is frittered away by detail. An honest man has hardly need to count more than his ten fingers, or in extreme cases he may add his ten toes, and lump the rest. Simplicity, simplicity, simplicity! I say, let your affairs be as two or three, and not a hundred or a thousand; instead of a million count half a dozen, and keep your accounts on your thumb nail. In the midst of this chopping sea of civilized life, such are the clouds and storms and quicksands and thousand-and-one items to be allowed for, that a man has to live, if he would not founder and go to the bottom and not make his port at all, by dead reckoning, and he must be a great calculator indeed who succeeds. Simplify, simplify. . . .

Why should we live with such hurry and waste of life? . . . When we are unhurried and wise, we perceive that only great and worthy things have any permanent and absolute existence, that petty fears and petty pleasures are but the shadow of the reality.

A man is rich in proportion to the number of things he can do without. Beware of all enterprises that re-quire new clothes.

Public opinion is a weak tyrant compared with our own private opinion. What a man thinks of himself, that it is which determines, or rather indicates, his fate.

Only that day dawns to which we are awake.

Every man is the builder of a temple, called his body. . . . We are all sculptors and painters, and our material is our own flesh and blood and bones. Any nobleness begins at once to refine a man's features, any meanness or sensuality to imbrute them.

Be not simply good; be good for something.

In the long run, men hit only what they aim at. Therefore . . . they had better aim at something high.

I know of no more encouraging fact than the unquestionable ability of man to elevate his life by conscious endeavor.

I learned this, at least, by my experiment: that if one advances confidently in the direction of his dreams, and endeavors to live the life which he had imagined, he will meet with a success unexpected in common hours.

The record of an experiment in serene living, *Walden* is as timely now as it was when Thoreau wrote it a hundred years ago. It has, in fact, steadily increased in popularity, and is today more widely read than ever—perhaps because the patterns of life have become more complex and confusing.

Simplify your life, Thoreau urged his readers. *Don't waste the years struggling for things that are unimportant. Don't burden yourself with possessions. Keep your needs and wants simple, and enjoy what you have. Simplify! Don't fritter away your life on nonessentials. Don't enslave yourself for luxuries you can do without. Don't destroy your peace of mind by looking back, worrying about the past. Live in the present, enjoy the present. Simplify!*

"Henry Thoreau's place in the common heart of humanity grows firmer and more secure as the seasons pass," wrote Elbert Hubbard, fifty years after *Walden* was written.

"Thoreau learned how to live a life, which is a thing rarely heard of," says Brooks Atkinson in his introduction to a recent edition of *Walden.*

In the peace and quiet of Walden Woods, Henry David Thoreau found what was for him, and has been for countless people since, a wise and tranquil approach to life. Out of his experiment in serene living has come a book of enduring beauty and inspiration, one of America's most beloved classics—*Walden,* named for the woods and the pond Thoreau so loved.

Those who want much are always much in need.

Horace

Riches are not from abundance of worldly goods,
but from a contented mind.   *Mohammed*

The World is too much with us; late and soon,
Getting and spending, we lay waste our powers;
Little we see in Nature that is ours;
We have given our hearts away, a sordid boon!

William Wordsworth

The little cares that fretted me,
    I lost them yesterday
Among the fields above the sea,
    Among the winds at play;
Among the lowing of the herds,
    The rustling of the trees,
Among the singing of the birds,
    The humming of the bees.

The foolish fears of what may pass,
    I cast them all away
Among the clover-scented grass,
    Among the new-mown hay;
Among the hushing of the corn
    Where drowsy poppies nod,
Where ill thoughts die and good are born,
    Out in the fields with God.

Author unknown

Half the confusion in the world comes from not
knowing how little we need. . . . I live more simply
now, and with more peace.

Admiral Richard E. Byrd

What is this life if, full of care,
We have no time to stand and stare?—

No time to stand beneath the boughs
And stare as long as sheep or cows:

No time to see, when woods we pass,
Where squirrels hide their nuts in grass:

No time to see, in broad daylight,
Streams full of stars, like skies at night:

A poor life this if, full of care,
We have no time to stand and stare.
                              William Henry Davies

Enjoy your life without comparing it with that of
others.   *Marquis de Condorcet*

A man may have a home, possessions, a charming
family, and yet find all these things ashy to his taste
because he has been outstripped in the marathon race
by some other runners to the golden tape line. It is
not that he does not possess enough for his wants but
that others possess more. It is the *more* that haunts
him, makes him deprecate himself, and minimize his
real achievements. This is the cancer eating away at
his serenity.
The time has come when a man must say to himself: "I am no longer going to be interested in how
much power or wealth another man possesses so long
as I can attain enough for the dignity and security of
my family and myself. I am going to break through
this vicious circle which always asks the question of
life in a comparative degree: 'Who is bigger?' 'Who
is richer?' 'Who has more?' I am going to set my goals
for myself rather than borrow them from others. I
will strive to achieve a mature attitude toward success
which is ambition for growth and accomplishment,
real accomplishment rather than spurious, decorative,
and vanity-filled acquisition. I refuse any longer to destroy my peace of mind by striving after wind, and I

will judge myself in the scale of goodness and culture as well as in the balance of silver and gold."

Such a man is on the road to avoiding the neurotic materialism of our age. He is like the poet who does not tear himself to pieces because his sonnet is not equal to that of Shakespeare. He is like the musician who does not always despise his little fugue because it lacks the magic of Bach. He is like the poet or musician who learns to accept himself and to be happy with his own growth from year to year rather than paralyze his gifted pen or his talented ear by contrast with the giants and the immortals.

Psychology will help religion to diminish the worship of the golden calf among men as it aids men to become free of their overexcessive demands upon themselves. When, instead of the pathological race for more houses and jewels, cars and refrigerators, bonds and stocks . . . when, instead of seeking these fictitious goals, men learn a certain modesty about things and become genuinely contented with their real contributions and achievements—only then is serenity achieved. Only when we harness our own creative energies to *goals which are of our own adult choice,* not imposed upon us by the compulsions of unresolved childhood competition, can we call ourselves mature and happy. *Joshua Loth Liebman*

PART EIGHT

LOVE

&

Family Life

"To be happy at home is the ultimate result of all ambition." SAMUEL JOHNSON

OF ALL HUMAN RELATIONSHIPS, none are more vital and enduring than those of home and family. Love and marriage, the joys of parenthood and family ties, are the basis of all that is best in life—the supreme happiness.

"The home is the empire!" said Cicero, two thousand years ago. "There is no peace more delightful than one's own fireplace."

"He is happiest who finds peace in his own home," wrote Goethe, centuries later.

A *happy* home ... A *peaceful* home ...

"The greatest of all arts is the art of living together!" said William Lyon Phelps in his famous essay on "Marriage."

In the intimate relationships of life, as in all human relationships, the Golden Rule is the basic principle. "If you wish to be loved, be lovable," says Benjamin Franklin. The only way you can ever hope to be loved, says Dale Carnegie, is to stop asking for it and start giving it; you get love only when you give it to others.

Here are some of the world's most inspiring quotations on love and marriage, on family ties and home.

1. ELIZABETH BARRETT BROWNING

HOW DO I LOVE THEE? LET ME COUNT
THE WAYS. . . .

ELIZABETH BARRETT BROWNING was supremely, unbelievably happy.

In the fog and chill of London she had been an invalid, almost a recluse. Here in the sunny warmth of Italy—here with her beloved husband, her new life, her new interests —she felt better than she had in years.

"I feel well; I feel almost strong!" she assured her anxious husband over and over again, that beautiful, unforgettable autumn in Italy.

Robert Browning had persuaded Elizabeth Barrett to leave her invalid's couch and elope with him, had brought her to this gentle climate for her health. And climate and love had worked their magic charm. She was still frail and delicate, but she was not an invalid now! She was able to move about, to see the world, to be a true wife and companion to the man she so admired, she so adored.

"How do I love thee? Let me count the ways. I love thee to the depth and breadth and height my soul can reach. . . ."

She thought of these lines from a sonnet she had written when Robert Browning came courting her in Wimpole Street, in London. She was ill then, nervous and distraught —completely dominated by a tyrannical father who had forbidden all his children to marry. But with unfailing devotion, Robert Browning had continued to visit her, to keep her room filled with flowers, to tell her of his love and beg her to marry him.

During this period of emotional strain and indecision, torn between love for Robert Browning and fear of her father's displeasure, Elizabeth Barrett wrote a sequence of love sonnets. She wrote them in secret, intending them for no eyes but her own.

"But I'll show them to him now," she thought, "I'll show them to him now, and they will tell him how much I love him!"

And so, one sunny day in Italy, one enchanted autumn afternoon, Robert Browning read his wife's secret love sonnets for the first time. He was profoundly moved by their beauty and power, recognizing the unmistakable quality of their genius. They were, he declared, "the finest sonnets since Shakespeare!"

She was pleased as a child by his praise—though she well knew his love warped his judgment, that Wordsworth's incomparable sonnets far surpassed any she had written or was ever likely to write. Still, she liked to hear his praise, liked to hear him say she was the finest woman poet England had produced.

"Which do you like best?" she asked him shyly, knowing these sonnets revealed her innermost thoughts and feelings.

"I like them all," he told her. "But there's one . . . 'How Do I Love Thee?' Let me read that one again."

She was delighted. "That's *my* favorite too, Robert!"

How do I love thee? Let me count the ways.
I love thee to the depth and breadth and height
My soul can reach, when feeling out of sight
For the ends of Being and ideal Grace.
I love thee to the level of every day's
Most quiet need, by sun and candle-light.
I love thee freely, as men strive for Right;
I love thee purely, as they turn from Praise.
I love thee with the passion put to use
In my old griefs, and with my childhood's faith.
I love thee with a love I seemed to lose
With my lost saints,—I love thee with the breath,
Smiles, tears, of all my life!—and, if God choose,
I shall but love thee better after death.

Robert Browning was so impressed with his wife's love

sonnets that he urged her to make them public, to give them to the world.

"We can't do that, Robert!" she said. "They were not intended for publication. They were written for you—for you alone."

"But they are too important to keep hidden," he insisted. "You *must* publish them."

At last she agreed, though she would have preferred to keep them secret. The poems were published under the title of *Sonnets from the Portuguese* to conceal their personal nature.* As Robert Browning expected, they enormously increased her fame and stature as a poet. Critics said the poems were "beautiful beyond praise"—that they were "the most inspiring love sonnets in English literature" —that they would "endure as long as love endured."

Written in secret and with no thought of publication, Elizabeth Barrett Browning's *Sonnets from the Portuguese* is today considered by many to be her finest poetry, and her greatest claim to immortality. With exquisite tenderness and feeling, these poems reveal her doubts and fears, her unwillingness to burden the man she loves with an ailing wife. But nowhere in the entire sequence, not in a single line or phrase, is there any doubt of her love for him, her great desire to be with him.

Sonnets from the Portuguese has some of the most famous of Elizabeth Barrett Browning's poems; and "How Do I Love Thee?" is perhaps the best-loved of the series. It was her own favorite, and his, and has been an inspiration to countless lovers since.

Love is strong as death. . . . Many waters canno͡ quench love, neither can the floods drown it.
                                        Song of Solomon 8:6, 7

When the one man loves the one woman and the one woman loves the one man, the very angels leave

---

* Elizabeth Barrett was a pronounced brunette, and her husband sometimes called her "my little Portuguese." This nickname suggested the title for her love sonnets when she put them together in book form.

heaven and come and sit in that house and sing for joy. *Brahma*

'Tis better to have loved and lost,
Than never to have loved at all.
Alfred Tennyson

Talk not of wasted affection, affection never was
    wasted,
If it enrich not the heart of another, its waters,
    returning
Back to their springs, like the rain, shall fill them full
    of refreshment;
That which the fountain sends forth returns again to
    the fountain.
Henry Wadsworth Longfellow

Two persons who love each other are in a place more holy than the interior of a church.
William Lyon Phelps

The most wonderful of all things in life, I believe, is the discovery of another human being with whom one's relationship has a glowing depth, beauty, and joy as the years increase. This inner progressiveness of love between two human beings is a most marvelous thing, it cannot be found by looking for it or by passionately wishing for it. It is a sort of Divine accident.
Sir Hugh Walpole

2. WILL DURANT

GLADLY I SURRENDER MYSELF TO
LOVE AND PARENTAGE

WILL DURANT had been asked to give his definition of that elusive, priceless quality of heart, soul, and mind called "happiness." He was a famous author and educator. He had studied the lives and ideas of the world's greatest philosophers. Surely he must have some interesting and helpful ideas on the subject.

What is happiness?

Will Durant looked back across the years. How could he best answer that provocative question? He himself had searched for happiness in so many ways since his earliest years. He had sought it in pleasure, in work, in travel, in friends. He had sought it in wealth, in knowledge, in honors and achievement. He had followed it along many winding trails, sometimes touching it briefly . . . only to lose it again. . . .

What is happiness?

He dipped deeply into the well of his lifetime's recollections. He looked back to his carefree boyhood, to the joys and mistakes of his early youth, to the pleasures of maturity. He looked back to the beginnings of his career, the early struggles and uncertainty, the disappointments, the bitterness—and the first sweet tastes of recognition and success.

His life had been a tangled stretch of dreams and hopes and disillusions, the good and bad together. But at last he had found what he had been seeking. At last he had come upon the quiet lane that led safely into the years ahead.

What is happiness?

There could be only one answer to that question! There

could be only one honest and sincere answer. He began to write:

Many years have I sought happiness. I found it first, perhaps, in the warmth of my mother's breast, and in the fond caress of her hands, and in the tenderness that shone in her eyes. I found it again in play; for even in the pain of defeat I knew the natural ecstasy of boyhood's games. I found it in first love; it came to me when a simple girl laid her hand upon my arm, and her braided hair, sweet with the fragrance of health, came so close to my lips that I kissed it without her knowing. And then she went from me, and happiness strayed away.

For I sought it next in remaking the lives of other men. I went forth to reform the world. I denounced the ways of mankind, and bemoaned the backwardness of time, and talked only of glories that were past, or were to come. I wanted many laws to make life easier for me, and for youth. But the world would not listen, and I grew bitter. I gathered anecdotes of human stupidity, and heralded the absurdities and injustices of men. One day, an enemy said, "You have in yourself all the faults which you scorn in others; you, too, are capable of selfishness and greed; and the world is what it is because men are what you are."

I considered it in solitude, and found that it was true. Then it came to me that reform should begin at home; and since that day I have not had time to remake the world.

Many years I lost happiness. I sought it in knowledge, and found disillusionment. I sought it in writing, and found a weariness of the flesh. I sought it in travel, and my feet tired on the way. I sought it in wealth, and I found discord and worriment.

And then one day, at a little station out on a wooded cliff near the sea, I saw a woman waiting in a tiny car, with a child asleep in her arms. A man alighted from a train, walked to her quickly, embraced her, and kissed the child gently, careful lest he should awaken it. They drove off together to some modest home among the fields; and it seemed to me that happiness was with them.

Today I have neglected my writing. The voice of a little girl calling to me, "Come out and play," drew me from my papers and my books. Was it not the final purpose of my toil that I should be free to frolic with her, and spend unharassed hours with the one who had given her to me? And so we walked and ran and laughed together, and fell in the tall grass, and hid among the trees; and I was young again.

Now it is evening; while I write, I hear the child's breathing as she sleeps in her cozy bed. And I know that I have found what I sought. I perceived that if I will do as well as I can the tasks for which life has made me, I shall find fulfillment, and a quiet lane of happiness for many years. Gladly I surrender myself to nature's imperative of love and parentage, trusting to her ancient wisdom, and knowing that, as Dante learned when he entered Paradise, *"La sua volontate è nostra pace*—in her will and service is our peace."

Dr. Will Durant has had a long and distinguished career as journalist, writer, and educator. He is perhaps best known for *The Story of Philosophy,* a book that was on the best-seller lists for months and which made the lives and opinions of the world's greatest thinkers familiar to many who had never even heard of them before.

It was not as a philosopher, however, that Dr. Will Durant wrote the quotation above, but as a man who looked back across the years and saw clearly what had the most significant and enduring value for him. It was not as a journalist or educator that he wrote, but as a husband and father—a man who had found his greatest happiness in the simple, familiar joys of family life.

There can be no real or lasting happiness without love. There can be no fulfillment of life's ultimate purpose without a successful marriage and a good family life.

That was the gist of Will Durant's message. That was his stimulating answer to the question, "What is happiness?" It has been widely published and discussed—and it has inspired many to seek their happiness where they are most likely to find it: in their own homes, in the rich fulfillment of marriage and the family relationship.

What therefore God hath joined together, let not man put asunder.
Mark 10:9

Perhaps the greatest blessing in marriage is that it lasts so long. The years, like the varying interests of each year, combine to buttress and enrich each other. Out of many shared years, one life. In a series of temporary relationships, one misses the ripening, gathering, harvesting joys, the deep, hard-won truths of marriage.
Richard C. Cabot

There's a bliss beyond all that the minstrel has told,
When two, that are link'd in one heavenly tie,
With heart never changing, and brow never cold,
Love on thro' all ills, and love on till they die.
One hour of a passion so sacred is worth
Whole ages of heartless and wandering bliss;
And oh! if there be an Elysium on earth,
It is this—it is this!

Thomas Moore

It was a wise man who said that it is important not only to pick the right mate but to *be* the right mate. And contrary to many popular love stories, it is not during the first year of bliss that most dangers crop up. Marriages do not, like dropped chinaware, smash as a result of that first quarrel which the newly married hope is unthinkable. Marriage is a rooted thing, a growing and flowering thing that must be tended faithfully.

Lacking that mutual effort, we are apt to find some day that our marriage, so hopefully planted, has been withering imperceptibly. Gradually we realize that for some time the petals have lost their luster, that the perfume is gone. Daily watering with the little gra-

cious affectionate acts we all welcome, with mutual
concern for the other's contentment, with self-watch-
fulness here and self-forgetfulness there, brings forth
ever new blossoms.   *Donald Culross Peattie*

The highest happiness on earth is in marriage. Every
man who is happily married is a successful man even
if he has failed in everything else.

William Lyon Phelps

3. RICHARD E. BYRD

AT THE END ONLY TWO THINGS REALLY MATTER TO A MAN . . . THE AFFECTION AND UNDERSTANDING OF HIS FAMILY

A BLIZZARD raged over the icy shelf of the Ross Barrier. The temperature plunged to seventy below; and the wind cut angry ridges into the ice. The night was filled with the fury of the Antarctic storm.

But inside the shack, buried beneath the ice for protection, it was strangely quiet. The sounds of the storm came only faintly, as though from a distance. But the dampness seeped in, and the bitter cold. And there was something else . . . oppressive, alarming.

The man on the cot knew what it was. Carbon-monoxide fumes were escaping from the stove. He had already been overcome by them but had miraculously revived, and discovering what was wrong, had tried to correct it. But the stove was still faulty; the fumes were still slowly escaping. Perhaps by the time the fire went out he would be strong enough to have another try at it—if he didn't freeze first in the seventy-below temperature. He was too sick to eat, or even to get up and light the lamp. He felt himself getting drowsy, and knew that if he fell asleep he might never waken again.

Facing death in this lonely outpost, Admiral Byrd's thoughts turned to those at home. He was filled with anxiety over the consequences to his family if he failed to return. He thought of the last words Captain Scott had written twenty-two years ago on this very Barrier, just before he died: "For God's sake look after our people!" And he suddenly realized how wrong his own sense of values had been, how in the end all that really matters to a man is his family.

"The family is an everlasting anchorage," he thought. "The family is a quiet harbor. . . ."

He must put those thoughts down before they escaped him, while his mind was still clear. *Harmony within oneself and the family circle:* that was an important part of the philosophy he had been working out for himself, alone here in the Antarctic. Perhaps if he started writing it would be easier to stay awake. He reached for the diary that was always just beside his cot.

Richard E. Byrd did not die, though he came very close to it. He managed to repair the faulty stove and to survive the noxious poisoning, though he was sick for weeks afterward. During those weeks the thoughts that had filled his mind as he lay on his cot, expecting to die, kept returning. He knew now that his ideas of success and happiness had changed. He knew now that the simple unpretentious things of life could be the most important. From the notes made in his diary during this period, he later wrote his famous book *Alone,* from which these four inspiring paragraphs,* the gist of his philosophy, are quoted:

"The universe is an almost untouched reservoir of significance and value," and man need not be discouraged because he cannot fathom it. His view of life is no more than a flash in time. The details and distractions are infinite. It is only natural, therefore, that we should never see the picture whole. But the universal goal—the attainment of harmony—is apparent. The very act of perceiving this goal and striving constantly toward it does much in itself to bring us closer and, therefore, becomes an end in itself. . . .

I realized how wrong my sense of values had been, and how I had failed to see that the simple, homely, unpretentious things of life are the most important. . . .

When a man achieves a fair measure of harmony

---

* In personal communication with the author, Admiral Byrd himself selected these paragraphs from *Alone* as the ones he felt most likely to be helpful to those seeking a philosophy of life.

within himself and his family circle, he achieves peace; and a nation made up of such individuals and groups is a happy nation. As the harmony of a star in its course is expressed by rhythm and grace, so the harmony of a man's life-course is expressed by happiness. . . .

At the end only two things really matter to a man, regardless of who he is; and they are the affection and understanding of his family. Anything and everything else he creates are insubstantial; they are ships given over to the mercy of the winds and tides of prejudice. But the family is an everlasting anchorage, a quiet harbor where a man's ships can be left to swing in the moorings of pride and loyalty.

For five long months Admiral Byrd lived alone on the Ross Barrier, literally buried in the shack beneath the ice-cap. He endured many hardships, faced grave dangers, very nearly lost his life. But he returned from that frozen outpost with far more than the valuable scientific data he had gone there to obtain. He returned with a deep and abiding faith;* and with a philosophy of life by which he has since lived, and which has proved an inspiration to many others.

Far from the confusions and complexities of modern life, in solitude and unhurried reflection, Admiral Byrd learned what philosophers of every age have taught—what Thoreau proved at Walden, and Gandhi demonstrated all his life—that "a man can live profoundly without masses of things." He learned that much of the bitterness and unhappiness in life comes from not knowing how little we need . . . and how very much we have when there are love and understanding within the family circle.

"I live more simply now, and with more peace," he wrote, when he was back in civilization.

The philosophy he brought back from the Antarctic has given many others a better sense of values and has helped them, too, live more simply and with more peace.

---

* See pages 38–40.

History teaches us that there is no substitute for the family if we are to have a society that stands for human beings at their best.　　　*Ray Lyman Wilbur*

Lord, behold our family here assembled. We thank Thee for this place in which we dwell; for the love that unites us; for the peace accorded us this day; for the hope with which we expect the morrow; for the health, the work, the food, and the bright skies that make our lives delightful; for our friends in all parts of the earth, and our friendly helpers in this foreign isle. . . .

Give us courage, gaiety, and the quiet mind. Spare to us our friends, soften to us our enemies. Bless us, if it may be, in all our innocent endeavors. If it may not, give us the strength to encounter that which is to come, that we be brave in peril, constant in tribulation, temperate in wrath, and in all changes of fortune and down to the gates of death, loyal and loving one to another. *Amen.*　　　*Robert Louis Stevenson*

The family is the nucleus of civilization.　*Will Durant*

The domestic affections are the principal source of human happiness and well-being. The mutual loves of husband and wife, of parents and children, of brothers and sisters, are not only the chief sources of happiness, but the chief springs of action, and the chief safeguards from evil.　　　　　*Charles W. Eliot*

The ideal which the wife and mother makes for herself, the manner in which she understands duty and life, contain the fate of the community. Her faith becomes the star of the conjugal ship, and her love the animating principle that fashions the future of all belonging to her. Woman is the salvation or destruction of the family. She carries its destinies in the folds of her mantle.　　　　　*Henri F. Amiel*

I regard marriage as the holiest institution among men. Without the fireside there is no human advancement; without the family relation there is no life worth living. . . .   *Robert Ingersoll*

4. JOHN HOWARD PAYNE

'MID PLEASURES AND PALACES THOUGH
    WE MAY ROAM,
BE IT EVER SO HUMBLE, THERE'S NO
    PLACE LIKE HOME

IT's LOVELY in Long Island in October. The trees are a brilliant red and gold; and in East Hampton, where John Howard Payne spent much of his boyhood, there was a crisp tang of the sea in the air.

But this was *Paris,* not Long Island. This was Paris, on a dull, gray day in October, in the year 1822. John Payne was far from family and friends, far from the rambler-covered cottage in East Hampton, the old homestead he remembered so well from his childhood . . . and had always loved. He had been living abroad now for nine years. As an actor and playwright he had been busy, successful, and in some ways happier than he had been at home. But he had always been lonely. In spite of his success, his travels, his fine new friends, he had been lonely. ·

In his room on the upper floor of a lodginghouse near the Palais Royal, Payne stood at the window and looked down at the happy, hurrying crowds in the streets below. Even on a gloomy day like this, Paris was gay. Everyone seemed to have somewhere to go, something to do. People laughed, and waved, and greeted each other, and hurried on . . . to their homes, their families, their loved ones. . . . Only *he* had nowhere to go but this lonely room! The depressing influence of the weather added to his mood, and he was suddenly homesick—completely, unutterably homesick.

He turned impatiently from the window. He had work to do! He had no time to stand mooning about the past, dreaming about East Hampton, wondering what the cottage looked like now, whether the pine woods were still as fragrant, the beach as white and dazzling in the sun. But the mood and the memories stayed with him, sat at his elbow as he wrote, filled his heart and mind so completely he could think of nothing else. *Home!* What strange, compelling magic that simple word possessed! How it brought memories rushing back, joyous and comforting, memories of family and fireside, of pleasures long since past. . . .

Home, sweet home! A man may travel the world over, may live in palaces, make new friends, find new pleasures. But there's no place like home!

He began writing the words of a new song. And into it he poured all his own aching loneliness, all his longing for the sights and scenes of his boyhood. Into it he poured all the lovely, lingering memories of a cottage in East Hampton where birds sang madly in the trees, and there was a crisp tang of the sea in the air:

> 'Mid pleasures and palaces though we may roam,
> Be it ever so humble, there's no place like home;
> A charm from the sky seems to hallow us there,
> Which, seek through the world, is ne'er met with
>   elsewhere.
>   Home, home, sweet, sweet home!
> There's no place like home, there's no place like
>   home!
>
> An exile from home, splendor dazzles in vain;
> Oh, give me my lowly thatched cottage again!
> The birds singing gaily, that came at my call—
> Give me them—and the peace of mind, dearer
>   than all!
>   Home, home, sweet, sweet home!
> There's no place like home, there's no place like
>   home!
>
> I gaze on the moon as I tread the drear wild,
> And feel that my mother now thinks of her child,
> As she looks on that moon from our own cottage
>   door

Thro' the woodbine, whose fragrance shall cheer
    me no more.
    Home, home, sweet, sweet home!
There's no place like home, there's no place like
    home!

How sweet 'tis to sit 'neath a fond father's smile,
And the cares of a mother to soothe and beguile!
Let others delight 'mid new pleasures to roam,
But give me, oh, give me, the pleasures of home,
    Home, home, sweet, sweet home!
There's no place like home, there's no place like
    home!

To thee I'll return, overburdened with care;
The heart's dearest solace will smile on me there;
No more from that cottage again will I roam;
Be it ever so humble, there's no place like home.
    Home, home, sweet, sweet home!
There's no place like home, there's no place like
    home!

In the early part of 1823, John Payne sold three plays
to the manager of the Covent Garden Theatre in London.
One of these was *Clari, or, the Maid of Milan;* and in the
first scene of this play, Payne had introduced the song he
wrote that lonely afternoon in Paris—the song he called
"Home, Sweet Home."

Clari opened in Covent Garden Theatre on May 8,
1823. The title role was played by Maria Tree, sister of
the famous Ellen Tree. As she stepped to the center of the
stage and began to sing, the audience—restless and even
unruly up to that point—was suddenly silent. The singer's
own voice choked up as she sang, her eyes filled with
tears, and by the time she reached the end of the song
there wasn't a dry eye in the audience. The tender words,
the plaintive melody, had tremendous appeal . . . and the
song was an instant, an overwhelming success.

Clari had a long run; and the words and music of its
"hit" song, "Home, Sweet Home," became famous. More

than a hundred thousand copies were sold in London alone during the first few weeks of the play. Millions of copies were sold before *Clari* came to the end of its extraordinary run. By then "Home, Sweet Home" had become one of the most famous songs in the world, and John Howard Payne returned to New York in 1832 as a celebrity.

Written in Paris, to be sung on a London stage, to a haunting Italian tune,* "Home, Sweet Home" was nevertheless essentially American; and America took the song to its heart. It was heard everywhere. Singers lavished their art on it. Ships' bands played it as they left port. Mothers crooned it to their babies. Choirs sang it in churches and schools. Even prisoners sang it in their cells, pouring out their souls in the song that sanctified the family fireside and home, promising themselves to live worthier lives. It was more than a song; it was a comfort, an inspiration, a compelling force for good.

On the night of December 17, 1850, Jenny Lind, "the Swedish Nightingale," sang in Washington for one of the most distinguished audiences ever seen in a concert hall in the United States. Among the notables were President Fillmore, Daniel Webster, Henry Clay, General Scott. At the end of the concert, Daniel Webster rose and bowed to the singer in public tribute to her great voice. She smiled and nodded, then turned to face a gentle, white-haired man seated obscurely in the audience. It was John Howard Payne, now nearly sixty years old. Without taking her eyes from his face, Jenny Lind sang "Home, Sweet Home"— just as Maria Tree had sung it on the stage of Covent Garden Theatre twenty-seven years before. The vast audience was electrified; all eyes were turned toward Payne, who was completely overcome by the tribute. As Jenny

---

* The music for "Home, Sweet Home" was composed by Sir Henry Rowley Bishop. The story is that Payne once heard an Italian peasant girl singing a tune he particularly liked. He asked her the name of it, but she didn't know; so he asked her to sing it again, and he carefully jotted down the notes. Later he gave them to Sir Henry Bishop, and the composer is said to have used them as the basis of the melody for Payne's verses.

Lind sang his famous song, he wept openly. And there were many in that great audience who wept with him—profoundly moved, as people always were, by the emotional impact of his song.

Payne died eighteen months later, his enduring fame assured. Though he had written much in his lifetime, a single song won him immortality—a song he wrote one gloomy afternoon in Paris when he was lonely and homesick. Few songs have had the universal appeal and compelling influence of "Home, Sweet Home." It has been translated into every language, sung in almost every land, known and loved by millions of people for more than a century. Its influence will continue as long as people love their homes and cherish their family ties.

Home is where the heart is.   *Pliny*

Happiness grows at our own firesides, and is not to be picked in strangers' gardens.   *Douglas Jerrold.*

> Peace and rest at length have come,
>   All the day's long toil is past,
> And each heart is whispering, "Home,
>   Home at last."
>
>   *Thomas Hood*

He is happiest, be he king or peasant, who finds his peace in his home.   *Johann von Goethe*

How dear to this heart are the scenes of my childhood,
When fond recollection presents them to view:—
The orchard, the meadow, the deep-tangled wildwood,
And every lov'd spot which my infancy knew.
                    Samuel Woodworth

> God gives all men all earth to love,
>   But since man's heart is small,
> Ordains for each one spot should prove
>   Beloved over all.
>
>   *Rudyard Kipling*

The happiest holidays are those people "go home" for. Going home may mean youngsters returning from school or job, sometimes bringing their own younger youngsters with them. It may mean going to "Grandma-and-Grandpa's." Home is where Father and Mother are, or where one of them was brought up. Home is a dreamland in which every effort is made to spoil children. Home is the fond memory held by parents of the days when they themselves were very young. Home is where the year's troubles and anxieties are forgotten. Home is where no unkind word is spoken, and where the good smells from the kitchen tell of deep affection. Home binds together the relatives by blood and the relatives by marriage and turns them into that most beautiful of human institutions —the family.

If trains are late or crowded, if planes can't get off, if Mother is worn out with packing and Father weary after his pre-holiday hours in the office, if many little things go wrong, who cares? When one is going home a bit of hardship on the way makes the arrival a greater joy. The Tree is lighted and waiting. The old folks are at the door, their faces beaming with pure welcome. The day's mirth does not hide its tenderness. The laughter comes closer than that of other days to the laughter of the angels; the joke is on those who maintain that it does not come natural to human beings to love one another.

Many who are elderly today remember such holidays from long ago, when jingling sleigh-bells were more familiar than automobile horns. Many who are now children will remember this day long years from now. The mechanisms of living change, the world changes, but the sweetness of family reunions, the bliss of "going home"—this abides.

The New York Times, December 25, 1948

PART NINE

CONTENTMENT

in

Later Years

"It is magnificent to grow old, if one keeps young."   HARRY EMERSON FOSDICK

THERE IS NO REASON to dread the passage of time. Age is, or should be, the rich and happy fulfillment of life—the shining consummation of all that has gone before.

"Don't be ashamed of your gray hair!" wrote William Lyon Phelps, when he himself was sixty-two. "Wear it proudly, like a flag. . . . Grow old eagerly, triumphantly!"

With age come wisdom and understanding. With age come many joys and compensations. "Each part of life has its own abundant harvest, to be garnered in season," said Cicero. "Old age is rich in blessings."

All through history we find convincing proof that mental powers increase with age, that artistic and intellectual powers are often intensified in later years. Michelangelo was still producing masterpieces at eighty-nine. Goethe completed the second part of *Faust* when he was eighty-two. Wagner finished *Parsifal* at sixty-nine, and Voltaire wrote *Candide* at sixty-five. Handel was still composing beautiful music, Longfellow was still writing immortal poetry, after seventy. Some of the greatest tasks ever undertaken by men were begun and carried through in what are called life's declining years. In *Life Begins at Forty,* Walter Pitkin points out that nine-tenths of the world's best work has been done by older people, well past their prime.

"To know how to grow old is a masterwork of wisdom, and one of the most difficult chapters in the great art of living," wrote Henri F. Amiel in his famous *Journal.*

This is truer today than it has ever been, with the life span lengthened and the opportunities for older people greater than ever before in history.

Following are some of the world's most famous quotations on old age, on contentment and security in later years, on keeping oneself young in heart and mind. Here are inspiring messages for those approaching what Robert Browning calls "the last of life, for which the first was made."

1. MARCUS TULLIUS CICERO

OLD AGE IS THE CONSUMMATION OF
LIFE, JUST AS OF A PLAY

Marcus Tullius Cicero was one of the greatest orators
and statesmen of Rome, in that seething period of moral
laxity and political corruption that was climaxed by the
murder of Julius Caesar.

Cicero was born in 106 B.C. and began his public career
when he was still little more than a youth. At twenty-five
he was already well known as an orator. He soon became
a public prosecutor, then consul, rising rapidly from one
public office to another until he was the outstanding leader
of the republican party in the senate.

At the height of his career, Cicero wielded great influence and power, and his ringing voice was heard often in
the senate. However, he made many enemies; and in 44
B.C., the year of Caesar's assassination (to which he was
not a party), he was forced out of public life by his political
opponents.

But even in retirement, Cicero's eloquent voice was not
stilled. He turned to literature and philosophy in this final
phase of his career, writing down the ideas and observations of a lifetime's fruitful experience. It was during this
period that he produced some of his most enduring works,
among them *de Senectute*—an essay in praise of old age
and its many blessings. It was written as a dialogue, a
favorite form of literary expression in those days. The
dialogue supposedly took place in 150 B.C. with Cato, the
aging censor, as one of the interlocutors. The following
selections, adapted from *de Senectute*, express—through
Cato—Cicero's own stimulating philosophy of old age.*

* The essay is known also as *Cato Major*, after Cato—the principal character in the dialogue.

I am in my eighty-fourth year. . . . As you see, old age has not quite enfeebled me or broken me down; the senate-house does not miss my strength, nor the rostra, nor my friends, nor my clients, nor my guests. For I have never agreed to that old and much-praised proverb which advises you to become an old man early if you wish to be an old man long. I for my part would rather be an old man for a shorter length of time than be an old man before I was one.

Life's race-course is fixed; Nature has only a single path and that path is run but once, and to each stage of existence has been allotted its own appropriate quality; so that the weakness of childhood, the impetuosity of youth, the seriousness of middle life, the maturity of old age—each bears some of Nature's fruit, which must be garnered in its own season. Each has something which ought to be enjoyed in its own time. . . .

I suppose that you hear, Scipio, what your grandfather's host, Masinissa, is doing at this day, at the age of ninety. When he has commenced a journey on foot, he never mounts at all; when on horseback, he never dismounts; by no rain, by no cold, is he prevailed upon to have his head covered. There is in him the greatest hardiness of frame; and therefore he performs all his duties and functions of a king. Exercise, therefore, and temperance, even in old age, can preserve some remnant of our pristine vigor. . . .

We must make a stand against old age, and its faults must be atoned for by activity. We must fight, as it were, against disease, and in like manner against old age. Regard must be paid to health; moderate exercises must be adopted; so much of meat and drink must be taken that the strength may be recruited, not oppressed. Nor, indeed, must the body alone be supported, but the mind and soul much more; for these also, unless you drop oil on them as on a lamp, are extinguished by old age. . . . Our minds are rendered buoyant by exercise.

As I like a young man in whom there is something

of the old, so I like an old man in whom there is something of the young; and he who follows this maxim will possibly be an old man in body, but he will never be an old man in mind.

Intelligence, reflection, and judgment reside in old men. . . . Age, especially an honored old age, has so great authority that this is of more value than all the pleasures of youth. . . .

Old age is the consummation of life, just as of a play. . . . The harvest of old age is the recollection and abundance of blessings previously secured. . . .

To those who have not the means within themselves of a virtuous and happy life, every age is burdensome.

Cicero was murdered in 43 B.C., just a year after Caesar. His head and hands were sent to Rome and gleefully nailed to the rostrum by his enemies, who thought they had silenced his golden tongue forever.

But they were wrong. Cicero kept careful copies of all his speeches, letters, essays, dialogues, and manuals; and though some were lost and some deliberately destroyed, most of them were found and preserved after his death. And these, together with his books on philosophy and politics, have talked to all the generations since—throwing a clear white light on the life and times in which he lived, and giving the world its chief source of information about that period.

Among the philosophical treatises that survive, few have had greater and more enduring influence than *de Senectute*. It expresses Cicero's ideas on old age with all the beauty of style, the brilliance and clarity that make him the most famous of the Latin prose writers.

Each part of life has its own pleasures, says Cicero. *Each has its own abundant harvest, to be garnered in season. We may grow old in body, but we need never grow old in mind and spirit. We must make a stand against old age. We must atone for its faults by activity. We must exercise the mind as we exercise the body, to keep it supple and buoyant. Life may be short, but it is long enough*

*to live honorably and well. Old age is the consummation
of life, rich in blessings. . . .*

Today Cicero's famous *de Senectute* remains not only
a classic of literature but one of the most inspiring essays
on old age ever written. It should be read in its entirety by
all who dread the passage of the years—who look upon
old age as a sad period of decline instead of the rich and
happy fulfillment of life.

The hoary head is a crown of glory. . . .
Proverbs 16:31

Many blessings do the advancing years bring with
them.   *Horace*

Nature gives to every time and season some beauties
of its own; and from morning to night, as from the
cradle to the grave, is but a succession of changes so
gentle and easy that we can scarcely mark their progress.   *Charles Dickens*

To express one's feelings as the end draws near is too
intimate a task. But I may mention one thought that
comes to me. . . . The riders in a race do not stop
short when they reach the goal. There is a little fin-
ishing canter before coming to a standstill. There is
time to hear the kind voices of friends, and to say to
oneself: "The work is done." But just as one says
that, the answer comes: "The race is over, but the
work is never done while the power to work remains."
The canter that brings you to a standstill need not
be only a coming to rest. It cannot be, while you still
live. For to live is to function. That is all there is to
living.   *Justice Oliver Wendell Holmes*

I strove with none, for none was worth my strife;
     Nature I loved, and next to Nature, Art;
I warmed both hands before the fire of life,
     It sinks, and I am ready to depart.
Walter Savage Landor

At forty, most men have not yet arrived and have not yet found themselves fully. The ablest are just coming into power and self-understanding. But even for them the peak of achievement is still more than seven years away. Then and not until then do they know themselves and what they can do. Not until then does the world take their measure and give them their due rank. Not until then, in the complete sense, can they truthfully say they know how to live.

Walter B. Pitkin

The best insurance against melancholia, depression, and a sense of futility in old age is the development of wide horizons and the cultivation of mental elasticity and interest in the world. Unlike the flesh, the spirit does not decay with the years. Many of the happiest individuals in the world are men and women in their sixties, seventies, or eighties, who have contributed richly to the world's work during their maturity, and at the same time have cultivated sufficient awareness and interest in the undying cultural activities to make their leisure a delight. . . .

The older men grow the more they realize that it is only by putting the focus of their activities in some movement or activity greater than their individual ego, that they can attain peace and security in old age.

W. Beran Wolfe

Growing old gracefully really depends most on an effective shifting of physical and emotional years. This necessitates a realization that every period of life has its rich compensations, and that only a fool fails to enjoy those of the period he is living in, because they are not the same as those of the past period. Personally, I think the achievement of happiness becomes easier as one grows older. Youth is so full of doubts and fears and needs that harass and worry constantly, but which happily largely disappear with the passing years. . . .

Happiness at the end of life demands some preparation beforehand. An assured income is not enough with which to meet old age. One must accumulate friends. One must lay up reserves of mental pleasures. One must plan for the health that is so extremely important to happiness in this period.

By the time a man is sixty he should be well enough acquainted with himself to know what he can and cannot do. He should know the varieties of self-expression which bring him the most happiness and should have attained some little skill in them. He should have a pretty good knowledge of how much he can expect of his body and of what his mental and spiritual capacities are.

Of the three watchwords for the happiness hunter—self-recognition, self-direction, and self-expression—it is the last that is most important for the graying years. The others also have their place in the sixties and seventies, but in not such a prominent place as before. Self-expression is the field to cultivate for later happiness. Then a man or a woman has more to express. Life begins at forty, yes, and it begins at sixty sometimes and even later. When all seems disappointing, when a review of one's life reveals no one great thing done, the man who takes inventory and devotes himself for some weeks and months to self-examination, may discover some neglected element which when brought out into its proper place may transform his life. Some desire he had in boyhood which got buried because of other interests may suddenly appear again. It may prove to have been his true bent, his real calling, and even the man of sixty, perhaps especially the man of sixty, ripened and strengthened by life experience, may take this boyhood ambition and in a surprisingly short time find himself doing more with the thing than he could have as a boy.

The technique of happiness for the elderly person is somewhat different from that for the youthful, but too much has been made of the difference between youth and old age. The human personality changes through the years, it is true, and yet it strangely remains the same. We have many second chances in life, sometimes even tenth chances. Let no man give up hope till the last breath is drawn.

Charles Francis Potter

2. SIR WILLIAM MULOCK

THE SHADOWS OF EVENING LENGTHEN
ABOUT ME, BUT MORNING IS IN MY
HEART

SMILING AND SERENE, Sir William Mulock, Chief Justice of Ontario, got up to acknowledge the great ovation. This distinguished gathering had come together in his honor, for he had reached an important milestone. It was his birthday . . . and he was ninety-five years old.

"Ninety-five," he thought as he stood before them, waiting for the applause to subside. "It sounds old. I must seem very old to most of them out there. But strangely enough, I don't feel old at all. It's just another birthday like all the others . . . another year behind me . . . and the best of life still ahead."

That had always been his philosophy: *The best of life is always ahead, always further on.* It was a philosophy that had served him well, that had kept him young in heart and spirit.

The great hall fell silent as he began to speak. What would Sir William say out of the long years of his experience? What would his message be to his friends and associates, out of the fullness and wisdom of his ninety-five years?

His voice was firm and clear as he spoke—the voice of a man who loved life, who loved his work and his fellow man, and who looked forward with pleasure to whatever still lay ahead.

I am still at work, with my hand to the plow, and my face to the future. The shadows of evening lengthen about me, but morning is in my heart. I have lived from the forties of one century to the thirties of the next. I have had varied fields of labor, and full contact with men and things, and have warmed both hands before the fire of life.

The testimony I bear is this: that the Castle of Enchantment is not yet behind me. It is before me still, and daily I catch glimpses of its battlements and towers. The rich spoils of memory are mine. Mine, too, are the precious things of today—books, flowers, pictures, nature, and sport. The first of May is still an enchanted day to me. The best thing of all is friends. The best of life is always further on. Its real lure is hidden from our eyes, somewhere behind the hills of time.

The simple dignity of Sir William Mulock's speech, his serene contentment at the age of ninety-five, touched the heart of every listener. For many there was an almost magical quality to his words. Men of fifty, of sixty, felt the weight of the years slip from their shoulders, felt somehow young in heart again . . . young in spirit. Men who had long lost sight of the true meaning of life, who had let themselves become tangled in the web of their own fears and confusions, listened to the words of this grand old statesman and jurist to whom life was still a thrilling adventure—and, as they listened, wistfully revalued their own dreams and ideals, their own aims and purposes. It was a comforting speech, and many later asked for a copy for their own use. It was widely printed and discussed in Canadian and American newspapers.

"Every man over forty should carry a copy of Sir William's speech in his pocket," declared one newspaper, discussing it editorially.

"His zest for life, his unfailing courage and good cheer, put many a younger man to shame," said another.

To greet each day without worry or confusion, to do one's appointed task, to be cheerful and unafraid, expectant, responsive—to live simply but fully, enjoying the many great blessings God had provided—that was his message on his ninety-fifth birthday. *Warm both hands before the fire of life,* he urged. *Live fully and happily. Make good friends and cherish good memories. And scorn the passage of time! Keep looking ahead, always ahead—for the best of life is always further on.*

Sir William Mulock died in 1944 at the age of one hundred, enjoying a rich and rewarding life to the very end. Though his voice is stilled, the message he gave the world on his ninety-fifth birthday lives on—inspiring us all to meet the challenge of the years with dignity and serenity.

As for old age, embrace and love it. It abounds with pleasure if you know how to use it. The gradually declining years are among the sweetest in a man's life; and I maintain that even when they have reached the extreme limit, they have their pleasure still.

Seneca

Winter is on my head, but spring is in my heart.

Victor Hugo

Age is a quality of mind.
If you have left your dreams behind,
If hope is cold,
If you no longer look ahead,
If your ambitions' fires are dead—
Then you are old.
But if from life you take the best,
And if in life you keep the jest,
If love you hold;
No matter how the years go by,
No matter how the birthdays fly—
You are not old.

Author unknown

If wrinkles must be written upon our brows, let them not be written upon the heart. The spirit should not grow old.
James A. Garfield

It is sad to see so many men and women afraid of growing old. They are in bondage to fear. Many of them, when they find the first gray hair, are alarmed. Now one really ought not to be alarmed when one's hair turns gray; if it turned green or blue, then one ought to see a doctor. But when it turns gray, that simply means there is so much gray matter in the skull there is no longer room for it; it comes out and discolors the hair. Don't be ashamed of your gray hair; wear it proudly, like a flag. You are fortunate, in a world of so many vicissitudes, to have lived long enough to earn it.   *William Lyon Phelps*

Youth is not a time of life—it is a state of mind. It is not a matter of ripe cheeks, red lips, and supple knees; it is a temper of the will, a quality of the imagination, a vigor of the emotions; it is a freshness of the deep spring of life.

Youth means a temperamental predominance of courage over timidity, of the appetite of adventure over love of ease. This often exists in a man of fifty more than in a boy of twenty.

Nobody grows old by merely living a number of years; people grow old only by deserting their ideals. Years wrinkle the skin, but to give up enthusiasm wrinkles the soul. Worry, doubt, self-distrust, fear, and despair—these are the long, long years that bow the head and turn the growing spirit back to the dust.

Whether seventy or sixteen, there is in every being's heart the love of wonder, the sweet amazement at the stars and the starlike things and thoughts, the undaunted challenge of events, the unfailing childlike appetite for what next, and the joy and the game of life.

You are as young as your faith, as old as your doubt; as young as your self-confidence, as old as your fear; as young as your hope, as old as your despair.

                                        Samuel Ullman

To me, old age is always fifteen years older than I am.
                                        Bernard Baruch

3. ROBERT BROWNING

**GROW OLD ALONG WITH ME!
THE BEST IS YET TO BE**

It was three years since Robert Browning's wife had died in his arms in the Casa Guida. Three years since he had left Italy and returned to England, to supervise his son's education and to take up his own shattered life again . . .

The poet got up and walked restlessly about the room. He had accomplished little in these three years. He was past fifty now, well past the line that separates youth from age.

Past fifty. . . . It was time to resume his work in earnest, if he were to accomplish what he had hoped to, what he had planned.

But after all, *a man's value is not measured by the years he has lived, or even the work he has done. A man's value is measured by the character he has molded.* Almost unconsciously, his mind had turned to the comforting philosophy of Rabbi ben Ezra. He had long admired that extraordinary twelfth-century scholar and had been influenced by his teachings—a sound and inspiring philosophy that belonged to no long-past era but to all time.

Abraham ben Meir ben Ezra was a celebrated Spanish rabbi, one of the most eminent of the Jewish literati of the Middle Ages. He was a man of such rare and noble character that he was affectionately known to his contemporaries as "The Admirable." Poet, physician, philosopher, astronomer, teacher—Rabbi ben Ezra was the spiritual leader of his people; and he taught them the true values of life, the enduring values of soul and spirit, the comforting values of faith and trust.

Approach the twilight of life with joy and hope,

preached Rabbi ben Ezra. *Approach the last of life with eagerness, not gloom. For the last of life is the best of life. Trust God and be not afraid.* . . .

The world has need of such a philosophy today, Robert Browning reflected. In the rush and hurry of our overly-ambitious lives, so many of us have lost our sense of perspective. We place too much stress on material things, and on personal achievement. Endlessly we worry and strive, watch the passage of time with dread, fear growing old—actually fear the *best* of life for which the first was made! Yes; the world sorely needed again the influence of a man like Rabbi ben Ezra who taught patience, serenity, the joy of a wise and chastened old age.

Robert Browning had a sudden inspiration. He would bring the twelfth-century rabbi back to life! He would make him the central figure in a poem, drawing the noble elements of character from the real man. It would be a poem of faith and courage . . . a paean of victory over approaching age. . . .

He became obsessed with the idea, lost himself in it completely. Even before he wrote the last stanza, Robert Browning knew that this was one of his finest poems. There was only one thing he could call it, of course, since its character and philosophy were taken right from the original source: "Rabbi ben Ezra." The first stanza leaped hot from his heart, an inspired interpretation of the rabbi's philosophy and religion:

> Grow old along with me!
> The best is yet to be,
> The last of life, for which the first was made;
> Our times are in his hand
> Who saith, "A whole I planned,
> Youth shows but half; trust God; see all, nor be afraid!"

In stanza after stanza, Browning depicted the learned rabbi as advising a young friend how to live a rich and re-

warding life. Be as ambitious as you wish, he tells the youth.
Strive for success and accomplishment while you are young.
Welcome and develop whatever talents you may have, the
divine spark that separates you from the clod. . . .

> Not for such hopes and fears
> Annulling youth's brief years,
> Do I remonstrate: folly wide the mark!
> Rather I prize the doubt
> Low kinds exists without,
> Finished and finite clods, untroubled by a spark.

But do not make worldly success the end and aim of
your existence, urges the rabbi. Do not live a life of the
flesh alone, content with material things.

> Poor vaunt of life indeed
> Were man but formed to feed
> On joy, to solely seek and find and feast.

The way may not be easy, the rabbi tells his young disciple. The way may be long and hard. But welcome the
strain and the struggle. For out of youth's struggle comes
strength, and out of youth's pain come wisdom and understanding.

> Then welcome each rebuff
> That turns earth's smoothness rough,
> Each sting that bids nor sit nor stand but go!
> Be our joys three-parts pain!
> Strive, and hold cheap the strain;
> Learn, nor account the pang; dare, never grudge the
> throe!

Live and learn, he advises the young man. Use the gifts
God gave you, and make the most of your life. But remember that youth shows but half, that God's perfect plan
includes the *whole* of life. See all—see the whole design—
and put your complete trust in God.

Yet gifts should prove their use:
I own the Past profuse
Of power each side, perfection every turn;
Eyes, ears took in their dole,
Brain treasured up the whole;
Should not the heart beat once, "How good to live
and learn"?

Not once beat, "Praise be thine!
I see the whole design,
I, who saw power, now see Love perfect too;
Perfect I call thy plan:
Thanks that I was a man!
Maker, remake, complete—I trust what thou shalt do!"

When youth is over, approach the last of life with dignity and repose. For this is the best of life, for which the
first was made. The struggles and mistakes of youth are
over; you are chastened now and wise. You have learned
the true values of life

Youth ended, I shall try
My gain or loss thereby;
Leave the fire ashes, what survives is gold;
And I shall weigh the same,
Give life its praise or blame:
Young, all lay in dispute; I shall know, being old.

Grow old along with me, says the rabbi. *Live my kind
of life, putting your faith and trust in God. Then you will
be serene and happy in your old age; you will not be afraid
of the end.*

. . . All that is, at all,
Lasts ever, past recall;
Earth changes, but thy soul and God stand sure.

Robert Browning's magnificent poem, "Rabbi ben Ezra,"
was published in 1864, in a group of poems which ap-

peared that year under the title *Dramatis Personae*. It was widely quoted and discussed, and became the subject of countless sermons and lectures. It was called "weighty and significant beyond anything Browning ever wrote," and "one of the most noble and inspiring poems in any language."

There are thirty-two stanzas to "Rabbi ben Ezra," but the first stanza is the best known and most frequently quoted. *"Grow old along with me, The best is yet to be. . . ."* The promise of these famous lines took a strong hold on the public; and they are today familiar to millions of people who have never read the poem in its entirety or even heard its name. The superb first stanza is complete in itself, a comfort to those approaching what Browning calls "the last and best of life."

Let me but live my life from year to year,
    With forward face and unreluctant soul.
    Not hurrying to, nor turning from the goal;
Not mourning for the things that disappear
In the dim past, nor holding back in fear
    From what the future veils; but with a whole
    And happy heart, that pays its toll
To youth and age, and travels on with cheer.
So let the way wind up the hill or down,
    O'er rough or smooth, the journey will be joy;
    Still seeking what I sought when but a boy,
New friendship, high adventure, and a crown,
    I shall grow old, but never lose life's zest,
    Because the road's last turn will be the best.
                     Henry van Dyke

As the bird trims to the gale,
I trim myself to the storm of time,
I man the rudder, reef the sail,
Obey the voice at eve obeyed at prime:
    "Lowly faithful, banish fear,
    Right onward drive unharmed;

The port, well worth the cruise, is near,
And every wave is charmed."
                                    Ralph Waldo Emerson

Let us see to it . . . that our lives, like jewels of great price, be noteworthy not because of their width, but because of their weight. Let us measure them by their performance, not their duration.   *Seneca*

Expect the best! It lies not in the past.
God ever keeps the good wine till the last.
Beyond are nobler work and sweeter rest.
    Expect the best!
                                    William Pierson Merrill

The seas are quiet when the winds give o'er;
So calm are we when passions are no more.
For then we know how vain it was to boast
Of fleeting things, so certain to be lost.
Clouds of affection from our younger eyes
Conceal that emptiness which age descries.

The soul's dark cottage, batter'd and decay'd,
Lets in new light through chinks that Time hath made;
Stronger by weakness, wiser men become
As they draw near to their eternal home.
Leaving the old, both worlds at once they view
That stand upon the threshold of the new.
                                    Edmund Waller

Life must be measured by thought and action, not by time.   *Sir John Lubbock*

I recognize a numbness—perhaps a diminution. Eyes are less keen; ears duller. . . . The important thing is that this equation between the urging of the soul and the obedience of the body should be maintained. Even while growing old, may I preserve within myself an undiminished harmony! I do not like the Stoic's proud stiffening of the lip; but the horror of death, of old age, of all that cannot be avoided, strikes me as impious. Whatever may be my fate, I should wish to return to God a grateful and enraptured soul.　*André Gide*

PART TEN

HOPE

for

The Future

"We are just at the beginning of progress in every field of human endeavor."

CHARLES F. KETTERING

THERE HAS NEVER BEEN AN AGE that did not applaud the past and lament the present.

"The illusion that times that were are better than times that are has probably pervaded all the ages," said Horace Greeley.

The *Prisse Papyrus,* dating back six thousand years or more—the oldest bit of known writing in existence—starts off with these startlingly familiar words: "Alas, times are not what they used to be!" And in one way or another people have been saying that same thing in all the centuries since.

"But no man who is correctly informed as to the past," says Thomas Macaulay, "will be disposed to take a morose or despondent view of the present."

For in the long panorama of man's progress through the centuries, the trend has been upward, always upward. The way has not been smooth or straight; it has been broken periodically by failures and mistakes, by crushing setbacks and catastrophes, by dark periods of war and depression. But always, irresistibly, the element of progress has been at work. Always, out of every great struggle or disaster, has come a new dawn, a rebirth of life and spirit, the powerful surge of progress carrying man onward and upward again.

Nevertheless, in times of crisis people tend to lose faith in the future. Today, too, there are many who feel we have reached the end of progress, perhaps the end of civilization. There are many who feel the future holds only darkness and despair. It is true, of course, that we are faced today with some of the most difficult and trying problems the nation has ever known. It is true that the recent past does not encourage confidence or peace of mind. With half the world in ruins, with millions of people worried and confused, haunted by the specter of atomic war, it is difficult to believe that there is an element of progress at work.

But we have come through serious crises before . . . and America has grown stronger with each succeeding crisis. The times may be "piled high with difficulty," as Lincoln said in another, earlier period of crisis, but "we must rise with the occasion. We cannot escape history!"

No; we cannot escape history. But we can learn much from the lessons of history. We can gain strength and courage and understanding from the past, to help us meet the challenge of our own times. "If we but learn the lessons that shriek from the pages of history," said Bernard Baruch in a recent address, "there is no handicap that cannot be overcome by will power, patience, and application!"

The ever-recurring evidence of history is that no time is as bad as it seems. *This time, like all other times, is a very good one, if we but know what to do with it.* Emerson's inspiring words are as true today as they ever were. The frontiers are never closed; the limits of progress are never reached. The future will be what we ourselves make it.

In the opinion of those best qualified to judge, the world is indeed far from "doomed." They tell us, in fact, that in spite of the problems and the chaos of the hour, the future is bright with promise. Spectacular advances are being made in science, invention, technology. In the United Nations the dream of centuries has at last taken shape, and hopeful beginnings have been made toward world unity and a lasting world peace. We are standing at the threshold of an exciting new era of development, at the beginning of enormous progress in every direction. The most challenging opportunity of all history lies before us.

If you doubt this, if you live in fear and dread of the future—there is nothing like a little perspective. Here are messages from outstanding personalities of our time, stirring words of faith and confidence. Here are selections from many sources, to calm your fears and lift your spirits. Here is hope for the future . . . the promise of a better world ahead.

1. ENDICOTT PEABODY

THE GREAT FACT TO REMEMBER IS
THAT THE TREND OF CIVILIZATION
ITSELF IS FOREVER UPWARD

OF ALL his many duties as Headmaster of Groton School, Dr. Endicott Peabody enjoyed most, he often told himself, these weekly talks in the chapel. Today again, as he took his accustomed place on the platform and looked into the rows of upturned faces, he thought as he had so many times before what a privilege it was to guide the boys' eager young minds, to help mold and shape their future lives.

He had given much thought to the preparation of today's talk. Many of these boys came from wealthy homes, from prominent families. Their lives were comfortable and secure. The times in which they lived were comparatively smooth and untroubled. But times changed; conditions changed; and it might be a far different world into which they matured from what it was today. They might be called upon to face grave problems, unforeseen dangers and difficulties. It was his duty as an educator to prepare them for the changes and chances of life, and for the possible challenge of the future.

The purpose of today's talk was to give them the perspective of history. He must try to impress them with the vital, the inescapable fact of *progress*. He must make them realize the importance of taking the long view of things, of thinking with courage and acting with faith—of keeping their ideals and moral principles intact—regardless of what conditions or what kind of world they might one day be called upon to face.

Progress is the law of nature, he told them. *It moves in long waves, but does not necessarily follow a straight line through the centuries. Sometimes there are setbacks and reverses, dark periods of trial and confusion. Sometimes there are supreme tests of courage, endurance, and resolve. But in the end the world always rights itself . . . and mankind moves ahead again. . . .*

As he spoke he saw that some of the boys were only half listening, some not listening at all as their eyes strayed to the windows and to the sunshine outside, their minds busy with thoughts of their own. But as usual there were a few who listened attentively; and if only these few were benefited—if only *one* remembered what he said today, and carried its influence into adult life—his talk would be worth the time and effort that went into its preparation.

He paused for a moment to give emphasis to his words, and to give the boys whose thoughts were wandering time to focus again on what he was saying. Then he summed up the day's message in these words:

Remember! Things in life will not always run smoothly. Sometimes we will be rising toward the heights—then all will seem to reverse itself and start downward. The great fact to remember is that the trend of civilization is forever upward; that a line drawn through the middle of the peaks and the valleys of the centuries always has an upward trend.

There was one young student in the chapel of Groton School that day who listened with particular interest, and who never forgot these words. So enduring was their influence that half a century later, when he had become a world-famous figure, he could still quote them exactly.

"I remember that my old schoolmaster, Dr. Peabody, said . . . Things in life will not always run smoothly. . . . The great fact to remember is that the trend of civilization itself is forever upward. . . ."

Millions of people in an anguished, war-weary world heard these words of Franklin D. Roosevelt on January 21, 1945, in his fourth inaugural address. Roosevelt never forgot the man who helped shape his early years, and whose faith in the progress of mankind so impressed him in youth that it remained an unfailing influence throughout life. In a letter to his old schoolmaster and friend, written in 1941, President Roosevelt said, "I count it among the blessings of my life that it was given me in formative years to have the privilege of your guiding hand and the benefit of your inspiring example."

Endicott Peabody became Headmaster of Groton School in 1884, and held that position for more than fifty years. He had a genius for teaching, and was widely recognized in his lifetime as one of the nation's outstanding educators. Thousands of boys came under his inspiring influence, and many went on to achieve unusual honors and distinction in adult life.

Today, of all Dr. Peabody's many talks with his boys in the dim old chapel of Groton, the one for which he is best remembered is the one from which we have here quoted, stressing the vital, inescapable fact of progress. Across the span of years his words still have the power to comfort and inspire; and in these anxious times, when many have lost faith in the future and in the very survival of civilization, his message is perhaps more significant than ever. Among all the voices of defeatism and despair, it is good to hear the old schoolmaster urging us to take the long view of things, to hold firmly to our courage and faith . . . and to remember that in our time, as in all times, though things may not run smoothly, though there may be periods of bitter struggle and trial, *the trend of civilization is upward, forever upward.*

We are reading the first verse of the first chapter of a book whose pages are infinite.   *Author unknown*

Say not thou, What is the cause that the former days were better than these? for thou dost not inquire wisely concerning this.   *Ecclesiastes 7:10*

If there exists a good and wise God, then there also exists a progress of mankind toward perfection.
     Plato

This time, like all other times, is a very good one, if we but know what to do with it.

Ralph Waldo Emerson

And step by step, since time began,
I see the steady gain of man.

John Greenleaf Whittier

Life is a fragment, a moment between two eternities, influenced by all that has preceded, and to influence all that follows. The only way to illumine it is by extent of view.   *William Ellery Channing*

Life travels upward in spirals. He who takes pains to search the shadows of the past below us, then, can better judge the tiny arc up which he climbs, more surely guess the dim curves of the future above him.

André Gide

Generations, succeeding to the pain of their predecessors, gradually elevate the status of mankind, as coral polyps, building one generation upon the work of the other, gradually elevate themselves from the bottom of the sea.   *Henry George*

We who now live are parts of a humanity that extends into the remote past, a humanity that has interacted with nature. The things in civilization we most prize are not ourselves. They exist by grace of the doings and sufferings of the continuous human community in which we are a link. Ours is the responsibility of conserving, transmitting, rectifying, and expanding the heritage of values we have received that those who come after us may receive it more solid and more secure, more widely accessible, and more generously shared than we have received it.

John Dewey

We are not the first generation to be discouraged by the contemporary scene. Victor Hugo reminds us that we now think of the sixteenth century as one of history's main turning points, with the Protestant Reformation and all the rest, but that Erasmus, who lived then, called it "the excrement of the ages"; that we see in the seventeenth century thrilling discovery and adventure, opening up the whole new world, but that Bossuet, in the thick of it, called it "a wicked and paltry age"; that to us the eighteenth century represents a stirring scene of political liberation, with the French and American Revolutions and the like, but that even Rousseau in a disheartened hour described it as "this great rottenness amidst which we live." So in the sixteenth, seventeenth, and eighteenth centuries the people who really fooled themselves were the skeptics, the cynics, while those who saw the possibilities and with a faith that moved mountains believed in them, were realistically right. Surely in this regard, history can repeat itself in our century, if we only stand by the best.   *Harry Emerson Fosdick*

We are marching along the endless pathway of unrealized possibilities of human growth.
Francis W. Parker

This is, of course, not the first time in the history of civilization that sensitive spirits, bred in a familiar culture, have declared, because that culture was changing, that all civilization was coming to an end. This is not the first time in the history of the West that the good and the reasonable saw nothing to do but to die or to shudder. It is sobering to our too hysterical fears to take, under the guidance of competent historians, a historical perspective. It requires a hard, even cruel effort at detachment, to take the long view, but only by taking such a view can we see our present plight in something like its true proportions, and find true proportions for our still persistent hopes. . . . Men in earlier ages, too, thought they were living at the end of the world. Nothing comes out of nothing, Lucretius once long ago informed his readers. . . .

The world seemed to a good many Athenians, too, to have ended with the Peloponnesian War.

Historical-mindedness may rescue us, then, from the sense that we are living in the twilight of the gods. . . .

The crisis of civilization through which we are living is . . . a moment only in the history of the cosmos, an episode only in the history of men. History moves in long waves; we are caught in the roughest surf today, and hurled about by it. But in the midst of the ocean it will be calm tomorrow. In its depths it is calm today. . . .

The darkness now seems absolute. Men before us have forgotten that it hides the morning star.

Irwin Edman

The world will right itself; take the long view and you are comforted.   *Lin Yutang*

2. DAVID E. LILIENTHAL

THE AGE IN WHICH WE LIVE CAN
BECOME ONE OF THE BLESSED
PERIODS IN ALL HISTORY

MILLIONS OF PEOPLE everywhere in the world had lost faith in the future. That, to David E. Lilienthal, was one of the most devastating aftereffects of World War II. The bombs that shattered Hiroshima and Nagasaki, ushering in the atomic age with such terrible impact, had shattered the world's peace of mind as well, had released a mounting flood of tensions and anxieties.

In America, as everywhere else, there was a breakdown of values and ideals, a creeping paralysis of fear and suspicion. People no longer felt secure. They no longer had faith or confidence in the future. Uneasily they contemplated the possibility of atomic attack . . . the destruction of American cities. . . . Was civilization doomed, they wondered? Could mankind survive an atomic war? Or were only darkness and destruction ahead?

The trouble, David E. Lilienthal reflected, was that most people saw only the destructive power of atomic energy. They saw it only as an incredibly potent and terrifying instrument of war. They did not see its enormous nonmilitary implications, its almost fantastic potentialities for constructive ends.

He himself had great faith in the future. As former Chairman of the United States Atomic Energy Commission, he knew that nuclear science opened up vistas of progress and achievement that fairly staggered the imagination with the promise of benefits to come. He knew that the technical and industrial developments likely to follow might usher in one of the most beneficent and remarkable periods in the history of mankind. And having been close to the problems of the nation, having watched democracy in action, he knew what was being done to strengthen democratic ideals, to advance the cause of world unity and peace.

The atomic age was a challenge, yes . . . but it was also an adventure, and a great opportunity. There were problems, of course; and there were great dangers. He would be the last person in the world to minimize those dangers! But the problems could be met; the dangers could be avoided. All that was necessary was to hold on to the principles that had made America strong and great. All that was necessary was to have faith, and to put that faith into action. The future was bright with promise. Democracy had never stood on firmer ground. The era in which we lived could become one of the blessed periods of all history. This he believed. This he firmly believed.

He thought about it a great deal. Working in his garden, riding his favorite horse, talking things over with his family and friends. David E. Lilienthal thought about his philosophy of faith. And at last he felt impelled to put it down on paper, for the benefit of those who saw nothing but chaos ahead—especially for the *youth* of America, the disillusioned and bewildered young men and women who were the chief victims of world tensions and anxieties. He wrote an inspiring testament of faith in America and in America's future, from which the following paragraphs are quoted:

Back of the dramatic discovery of atomic energy is a long history of generation after generation of inquiring minds, restlessly questioning, testing, doubting, probing, seeking the truth about the nature of the physical world, about the procession of the seasons, about the sun in its power and warmth, about the very stars in their courses.

Was this release of the basic energy of matter an event over which we should rejoice, or should we tremble with apprehension that man had at last let out of the bottle an evil jinni too powerful to be tamed? We are not yet in a position to judge of this question, for the time has been far too short. We would not say today that the discovery of fire is to be regretted. There is hardly a force more beneficent in the life of man. When fire is out of control, however, it can and does cause catastrophes of the most horrible kind. We have learned to live with fire. Indeed, we can hardly imagine our civilization in its best aspects without it. If, however, the only time we had ever seen fire was in battle, pouring out of a flame thrower, consuming human life, or dropped from airplanes to burn to a cinder a city of a million people, could we be sure that it had been a good discovery?

Whatever answer the future holds, this much I believe we must accept: There can be no putting the jinni back into the bottle. To try to bury or to suppress new knowledge because we do not know how to prevent its use for destructive or evil purposes is a pathetically futile gesture. It is, indeed, a symbolic return to the methods of the Middle Ages. It seeks to deny the innermost urge of the mind of man—the desire for knowledge. . . .

Greater knowledge about the world will, I think, be the keystone of the immediate future. But greater knowledge alone will not be enough. There must also be greater love and understanding among men. And there must also be greater faith in humankind and in the purposes of the Creator of the Universe. Knowledge, love, faith—with these three the atomic age, the age in which we live, can become an age of mercy, of joy, and of hope, one of the blessed periods of all history. . . .

We have great visions today. We are going to have more of them. From our strengths have come great actions. We can move forward to even greater achievements. In our hearts we know we have heard only the opening bars of the New World Symphony.

Ours is a time of great expectations. . . . There is open before us an unparalleled opportunity to build new and firmer foundations under our feet. We stand at the gateway of an age of expansion, of the flowering of modern imagination and the new skills and knowledge of mankind.

The task ahead may prove to be the boldest and most stirring adventure of the human spirit since the circumnavigation of the globe. That will be true if it can release a flood of pent-up genius, not alone in our works of hands and skills in management but in the development of the free spirit.

What I have in mind in such an era of American development is not an ideal world lying somewhere in the remote future, peopled by a different kind of human beings than we are now, or living under an imaginary social system. I am speaking of something that can be done with tools of understanding and organization already ours. I have in mind that reservoir of knowledge that gives us in our time the power to mold the very face of things.

The necessary skills of organization and technology exist today, but this is not to say that it is automatic or inevitable that they will be used for an age of creation. We must have the will to set out boldly on the adventure, the resolution to begin from where we are. We need the will and the faith, we need a sense that *this* is the historic hour to turn the first shovel, to take the first steps.

The kind of American development I have outlined will depend upon all of us. It will depend on our thinking and uttering, almost lovingly, words that speak of pine and cedar, of streams and turbines, of aircraft factories and steel billets; of coal and copper ore; of red clay and black loam and fields of wheat, wave after wave; of river barges and electric power lines; of construction workers and miners; woodsmen and farmers, doctors and teachers—of things and of people. The outcome turns upon whether ours is a static nation resting on its laurels, holding fearfully to what we have, or a land which forever renews its youth by magnificent dreams and noble plans turned into great deeds.

Many stimulating messages of faith and hope have been written since the world emerged, shaken and bemused, from the devastating upheaval of World War II. But because of his close association with the development of atomic energy, because he is one of the nation's best-informed men on the potentialities of nuclear science, David E. Lilienthal's message has had unusual influence.

"This I Do Believe" is his answer to all the gloomy, long-faced prophets of doom who predict a terrifying future and the end of civilization. To them he says: *Civilization will survive and will flourish . . . the future will be better than ever . . . we stand at the gateway of vast developments, widening horizons.*

To the anxious youth of America, infected with the virus of defeatism and despair, he says: *Enormous technological progress is on the way . . . opportunities for individual achievement will be greater than ever . . . an era of challenging promise lies ahead.*

And to the panicky who dread atomic war, who live in terror of attack, he says: *Atomic energy can be a greater force for good than for evil . . . we have the knowledge and the power to mold the very face of things . . . what we need is the will and the faith. Faith,* says this man who has been close to the development of atomic energy and who knows better than most what its potential hazards are— *faith is greater than any bomb! Faith is the most potent weapon ever devised. Faith in action is the wellspring of America's great strength, the source of America's great power and achievement. Do not lose faith in mankind, and in the purposes of the Creator. Do not lose faith in the future. Much is being done to promote brotherhood, understanding, and peace. . . .*

Like Walt Whitman, whom he so greatly admires, David Lilienthal believes in the nation and its people, and in the capacity of democracy to survive and grow stronger. His faith is deeply rooted in the background and traditions of American democracy. His message is not for these times alone, but for *all* times of doubt and despair—an inspiring message of hope and faith to help people face the future with courage.

No one can see, even in outline, the shape of things to come. History has been stepped up incredibly and is now exceeding the speed limit. Still, it is my belief, in spite of old rancors, new envies, and the chaos of the hour, that we are entering the greatest era in the story of man, destined to see changes such as man has never seen.   *Joseph Fort Newton*

I believe that we will go on to realize a way of life better than has ever existed before. America . . . has never been so strong. Its truly great achievements lie ahead of it.   *William O. Douglas*

If we have the courage to lift our eyes above the agony of the moment, we may see a world in which the forces of applied science and the diffusion of knowledge offer to all men and nations a plane of living, a freedom and richness of spiritual, cultural, and economic attainment that can scarcely be imagined at the present moment.   *James T. Shotwell*

Never before in the history of the world has life been so eminently worth living, and never before so thrilling. The morning newspaper and the monthly magazine are a veritable storehouse of challenges and stimuli. Never before has the opportunity for living life at a high conscious and intellectual level been so apparent. Never before have there been so many profoundly important causes crying for intelligent social co-operation from adult men and women. Never before has the challenge of living fully been so clear. You can hardly name a sphere of human activity, be it transportation or international peace, be it economics or sociology, be it commerce or medicine, politics or philosophy, in which old values are not

tumbling, in which there is not a cry for leaders and
for soldiers in a good cause.   *W. Beran Wolfe*

The future fairly startles me with its impending greatness. We are on the verge of undreamed progress.
                                        Henry Ford

Youth today is better off in America than ever before
in my memory. . . .
Today the field of choice for an able youngster is
vastly wider than it was when I was a boy. Today,
with technology on the march, the opportunities
have widened; there are dozens of specialties we had
never heard of when I was young—electronics and
nuclear physics and a dozen more. These are careers
of the future that stir the imagination.
                        Admiral Chester W. Nimitz

It is well to stand off and look at America and its
opportunities. . . . It is stimulating to realize that ten
or twenty years from now . . . there will be in our
homes products and articles of convenience and
luxury which are not to be found in any store today;
that new professions will have been developed; that
there will be new services which are as yet only em-
bryonic ideas in the minds of observing or imaginative
men and women. . . .
First of all, we must realize that a generation belongs
to those who know what to do with it. The people,
the situation, the very times, serve those who understand and can command them.   *Robert R. Updegraff*

Careers never dreamed of lie ahead for the young
man or woman with ideas, ambition, and ability. . . .
Of course, there are those who say there is nothing
new ahead. Twice in my lifetime, responsible people
thought that physics had reached the end of its development. The first time was around 1890, when most
top physicists were convinced that there was nothing
new to come to this science. Yet, in 1895, the X-ray

was discovered; a year later came radioactivity, and it was followed in 1897 by the electron. These discoveries sent physics off in entirely new directions and created thousands of new opportunities.

Then in 1940, one of the world's outstanding physicists made a statement in an address to the effect that he saw nothing new ahead for physics. Quite a few people agreed with him. But at the very moment he was speaking, nuclear fission was being developed and we were on our way to the atom bomb and the now dawning atomic age.

The point to remember is that new scientific developments create new industries and find new outlets for established businesses. The steam engine and the opening of the West by railways were the foundation of practically every job in America. They sent thousands into a new empire—bankers, builders, merchants, lumbermen, and cattlemen, to name a few. They carried goods from this new empire across the country to be shipped around the world and they carried goods from Europe and the Orient back. Both ways, countless jobs and opportunities were made.

The gasoline engine opened opportunities for everybody, from salesmen to upholstery fabric makers, to small parts and accessory manufacturers. Then there were the airplane and the radio, which made entirely new industries. The head of one of the top radio networks came from a Midwest farm and when he left the farm there was no radio and he never dreamed of what was ahead for him.

Now there are television and plastics pointing the way to new avenues of achievement, and so it will be with electronics and atomic fission. . . .

No young man today need fear for the future. I believe that the young man of ideas, ambition, and ability can look forward to the greatest opportunities in history. . . .

I have great confidence in our young people. I do not go along with the prophets of doom who believe the world is going to pot. They've been saying that for years. We've always had trouble and scandal and strife. We had them in the so-called "good old days" of the '20s, the '90s, the '60s, and as far back as runs the mind of man. One of the weaknesses in our system of studying history is that too much time is spent learning about the heroes and the great victories and not enough about the troubles and weaknesses that existed then as today.

Similar problems existed centuries ago as are found at the present. They were solved then and they will be solved now. . . .

In thinking of the future, I am reminded of a travel experience I had several years ago. It was late in the afternoon and I was aboard a ship going from Seattle, Washington, toward Victoria, on Puget Sound. It was a day of rare visibility and I could see Mt. Rainier a hundred and twenty miles away, looking up high in the sky like a golden monument, with range upon range of islands and foothills extending, dimly outlined, through the intervening reaches.

In this way, I like to think, stands the future of America—a golden future that is accessible to us if we have the skill and courage to surmount the foothills!

Karl T. Compton

Fortunately for us and our world, youth is not easily discouraged. Youth with its clear vista and boundless faith and optimism is uninhibited by the thousands of considerations that always bedevil man in his progress. The hopes for the world rest on the flexibility, vigor, capacity for new thought, the fresh outlook of the young. Age grows cautious, overly conscious of difficulties, enmeshed in the conflict of personal problems and changing sense of values.

Youth must always carry the burden of enforcing and realizing bold decisions. Older men, drawing on years of experience and knowledge of the world, may fix the line we must attain, behind which we may not compromise. But it is the young who must maintain that line.

In Lincoln's war, the masses of enlisted ranks on both sides were made up in the end of beardless youths. During this last war, many of you present were on the battle line. All of you had brothers or relatives or friends who fought to maintain the line for the freedom of man. Had you failed, we and no other nation could have continued to live as a free people.

Thanks to the youth of our nation and our Allies the line was firmly held. Unconditional surrender of those who sought to wipe it out was achieved. Today's problem is to see that indecision and confusion and pessimism may not threaten the permanence of the victory. Free people who, in massed strength, crossed the oceans to beat into submission two huge military machines, must not become prey of fears and doubts and misgivings. We must not permit present problems to form a wall of bewilderment that shuts off our view of great futures. The future is the special province of the young, of you and your companions throughout the land! Schooled in the lessons of the past, unaffrighted by the present, you look ahead with confidence.   *Dwight D. Eisenhower*

The human race is not a spineless, brainless species to be pushed around and finally exterminated by forces which it has itself created. In spite of the atomic bomb we are still the captains of our own destiny, and we can make that destiny anything we desire.
The twentieth century is the bloodiest century in history, but we can yet retrieve it. The last half of the century could produce a world-wide flowering of the human spirit such as we have not known since the Renaissance—or, more accurately, since the twelfth century—a flowering that would be fertilized by the blood and sorrow of these last calamitous decades. We know that science and medicine are on the threshold of great events. It can be a time, too, of great literature, of creative art and drama. With intelligence and conscience to guide us, we can also make gigantic strides in social control, bringing our de-

structive weapons within the orbit of a world authority, and harnessing their powers to enhance the
happiness of men and increase the dignity and worth
of the human person.

This is not an idle dream. Its realization is distinctly
possible, but only on the condition that we fight for it
—fight for it with undiscouraged faith and grim tenac-
ity. If men . . . can develop the wisdom to use their
technology only for constructive ends, if they will
act on the principle that racial intolerance of every
kind threatens the safety of the future, if they will
move out into a new world society with decisiveness
and daring, then the twentieth century can be re-
deemed.   *Raymond B. Fosdick*

Even in times as troubled and uncertain as these, I
still hold to the faith that a better civilization than
any we have known is in store for America and, by
our example, perhaps for the world. Here destiny
seems to have taken a long look. Into this continental
reservoir there has been poured untold and untapped
wealth of human resources. Out of that reservoir, out
of the melting pot, the rich promise which the New
World held out to those who came to it from many
lands is finding fulfillment.

The richness of the promise has not run out. If we
keep the faith for our days as those who came before us kept the faith for theirs, then you and I can
smile with confidence into the future.

Franklin D. Roosevelt

3. WENDELL WILLKIE

OUR THINKING IN THE FUTURE MUST
BE WORLD-WIDE

ON AUGUST 26, 1942, a bomber operated by United States Army officers took off from Mitchel Field, in New York. The world was at war; but this plane was not on a war mission. Aboard was Wendell Willkie, private citizen, authorized by the President to make a world tour in the interest of global unity and peace.

As the plane roared over the Atlantic, Willkie considered his itinerary. His plan was to see as much as he could of the world and the war, its battlefronts, its leaders, and its people. His hope was to help translate into reality the dream of a world without violence—the age-old dream of peace and harmony among nations.

It was a unique, a challenging, assignment, and one that Willkie eagerly welcomed. He was to have the opportunity of seeing the world at war . . . and of visualizing the world at peace. He was to have the opportunity of observing the nations of the world as though on a giant chessboard, and of contemplating the best moves in the direction of international understanding and co-operation.

He talked with Montgomery in El Alamein, and with de Gaulle in Beirut. He discussed world problems with Stalin in Moscow, and with Chiang Kai-shek in Chungking. He talked with soldiers at the fighting fronts, and with their families behind the lines—with teachers, farmers, and factory workers—with generals, prime ministers, and kings.

He visited more than a dozen countries, traveled a total of thirty-one thousand miles, talked with hundreds of people around the world. And the impression he got was not of *distance* from these people, but of *nearness* to them. The more he saw of the world, the smaller it seemed to him; and the greater his desire to see the nations of the world united in a just and lasting peace. "If I had ever had any doubts that the world has become small and completely interdependent," he said later, "this trip would have dispelled them altogether."

In seven weeks he was back in the United States; and on October 26th, just two months after his plane took off from Mitchel Field, he reported to the nation in a radio broadcast on "Global War and Peace." He reported on a world transformed by swift communication and economic interdependence, a world of shrinking boundaries, of revolutionary new values and ideas. He stressed the need for broader vision and better understanding, insisted that our thinking and planning in the future must be world-wide. "There can be no peace for any part of the world," he said, "unless the foundations of peace are made secure throughout *all* parts of the world."

Later he published a more detailed report of his findings in book form. The gist of his message is summed up in this paragraph from the first chapter—a simple, unadorned statement of fact which millions have nevertheless found memorable and provocative. It is the keynote of the book, and the inspiration of its title: *One World.*

> There are no distant points in the world any longer. I learned by this trip that the myriad millions of human beings of the Far East are as close to us as Los Angeles is to New York by the fastest trains. I cannot escape the conviction that in the future what concerns them must concern us, almost as much as the problems of the people of California concern the people of New York. Our thinking in the future must be world-wide.

Wendell Willkie's report on his global tour dramatized the idea of *One World,* and clarified its meaning for the average person. He made the phrase familiar and inspiring to millions who had never heard it before. He gave them a clearer perspective of the world today, and America's relationship to it. He gave them a better understanding of what must be done to promote and maintain a world society—a world in which all men everywhere can be free, in which all can live in security and peace.

We are members of a world team, he reported to the nation. *We are partners in a grand adventure. We are offered the most challenging opportunity of all history: the chance to help create a new society in which men and women the world around can live and grow invigorated by independence and freedom.*

These words are based not on some vague humanitarian hope or dream but on firsthand observation of the world and its people in the middle of a devastating war. Wendell Willkie's message is as significant now as it was in 1942, perhaps even more so. *Our thinking must be world-wide. . . . There can be no peace for any part of the world unless the foundations of peace are made secure throughout all parts of the world.*

I am a citizen, not of Athens or Greece, but of the world.
Socrates

God grant that not only the love of liberty but a thorough knowledge of the rights of man may pervade all the nations of the earth, so that a philosopher may set his foot anywhere on its surface and say: "This is my country!"
Benjamin Franklin

I believe that our Great Maker is preparing the world, in His own good time, to become one nation, speaking one language, and when armies and navies will be no longer required.
Ulysses Simpson Grant

For I dipt into the future, far as human eye can see,
Saw the vision of the world, and all the wonder that
would be,
Saw the heavens fill with commerce, argosies of magic
sails,
Pilots of the purple twilight dropping down with costly bales. . . .

Heard the heavens filled with shouting, and there
  rained a ghastly dew
From the nation's airy navies grappling in the central blue. . . .
Far along the world wide whisper of the south wind
  rushing warm
With the standards of the peoples plunging through
  the thunder storm
Till the war drum throbbed no longer, and the battle
  flags were furled
In the parliament of man—the federation of the world.
                                    Alfred Tennyson

The American who cares about freedom will have to
discipline his mind to a new way of thinking. He will
have to pass beyond his easy, confident localism and
learn to think in world terms. This will be a much
harder way for him to think, for the world patterns
are still unformed. But if he cares about making freedom grow in strength and grandeur, he will have to
accustom himself to think in this broader way. The
day for provincial Americanism is past. To save the
freedom of America, we shall have somehow to help
achieve the freedom of the peoples of the world.
                                    Harry A. Overstreet

The day will come when . . . victorious nations will
plan and build in justice and freedom a house of
many mansions, where there will be room for all.
                                    Winston Churchill

In the future days, which we seek to make secure,
we look forward to a world founded upon four essential human freedoms.

The first is freedom of speech and expression—everywhere in the world.

The second is freedom of every person to worship
God in his own way—everywhere in the world.

The third is freedom from want—which, translated into world terms, means economic understandings which will secure to every nation a healthy peacetime life for its inhabitants—everywhere in the world.

The fourth is freedom from fear—which, translated into world terms, means a world-wide reduction of armaments to such a point and in such a thorough fashion that no nation will be in a position to commit an act of physical aggression against any neighbor—anywhere in the world. *Franklin D. Roosevelt*

We, the peoples of the United Nations
Determined to save succeeding generations from the scourge of war, which twice in our lifetime has brought untold sorrow to mankind, and
To reaffirm faith in fundamental human rights, in the dignity and worth of the human person, in the equal rights of men and women and of nations large and small, and
To establish conditions under which justice and respect for law and the pledged word can be maintained, and
To promote social progress and better standards of life in larger freedom, and for these ends
To practice tolerance and live together in peace as good neighbors, and
To unite our strength to maintain international peace and security, by the acceptance of principles and the institution of methods to insure that armed force shall not be used, save in the common interest, and
To employ international means for the economic and social advancement of all peoples,
Have resolved to combine our efforts to accomplish these aims.
Accordingly, our respective governments, through representatives assembled in the City of San Francisco, who have exhibited their full powers found to be in good and due form, have agreed to the present

Charter of the United Nations and do hereby establish an international organization to be known as the United Nations.

Preamble of the United Nations Charter

4. OLIVER WENDELL HOLMES

BEYOND THE VISION OF BATTLING
RACES AND AN IMPOVERISHED EARTH,
I CATCH A DREAMING GLIMPSE OF PEACE

RELUCTANTLY Justice Oliver Wendell Holmes left his comfortable old house in Washington for the railroad station. He hated leaving his pleasant book-lined study, where he spent so many relaxed and happy hours. But he had promised to speak at a dinner of the Harvard Law Association in New York, and he did not propose to disappoint his old friends.

All the way up in the train he thought about what he would say at the dinner. The times were out of joint, and people were troubled, uneasy. There was a growing discontent; and as always, in times like these, people talked as though civilization were doomed, as though there were no hope for the future—as though peace on earth and good will toward men were an impossible dream.

But there had been bad times before. There had been anxious, unhappy times before. He had lived through nearly half his country's history, and he had seen many dark hours, many periods of trials and crisis, of blazing hatreds and distrust. But he had never lost faith in the future; and now, as he grew older, that faith was stronger than ever.

He took an envelope from his pocket and made some notes on the back of it. *We must search behind the popular discontent to find its cause. We must attack our problems with courage and with faith. We must look ahead—plan and build for a better world—blaze new trails of brotherhood and understanding.*

He leaned his head back against the pillow and closed his eyes. There were problems in every period, ferments of hope and fear in every generation. He thought of something Emerson once said, in times that were much like these. It was in Boston, in 1841—he had a copy of the lecture somewhere among his papers. He had, in fact, quoted from it not very long ago. "A great perplexity hangs over us like a cloud," Emerson had said. "We mistrust every step we take. . . . It is not that men do not wish to act; they are paralyzed by fear and uncertainty. . . . We must think with courage."

Yes, *we must think with courage*. That was as true now as it had been in Emerson's day—as it would always be! There could be no better philosophy for any generation, regardless of what problems or dangers it might be called upon to face. *Think with courage; look forward with hope; act with faith and confidence in the future of mankind*.

The night of the dinner he stood in the crowded, smoke-filled dining room—tall and straight for all his seventy-two years, a handsome, distinguished-looking man with his great mane of silver hair shining in the light. He had lived through wars, crises, panics, depressions. He had lived through many changing eras, many changing patterns of life and thought. But nothing had ever shaken his faith in the future, his firm belief that civilization would survive and grow stronger. He saw life as an endless, flowing stream of progress and development. He saw the future as through a door, bright with promise. . . .

Slowly he looked around the room. Many of these men were old friends whom he had known for years. They had been listening attentively to his speech; and as he summed up, his voice was deep with emotion. This was the thought he wished most to leave with them. This was the hope and the dream he wished to share.

As I grow older, I grow calm. . . . I do not lose my hopes. . . . I think it probable that civilization some-how will last as long as I care to look ahead—perhaps with smaller numbers but perhaps also bred to splendor and greatness by science. I think it not improbable that man, like the grub that prepares a chamber for the winged thing it never has seen but is to be—that man may have cosmic destinies he does not understand. And so beyond the vision of battling races and an impoverished earth, I catch a dreaming glimpse of peace.

Justice Oliver Wendell Holmes was one of the most outstanding men of his time. The nation's press often referred to him as "the greatest living American." Chief Justice Taft called him "the most brilliant and learned member of the Court." He was a man whose roots were deep in American tradition, a man who loved life, believed in people, and had enormous faith in the future.

His speech before the Harvard Law Association in February, 1913, was widely quoted—especially his closing message of faith in a high and splendid destiny for man, his vision of an enduring civilization and peace. These were stirring words of hope and promise, at a time when such words were gravely needed. Many were inspired by his message, and carried its influence into their own lives.

When Justice Holmes was in his eighties, a young man wrote to him for some advice; and in his reply he said, "If I were young, my last words would be: Have faith and pursue the unknown end." The famous Supreme Court Justice lived to be ninety-four; but he never lost his faith in the future, his vision of a better, more peaceful world to come.

"Beyond the vision of battling races . . . I catch a dreaming glimpse of peace."

Two great wars have been fought since Justice Holmes spoke these words—wars more terrible than any the world has ever known. But the first steps have been taken to create a world society, and to maintain a just and lasting peace among the nations. We are at last, for the first time in history, beginning to realize the kind of world that has been the vision and the hope of man for centuries.

So is the faith of Justice Oliver Wendell Holmes justified. So do his words have vital meaning for us today— even more meaning than in 1913, when Justice Holmes stood at the end of an era and spoke the words that seem strangely prophetic to us now: *I catch a dreaming glimpse of peace.*

They shall beat their swords into plowshares, and their spears into pruning-hooks; nation shall not lift up sword against nation, neither shall they learn war any more.   *Isaiah 2:4*

I believe without a shadow of doubt that science and peace will finally triumph over ignorance and war, and that the nations of the earth will ultimately agree not to destroy but to build up.   *Louis Pasteur*

I firmly believe that the future of civilization is absolutely dependent upon finding some way of resolving international differences without resorting to war.
                              Dwight D. Eisenhower

We have learned that we cannot live alone, at peace; that our own well-being is dependent upon the well-being of other nations, far away.
We have learned that we must live as men, and not as ostriches, nor as dogs in the manger.
We have learned to be citizens of the world, members of the human community.
We have learned the simple truth, as Emerson said, that "the only way to have a friend is to be one."
We can gain no lasting peace if we approach it with suspicion and mistrust—or with fear.
We can gain it only if we proceed with the understanding and the confidence and the courage which flow from conviction.   *Franklin D. Roosevelt*

Those dangers ahead—a new world war—need not happen, nor will ever happen, if we use the powers that have been given us for life and not for death. The Destroyer will not get his chance, the Four Horsemen will not come riding out again, if we have a wider sense of comradeship with other peoples— stricken like ourselves, bewildered like ourselves, and searching like ourselves for some way of escape out of this ruin. We need not use poison gas, nor see great cities smashed by high explosives, if the best intelligence amongst us will give a lead to the world. Let us love life and laughter and tolerance and good-fellowship. Let us hate cruelty. Let us dedicate ourselves to the children of the world, so that they may get a decent chance of happiness. Let us have courage above all to face this life, this strange adventure, whether it brings in hardship or peril.

Throughout all the struggles and strivings of the human race, all its blunderings and conflicts, all its stupidities and failures, those ideals lived in many simple and noble minds—before and after Socrates and Plato—and that faith helped them through. Only by such faith again—reawakened and strengthened by new knowledge, reaching out across the world, controlling the machines and instruments of power, distributing more fairly the fruits of toil, working for peace, and raising the standard of charity—may we go forward to meet the unknown future, unafraid.

Philip Gibbs

The President of the United States of America and the Prime Minister, Mr. Churchill, representing His Majesty's Government in the United Kingdom, being met together, deem it right to make known certain common principles in the national policies of their respective countries on which they base their hopes for a better future for the world.

1. Their countries seek no aggrandizement, territorial or other.

2. They desire to see no territorial changes that do not accord with the freely expressed wishes of the peoples concerned.

3. They respect the right of all peoples to choose the form of government under which they will live; and they wish to see sovereign rights and self-government restored to those who have been forcibly deprived of them.

4. They will endeavor, with due respect for their existing obligations, to further the enjoyment by all

States, great or small, victor or vanquished, of
access, on equal terms, to the trade and to the raw
materials of the world which are needed for their
economic prosperity.

5. They desire to bring about the fullest collaboration
between all nations in the economic field with the
object of securing, for all, improved labor standards, economic advancement, and social security.

6. After the final destruction of the Nazi tyranny,
they hope to see established a peace which will
afford to all nations the means of dwelling in safety within their own boundaries, and which will
afford assurance that all the men in all the lands
may live out their lives in freedom from fear and
want.

7. Such a peace should enable all men to traverse the
high seas and oceans without hindrance.

8. They believe that all of the nations of the world,
for realistic as well as spiritual reasons, must come
to the abandonment of the use of force. Since no
future peace can be maintained if land, sea, or
air armaments continue to be employed by nations
which threaten, or may threaten, aggression outside of their frontiers, they believe, pending the
establishment of a wider and permanent system of
general security, that the disarmament of such
nations be essential. They will likewise aid and
encourage all other practicable measures which
will lighten for peace-loving peoples the crushing
burden of armaments.

Franklin D. Roosevelt, Winston S. Churchill:
The Atlantic Charter

It is given to us, of this generation, to achieve real
peace—if not for ourselves, for our children.

It is given to us to reassert the right of man to live as
the image of God. To those who say that these unlimited objectives are unthinkable, impossible, let us
reply that it is the alternative to them which is unthinkable, impossible for Americans to contem-

plate. Let us dedicate ourselves to the achievement of these unlimited objectives as boldly and as surely and as confidently as did Columbus and Washington and all the countless millions of Americans, from the Pilgrims to the pioneers, who have proved that in this unconquerably and justifiably optimistic nation *nothing* undertaken by free men and free women is impossible.   *Robert E. Sherwood*

5. FRANKLIN D. ROOSEVELT

THE ONLY LIMIT TO OUR REALIZATION
OF TOMORROW WILL BE OUR DOUBTS
OF TODAY. LET US MOVE FORWARD
WITH STRONG AND ACTIVE FAITH

IT WAS APRIL, 1945—and now at last the end of the war was in sight. The German armies were tottering. American and Russian troops were converging on Berlin from opposite directions. Japan, too, was losing ground. American forces had driven back the enemy on Okinawa . . . with Tokyo only three hundred miles away. It would soon be over.

Eagerly President Roosevelt looked forward to the end of hostilities, and to a world at peace again. It was his greatest wish to see a strong and enduring peace structure that would safeguard the world for generations to come from the scourge of war. He envisioned a world in which people everywhere could live without fear, in peace and security —a world founded on fundamental human rights and freedoms.

The President had already returned from Yalta, where he had conferred with Churchill and Stalin on plans for victory and peace. They had agreed to co-ordinate their military efforts for a swift and decisive victory. They had agreed to reorganize Poland, to share the administration of Germany, to let the liberated countries create "democratic institutions of their own choice." And most important for the future welfare of the world, they had agreed to support the United Nations—had set the scene for an international conference in San Francisco to draw up a charter that would help insure a lasting peace.

Much had been accomplished at Yalta, but much still remained to be done; and the President was tired. The grueling burdens and problems of the war years had taken their toll, and for some time now he had been ailing. The sixty-seven-hundred-mile trip to the Crimea, and the strenuous sessions of the conference, had further sapped his waning strength. He felt worn out, drained of energy.

For the past two weeks he had been at his cottage in Warm Springs, resting and getting in shape for the meeting of the United Nations in San Francisco. He must be at his best for that meeting. The representatives of fifty nations would be there, and they would look to him for leadership. So much depended on the success of the conference! It was the hope of hundreds of millions of people everywhere in the world—the promise of a lasting peace, a better and happier future for mankind.

He tried to relax at Warm Springs, to get as much rest as he could in preparation for the busy weeks ahead. It was perfect weather, and he took long drives in the familiar countryside, enjoying the broad, pine-filled Georgia valley, the budding trees, the fresh green promise of spring. He tanned a healthy brown in the outdoors. He took time to enjoy his stamp collections, to pose for his portrait, to visit and talk with old friends.

But there was work to be done, too. A small staff of associates had accompanied him to Warm Springs, and a remarkable amount of activity went on in the little white pine cottage. The President was in constant communication with Washington and world affairs. There were problems that weighed heavily on his mind, and he gave them much time and thought. Daily there were reports to read, documents to sign, letters and official papers to dictate. And as usual there were speeches to think about and plan —among them, a radio address to be given on April 13th in honor of the Annual Jefferson Day Dinner.

The President completed his draft of the Jefferson Day address on Wednesday evening, April 11th. It had been an unusually pleasant and relaxing day, and he felt better than he had in some time. The war news had been very good this past week; he hoped for and soon expected a crushing Allied victory. Then there would be another conference with Churchill, perhaps in London, perhaps in Berlin. . . .

He picked up the brief address and read over what he had written. *Americans are gathered together this evening in communities all over the country to pay tribute to the living memory of Thomas Jefferson. . . .* The first part of his speech eulogized Jefferson, champion of liberty and defender of the rights of man.

Today this nation, which Jefferson helped so greatly to build, is playing a tremendous part in the battle for the rights of man all over the world. He expressed his high hopes for the future, his dream of a firm and lasting peace, of a better, happier life for all people, everywhere in the world.

We must conquer doubts and fears. . . . We must cultivate the science of human relationships. . . . He concluded the address with these characteristic words, an inspiring message of faith and hope:

Let me assure you that my hand is the steadier for the work that is to be done, that I move more firmly into the task, knowing that you—millions and millions of you—are joined with me in the resolve to make this work endure.

The work, my friends, is peace; more than an end of this war—an end to the beginnings of all wars; yes, an end, forever, to this impractical, unrealistic settlement of the differences between governments by the mass killings of peoples.

Today as we move against the terrible scourge of war, as we go forward toward the greatest contribution that any generation of human beings can make in this world—the contribution of lasting peace—I ask you to keep up your faith. I measure the sound, solid achievement that can be made at this time by the straight edge of your own confidence and your resolve. And to you, and to all Americans who dedicate themselves with us to be making of an abiding peace, I say:

The only limit to our realization of tomorrow will

be our doubts of today. Let us move forward with strong and active faith.

These were the last words Franklin D. Roosevelt wrote for public utterance. This was his final message to America —and to the world.

For the next day a stunned nation learned that the President was dead. While at work on some official papers, and posing for his portrait at the same time, he suddenly clapped his hand to his head and said, "I have a terrible headache!" Then he slumped forward, unconscious—and a few hours later was dead of a cerebral hemorrhage.

And so the Jefferson Day address was never delivered. Death stilled the famous voice that was to have spoken on April 13th in honor of Jefferson . . . and in hope of an enduring peace. But his words remain, eloquent and inspiring: *I ask you to keep up your faith.*

Franklin D. Roosevelt did not live to see the day of final victory. He did not live to see his dreams of world unity and a strong peace structure realized. But he never lost faith that out of the agony of war a new and better world would be born.

Faith in the future is part of the common faith of America; and never has it been more unforgettably expressed than in these last words of Franklin D. Roosevelt: *The only limit to our realization of tomorrow will be our doubts of today. Let us move forward with strong and active faith.*

I steer my bark with Hope ahead and Fear astern.
Thomas Jefferson

Here in America we the people have a continent on which to work out our destiny, and our faith is great that our men and women are fit to face the mighty days. Nowhere else in all the world is there such a chance for the triumph on a gigantic scale of the great cause of democratic and popular government.
Theodore Roosevelt

None of us knows what is ahead. . . . The important
thing is to use today wisely and well, and face tomorrow eagerly and cheerfully and with the certainty
that we shall be equal to what it brings.

Channing Pollock

I think the true discovery of America is before us. I
think the true fulfillment of our spirit, of our people,
of our mighty and immortal land, is yet to come.
I think the true discovery of our own democracy is
still before us. And I think that all these things are
certain as the morning, as inevitable as noon. I think
I speak for most men living when I say that our
America is Here, is Now, and beckons on before us,
and that this glorious assurance is not only our living
hope, but our dream to be accomplished.

Thomas Wolfe

When I look back on the processes of history, when
I survey the genesis of America, I see this written
over every page: that the nations are renewed from
the bottom, not from the top; that the genius which
springs up from the ranks of unknown men is the
genius which renews the youth and energy of the people. Everything I know about history, every bit of
experience and observation that has contributed to
my thought, has confirmed me to the conviction that
the real wisdom of human life is compounded out of
the experiences of ordinary men. The utility, the vitality, the fruitage of life does not come from the top
to the bottom; it comes, like the natural growth of a
great tree, from the soil, up through the trunk into
the branches to the foliage and the fruit. The great
struggling unknown masses of the men who are at the
base of everything are the dynamic force that is lifting
the levels of society. A nation is as great, and only
as great, as her rank and file. . . . The hope of the
United States in the present and in the future is the
same that it has always been: it is the hope and the
confidence that out of the unknown homes will come

men who will constitute themselves the masters of industry and of politics. . . .

It behooves this nation to remember that a people shall be saved by the power that sleeps in its own deep bosom, or by none; shall be renewed in hope, in conscience, in strength, by waters welling up from its own sweet, perennial springs. Not from above; not by patronage of its aristocrats. The flower does not bear the root, but the root the flower. Everything that blooms in beauty in the air of heaven draws its fairness, its vigor, from its roots. Nothing living can blossom into fruitage unless through nourishing stalks deep-planted in the common soil. The rose is merely the evidence of the vitality of the root; and the real source of its beauty, the very blush that it wears upon its tender cheek, comes from those silent sources of life that lie hidden in the chemistry of the soil. Up from that soil, up from the silent bosom of the earth, rise the currents of life and energy. Up from the common soil, up from the quiet heart of the people, rise joyously today streams of hope and determination bound to renew the face of the earth in glory.

Woodrow Wilson

Considering the resources with which nature and the accumulated achievements of the past have endowed America, there ought to be no question in anyone's mind about the American future. . . .

The American people will move forward again, and feel once more the exhilaration and the confidence that have made them what they are, when they allow themselves to become conscious of their greatness, conscious not only of their incomparable inheritance but of the splendor of their destiny.

Walter Lippmann

Our national history, short in years, rich in manifold development and growth, has been seventeen decades crammed with achievement. Men and women, inspired by faith in man's dignity, goaded by conviction in man's responsibility, labored that this land might be a better home for those who followed them. Because every American generation attacked its problems with fresh vigor, we have peopled a continent, subdued its prairies and wilderness, tamed its rivers and devoted its resources to the betterment of those who dwell in it. The concepts of government, designed by our forefathers to assure all men freedom, justice and equality before the law, have been sustained and amplified in this land of vast resources so that the United States is today the world's most prominent citadel of human rights and the greatest provider of human opportunity. . . .

Today the future holds for us goals that exceed our past accomplishments and its imposes responsibilities weighty beyond those we have borne. Twice in our generation we have had to defend our heritage by resort to arms. The time approaches, however, when resort to arms may leave the wilderness as the only conqueror. But the certainty is also here that if we can eliminate wars from from the face of the earth, this country, and all the world, can reach new heights of prosperity and happiness, exceeding even the most sanguine dreams of our forebears. Between us and the attainment of all the hopes represented in a permanently peaceful world runs a tortuous and even dangerous path; its successful negotiation will demand all we have of faith in ourselves and in democracy; all the labor of our hearts and minds and bodies; all our moral and material strength. . . .

On the solid foundation of human rights established by our forefathers has been built a mighty structure which stands before the world as a stronghold of freedom and democracy. Its girders are the pioneer traits of initiative, resourcefulness, self-reliance, and pride in achievement. . . . If our youth and the generations to come clearly understand the relationship between individual effort and common good; if they perceive that our privileges and advantages in this great country, won by the toil and sacrifice of generations before them, can be retained only by a comparable expenditure on their part; if they appreciate that a corollary to our premise of man's dignity is his individual responsibility to maintain it against any threat; then the future of our country is secure.

And in broader fields, a vibrant, purposeful America will be the greatest single factor in the progress toward world order. Leadership for peace cannot be attained by armed strength alone, any more than it can merely by lofty words. But with a clear moral probity evident in all our international dealings, a unified, productive nation can demonstrate the manifest advantages of co-operation over coercion. If we will it, this land shall remain proof and example to all the world that men, of themselves, for themselves, may build in concord a better dwelling place, whether it be a city or continent or globe.

Dwight D. Eisenhower

For our encouragement, as we examine the current scene about us and are sometimes dismayed at the difficulties we face, we can look back on the performance of the last decade. In war and peace we have accomplished much that no dictatorship could ever match. We fought a war well and applied science in the process in ways that startled the world. When peace returned we created an internal vigor and prosperity that enabled us to lend a helping hand to those, our friends, who suffered more grievously, as they started their climb back to national health. We have not come to the end by any means. The applications of science yet to come are manifold and far-reaching. With them we can establish a standard of living in this country far higher than we have ever had; we can make more goods and have them more generally available throughout the population. We can prolong our lives and escape the ravages of old age, overcoming the scourges of mankind, epidemic disease, cancer, senility, to an extent that we can now barely grasp. We can create an environment in which the

creative arts can flourish, in which the human spirit
has an opportunity to rise and aspire. We can build a
society in which there will be justice and good will.
All this is within our grasp; we know it, for the performance of the past two years is a guarantee of the
effectiveness of the system under which we operate
and of the fundamental principles to which we adhere. All we have to do to bring it about is to preserve that system and improve it and hold fast to
those ideals and the faith from which they arise.

Vannevar Bush

For centuries my ancestors lived in Central Europe.
Some of them were peasants, some were artisans,
others were landed proprietors; but all of them through
those centuries had been restricted in their opportunities to the group in which they were born, and no
one of them had ever known the true meaning of
liberty. They were led to these shores, as were millions before and after them, by a special reputation
that the United States has had among nations. This
reputation is founded upon one simple fact: in the
United States the plain man has always had a chance.
My father and mother were the first generation in
their families to grow up in America. My mother became a lawyer. My father was also a lawyer. Of
course, in Europe my mother would have found it
impossible to practice a profession; and my father
would have found it difficult to get out of the groove
worn by his ancestors. Furthermore, it would have
been utterly impossible for them to have given their
six children the education which we received in
America. We went to high school and college.
And with schooling finished, there were no doors
closed to their children just because they came from
a plain family in a small town. No class distinction,
no law interfered with their effort to earn a living in
the occupation of their choice, or to express their
opinions as they pleased.
This family record is the record of any number of

American families. For us the value of freedom has had a practical demonstration. Freedom means for us not only a theoretical ideal, but definite practical rights. Freedom means that if you are a professor, you don't have to alter science or history as a bureaucrat prescribes. If you own a newspaper, you don't limit your editorial opinions to what an official censor approves. If you are a laborer, you can leave your job when you feel like it for any other job you prefer; you and your fellow workers can bargain collectively concerning the conditions of your work. If you think taxes are too high, you can vote against those officials you think responsible. And there is no limitation upon your inherent American right to criticize anybody, anywhere, at any time. . . .

My creed, if I were asked to define it, would run something like this: I believe in America because in it we are free—free to choose our government, to speak our minds, to observe our different religions;

Because we are generous with our freedom—we share our rights with those who disagree with us;

Because we hate no people and covet no people's land;

Because we are blessed with a natural and varied abundance;

Because we set no limit to a man's achievement: in mine, factory, field, or service in business or the arts, an able man, regardless of class or creed, can realize his ambition;

Because we have great dreams—and because we have the opportunity to make those dreams come true.

Wendell Willkie

INDEX

A

Abbott, Lyman, 62
Adams, George Matthew, 170
Adams, John Quincy, 150
Adams, Sarah Flower, 51-54
Addison, Joseph, 8, 44, 248
Allen, James Lane, 44, 108,
    181-85
Amiel, Henry F., 112, 215-16,
    272
Antiphanes, 65-66
Aristotle, 25, 101, 195, 203
Atlantic Charter, 335-36
Aurelius, Marcus, 12, 49, 84-85,
    122, 179, 186, 235

B

Babcock, Maltbie D., 248
Bacon, Francis, xiii, 226
Bailey, Philip James, xiii, 25, 48
Barrie, Sir James M., 79
Baruch, Bernard, 295
Beecher, Henry Ward, 216
Beethoven, Ludwig van, 196
Bennett, Arnold, xiii, 152-55
Bhagavad Gita, 176
Bible, xiii, 12, 40, 43, 44, 48,
    49, 54, 57, 72, 77, 84, 95,
    112, 150, 162, 203, 206, 211,
    215, 221, 235, 262, 267, 288,
    310, 334

Bok, Edward, 21
Bolton, Sarah K., 96
Brahma, 262-63
Brande, Dorothea, 147, 170
Brontë, Charlotte, 216
Brontë, Emily, 58
Brooks, Phillips, 213-15
Browning, Elizabeth Barrett,
    260-62
Browning, Robert, 41, 63-65,
    177, 296-300
Bruyère, Jean de la, 150
Bryant, William Cullen, 48,
    117-22
Buddha, 185
Burke, Edmund, 132, 137
Burroughs, John, 5-8, 245-47
Bush, Vannevar, 345-46
Butts, Mary Frances, 243
Byrd, Richard E., 38-40, 254,
    269-71
Byron, Lord, xii

C

Cabot, Richard C., 137, 267
Carlyle, Thomas, 144-45, 156-
    57, 191
Carnegie, Dale, 33
Carrel, Alexis, 72-73
Channing, William E., 180, 186,
    311

349

ABOUT THE EDITOR

Lillian Eicher Watson is a well-known writer with many years of experience of helping people help themselves. She is one of the most widely read authorities on social usage in the world—author of the fabulous best seller, the original Book of Etiquette, *and of* Customs of Mankind, Well-Bred English, *and a dozen other inspirational and self-improvement books.*

Light from Many Lamps *represents years of research, is the culmination of a lifetime's ambition: to produce a book that would give people comfort, guidance and inspiration* when they need such help most.

Pocket Bibles and
inspirational writing to carry
with you always—comforting you
through troubled times,
bringing you

JOY and STRENGTH.

____82385	ART OF CHRISTIAN MEDITATION, David Ray	$1.95
____81624	BIBLE THERAPY, E.C. Wittman & C.R. Bollman	$2.50
____83597	GOOD NEWS FOR MODERN MAN: The New Testament in Today's English Version. American Bible Society	$2.95
____41653	GO OUT IN JOY!, Nina Herrmann	$2.50
____81636	HE WALKS WITH ME, David Graham	$1.75
____81048	I'M OUT TO CHANGE MY WORLD, Ann Kiemel	$1.50
____82626	LET THE HAMMER DOWN, Jerry Clower	$1.95
____41016	PLEASE LOVE ME, Keith Miller	$2.75
____48784	POCKET AQUINAS, V. Bourke, Ed.	$1.95
____41889	SACRED SHROUD, Thomas Humber	$2.50